Palgrave Studies in Governance, Leadership and Responsibility

Series Editors
Simon Robinson
Leeds Business School
Leeds Beckett University
Leeds, UK

William Sun
Leeds Business School
Leeds Beckett University
Leeds, UK

Georgiana Grigore
Henley Business School
University of Reading
Henley-on-Thames, Oxfordshire, UK

Alin Stancu
Bucharest University of Economic Studies
Bucharest, Romania

The fall-out from many high profile crises in governance and leadership in recent decades, from banking to healthcare, continues to be felt around the world. Major reports have questioned the values and behaviour, not just of individual organizations but of professionals, industries and political leadership. These reports raise questions about business corporations and also public service institutions. In response this new series aims to explore the broad principles of governance and leadership and how these are embodied in different contexts, opening up the possibility of developing new theories and approaches that are fuelled by interdisciplinary approaches. The purpose of the series is to highlight critical reflection and empirical research which can enable dialogue across sectors, focusing on theory, value and the practice of governance, leadership and responsibility.

Written from a global context, the series is unique in bringing leadership and governance together. The King III report connects these two fields by identifying leadership as one of the three principles of effective governance however most courses in business schools have traditionally treated these as separate subjects. Increasingly, and in particular with the case of executive education, business schools are recognizing the need to develop and produce responsible leaders. The series will therefore encourage critical exploration between these two areas and as such explore sociological and philosophical perspectives.

More information about this series at
http://www.palgrave.com/gp/series/15192

Francisca Farache · Georgiana Grigore ·
Alin Stancu · David McQueen
Editors

Responsible People

The Role of the Individual in CSR, Entrepreneurship and Management Education

Editors
Francisca Farache
Brighton Business School
University of Brighton
Brighton, UK

Georgiana Grigore
Henley Business School
University of Reading
Henley-on-Thames, Oxfordshire, UK

Alin Stancu
Bucharest University of Economic Studies
Bucharest, Romania

David McQueen
Faculty of Media and Communication
Bournemouth University
Poole, Dorset, UK

ISSN 2662-1304   ISSN 2662-1312   (electronic)
Palgrave Studies in Governance, Leadership and Responsibility
ISBN 978-3-030-10739-0   ISBN 978-3-030-10740-6   (eBook)
https://doi.org/10.1007/978-3-030-10740-6

Library of Congress Control Number: 2019931744

This Palgrave Macmillan imprint is published by the registered company Springer Nature Switzerland AG
The registered company address is: Gewerbestrasse 11, 6330 Cham, Switzerland

Contents

Notes on Contributors

Maria Teresa Bosch Badia is Research Director of Finance, Corporate Social Responsibility, and Ethics at the Universitat de Girona, where she is Vice-Dean of Quality of its Faculty of Economics and Business Studies. She lectures compulsory and elective courses in undergraduate and graduate groups in Finance, in subjects both financial-market as well as corporate-finance orientated. Her main research interests are Corporate Social Responsibility, asset valuation, investments efficiency, financial performance analysis, capital budgeting and real options. Among other academic journals she has published in *International Journal of Accounting & Information Management, Información Commercial Española, ICE: Revista de Economia, Journal of Banking and Finance, Engineering Economist, PlosOne, Review of Managerial Science, Cogent Economics & Finance, Journal of European Real Estate Research,* and *Sustainability.*

Véronique Boulocher-Passet is Senior Lecturer in Marketing at the University of Brighton. She received her Ph.D. degree in Education and Marketing from Université Charles de Gaulle in Lille, France. Her major research focuses on marketing education, and how writing teaching case studies can enhance students' learning of marketing.

Teresa Chahine is the inaugural Sheila and Ron '92 B.A. Marcelo Lecturer in Social Entrepreneurship at Yale School of Management. She is the author of *Introduction to Social Entrepreneurship*, a twelve-step framework for building impactful ventures in new and existing organizations. Dr. Chahine's research focuses on developing tools to characterize and advance social and environmental determinants of health. She launched the first social entrepreneurship program in the context of public health, at Harvard University. She was also responsible for launching the first venture philanthropy organization in her home country of Lebanon, providing tailored financing and critical management support to social enterprises serving marginalized populations through education and job creation for youth and women.

Nobuyuki Chikudate, Ph.D. is Professor of Organization Theory and CSR at Hiroshima University in Japan. He also has been jointly appointed to Professor of Phoenix Leader Education Program for Renaissance from Radiation Disaster. He received Ph.D. from University at Buffalo-State University of New York and was a postdoctoral fellow at the Johns Hopkins University in the United States. His articles are included in such journals as *Human Relations, Journal of Business Ethics, Journal of Management Studies*, and others. He also published a book entitled, *Collective Myopia in Japanese Organizations: A Transcultural Approach for Identifying Corporate Meltdowns* in 2015 from Palgrave Macmillan. Furthermore, he received O.N.E.-Kedge Unorthodox Paper Award in 2016, Academy of Management Annual Meetings, Anaheim, California.

Gwyneth Edwards studies the creation and transfer of strategic practices in high tech firms. She has over 20 years of industry experience in senior management positions and, since earning her Ph.D., has presented in numerous international conferences and published a number of journal articles focused on MNE strategy. She was awarded Canada's Governor General Academic Gold Medal in 2014. www.gwynethedwards.com.

Francisca Farache is a Principal Lecturer in Marketing and Course Leader of the M.Sc. Marketing at Brighton Business School. She holds an M.A. in Marketing and a Ph.D. in Business, both of which are from the University of Brighton. Her research is in the field of Corporate Social Responsibility, CSR communication and Business Ethics. She has published in *Journal of Business Ethics, Journal of Business Research, Corporate Communication: An International Journal, Journal of Consumer Market* and *Latin American Business Review*.

Yulia Fomina is Associate Professor at Dostoevsky Omsk State University (Russia). She received her Ph.D. from Omsk State University and continued her postdoctoral research at the University of Natural Resources and Applied Life Sciences, Vienna. Her research interests include Innovations and Entrepreneurship, Social Entrepreneurship, Economic Methodology, and Schumpeter's theory.

Irene Garnelo-Gomez is a member of the John Madejski Centre for Reputation and Lecturer in Reputation and Sustainability at Henley Business School, University of Reading. She completed a doctorate in Management at Henley Business School on sustainable living. In particular, she researched the interplay between identity and motivations among those following sustainable lifestyles, trying to understand why individuals are differently motivated to live sustainably depending on the expression of their identity. Irene teaches CSR and Reputation and Responsibility at undergraduate and MBA level. She is involved in several research projects, mostly related to pro-social behaviors. Her research interests include sustainable behavior, CSR and social marketing.

Georgiana Grigore is a lecturer in marketing at Henley Business School. She is co-founder and chair of "Social Responsibility, Ethics and Sustainable Business" conference. Her major area of research is in marketing and corporate responsibility concepts and practices, including changes that result from digital media. She has published several books, including *Corporate Responsibility and Digital Communities* and *Corporate Social Responsibility in the Digital Age* that explores a contemporary intersection of two contemporary fields: corporate responsibility and digital technology. Her research has appeared in international journals including *Marketing Theory, Journal of Business Research*, and

Internet Research. She currently leads a British Academy/Leverhulme grant that aims to understand new responsibilities in the digital economy.

Kazue Haga has been an associate professor at Bunkyo Gakuin University in Tokyo since April 2017. She received her Ph.D. degree from the Faculty of Business Administration and Economics of Philipps University of Marburg (Germany) in 2012 and was a Senior Research Fellow at the German Institute for Japanese Studies (DIJ) in Tokyo from May 2013 to April 2016. Her research focuses on entrepreneurship in older age, innovation in aging regions, and improvements in health for a productive long life. One of her current research questions is how the economies of rural, agricultural regions facing demographic change (aging) and declining populations can be redeveloped by the residents themselves. She works on the issue in a holistic sense and her research concerns the social responsibilities and social entrepreneurship of local enterprises and their role in increasing the quality of life and satisfaction of the residents. She has conducted case studies about "olderpreneurship" in Japan and Germany, and from her participant observations she has developed a deep insight into the potential of innovative small enterprises which are deeply embedded in the local community to provide social innovation in a holistic sense.

Nadia Lonsdale is a Lecturer at the University of Brighton. She teaches Marketing and CSR. Her doctoral research is concentrated on implementation of Environmental CSR practices in Russian companies as well as integration of principles of Education for Sustainable Development in the Russian Tertiary Education system.

Anders Lundström is professor emeritus in business administration. He is working as managing director at the Institute of Innovative Entrepreneurship—IPREG. His current research interests are policies for entrepreneurship and small business as well as social entrepreneurship. He set up the Swedish Foundation for Small Business Research as well as the international network IPREG consisting of research organizations in 14 EU countries. He created an international research group of outstanding researchers and EU representatives in the field of entrepreneurship. He also founded the International Award for Entrepreneurship Research, chaired three international conferences and has been president of ICSB (International Council of Small Business) a worldwide network. He has published extensively on entrepreneurship and small business issues. His thesis was about heuristic models to solve complex problems. Anders Lundström has been involved in introducing a number of EU programs in Sweden. He has also published one novel and three poetry books.

David McQueen is a lecturer at Bournemouth University and his research interests include questions of media & power, conflict coverage and PR. David's recent publications include Fear, loathing and shale gas. The introduction of fracking to the UK: a case study. In Theofilou, A., Grigore, G. and Stancu, A. (eds) 2016. *Corporate Social Responsibility in the Post Financial Crisis*; Panorama and 9–11. In Lacey, S. and Paget, D. (eds) 2015. *The War on Terror: Post-9/11 Drama, Docudrama and Documentary*; Media Democracy and Reform in Latin America: The Policy Lessons for Europe for *The International Political Economy of Communication: Media and Power in South America* (2014) edited by Vivares, E., Cheryl Martens, C., McChesney R. Palgrave.

Rick Molz performs research in international strategy within the context of developing, emerging and transitional economies. He was co-founder and chair of the Montreal Local Global Research Group and has published four books and 25+ refereed journal articles. Dr. Molz has been invited to speak, lecture and research in China, Austria, Germany, Morocco, Tunisia, Czech Republic, India, Poland, and the United States.

Joan Montllor-Serrats is Professor of Finance at the Universitat Autonoma de Barcelona, where he has been Dean (1990–1992 and 2005–2010) of its Faculty of Economics and Business Studies. He lectures compulsory and elective courses in undergraduate and graduate groups in Finance, in subjects both financial-market as well as corporate-finance orientated. His main research interests are asset valuation and corporate social responsibility, including capital budgeting and real option valuation; performance analysis of financial strategies; corporate financial policy, capital structure, and value creation. Among other academic journals he has published in *Journal of Banking and Finance, Engineering Economist, PlosOne, Review of Managerial Science, Journal of Applied Finance, Cogent Economics & Finance, Journal of European Real Estate Research,* and *Sustainability.*

Salma Msefer is an industry marketing professional and experienced qualitative researcher with an M.Sc. in International Management. She is currently a Learning Officer at the Business Development Bank of Canada and holds significant expertise in web marketing analytics. She is skilled in Search Engine Optimization (SEO), Digital Strategy, Translation, Market Research, and Search Engine Marketing (SEM).

Wybe Popma is a Principal Lecturer at the University of Brighton. He teaches Marketing and Innovation Management. His research focuses on CSR and organizational ethics.

Anastasiya Saraeva is a member of the John Madejski Centre for Reputation and a Lecturer in Reputation and Responsibility at Henley Business School, University of Reading. Anastasiya has been teaching Reputation and Responsibility and supervising dissertations on topics related to CSR at MBA level. She recently completed her Ph.D., which explored the impacts of communication on corporate reputation and stakeholder behavior. Anastasiya is currently involved in a number of research projects, which are related to CSR, communication and stakeholder behaviors. Her research interests include corporate responsibility, reputation, communication, and behavioral psychology.

Nizar Shbikat is a doctoral student in the School of Business and a member of Social Human Rights Graduate School (ProSoM) at the University of Kassel, Germany. His research centers on labor governance, power resources approach, and ethical sourcing in global supply chains.

Alin Stancu is Associate Professor of Corporate Social Responsibility and Public Relations in the Department of Marketing from The Bucharest University of Economic Studies. His main areas of research include: business ethics, corporate responsibility and public relations. He is the co-founder of The International Conference on Social Responsibility, Ethics and Sustainable Business (www.csrconferences. org) and editor of several books in *Palgrave Studies in Governance, Leadership and Responsibility*.

Maria-Antonia Tarrazon-Rodon is Associate Professor of Finance at the Universitat Autonoma de Barcelona, where she has been Deputy Director of the Olympic Studies Centre CEO-UAB (2006–2007). Since 1996–1997 she also serves under the *Programme Tutoresport-UAB* as academic tutor of high-level sportsmen and sportswomen studying at the Faculty of Economics and Business. She lectures compulsory and elective courses in undergraduate and graduate groups in Finance, in subjects both financial-market as well as corporate-finance orientated. Her main research interests are asset valuation, corporate social responsibility and gender questions, including capital budgeting and real option valuation; performance analysis of financial strategies; weather derivatives pricing and strategies; corporate financial policy, capital structure, and value creation. Among other academic journals she has published in *Journal of Banking and Finance, Engineering Economist, PlosOne, Review of Managerial Science, Cogent Economics & Finance, Journal of European Real Estate Research, Sustainability*, and *Journal of Developmental Entrepreneurship*.

Besrat Tesfaye is Associate Professor in Business Studies at the Department of Social Sciences, at Södertörn University. Her research focuses primarily on entrepreneurship and small business. She has studied entrepreneurship from different perspectives, including gender and ethnicity, and in contexts such as academic institutions and low income economies. At present, she is researching the role of the patent system on smaller enterprises, with emphasis on how the SMEs use and benefit from the patent system. In another multidisciplinary project, "Re-inventing the suburbs", Besrat is studying the emergence (or lack of) high-technology clusters in knowledge-intensive environments in the southern suburbs of Stockholm City.

Gianpaolo Tomaselli is a Research Support Officer at the University of Malta within the Department of Health Services Management (Faculty of Health Sciences)—and previously within the Institute for European Studies. He holds a Ph.D. in Economics and Management in Health Care, a Master in Public Administration and a Bachelor in Administration from University Magna Græcia of Catanzaro, Italy. Dr. Tomaselli collaborates also with the Marco Vigorelli Foundation in Milan (Italy). He has been a Visiting Research Fellow at the University of Malta at Faculty of Information & Communication Technology (ICT). His main research interests involve Corporate Social Responsibility Communication, Health Services Management & Policy and Health Innovation. His Ph.D. thesis was on "Corporate Social Responsibility Communication. Dimensions and Perspectives".

List of Figures

List of Tables

1

The Role of the Individual in Promoting Social Change

Francisca Farache, Georgiana Grigore, David McQueen and Alin Stancu

We are all very familiar with the power of the individual. Rosa Parks, perhaps one of the best-known examples, was a black woman in a highly segregated Alabama, USA, who refused to give up her seat to a white person. Her actions inspired the Montgomery Bus Boycott and she is regarded as 'the first lady of the civil rights movement'. This was

F. Farache (✉)
Brighton Business School, University of Brighton, Brighton, UK
e-mail: f.farache@brighton.ac.uk

G. Grigore
Henley Business School, University of Reading, Henley-on-Thames, UK
e-mail: g.f.grigore@henley.ac.uk

D. McQueen
Faculty of Media and Communication,
Bournemouth University, Poole, UK
e-mail: dmcqueen@bournemouth.ac.uk

A. Stancu
Bucharest University of Economic Studies, Bucharest, Romania
e-mail: alinstancu@mk.ase.ro

© The Author(s) 2019
F. Farache et al. (eds.), *Responsible People*, Palgrave Studies in Governance,
Leadership and Responsibility, https://doi.org/10.1007/978-3-030-10740-6_1

back in 1955. Interesting enough, the civil rights movement, together with other social movements of the 60s—consumer, environmental and women's movements—are intrinsically related to refinements and applications of Corporate Social Responsibility (CSR) (Carroll 2016). So, where are we now? Can the power of the individual change the way we deal with environmental issues? Can it impact the way corporations understand their obligations and responsibilities towards society? Can teachers and lecturers shape the managers of the future? Can entrepreneurship provide an answer to social problems?

David Attenborough, the English broadcaster and naturalist, exposed the damage plastic is causing to marine life in his BBC TV series, *Blue Planet II*. He urged the world to cut back plastic usage in order to protect the oceans. And, at least in the UK, he was listened to. The impact of *Blue Planet* was enormous. The 'plastic issue' has become a national and political talking point. It even caused the issue to be highlighted in the 2017 Budget speech and lead to change in the government environmental policy (BBC 2018). It also made a huge impact on society. After the final episode of the series, 62% of viewers surveyed wanted to make changes to their daily life. David Attenborough was also astonished with its effect, as he would not expect that the documentary could inspire so many people to want to change. He summarised the importance of the individual in leading change as follows:

> The actions of any just one of us may seem to be trivial and to have no effect. But the knowledge that there are hundreds of thousands of people who are doing the same thing - that really does have an effect. (BBC 2018)

Super Size Me, the 2004 documentary by the American Morgan Spurlock impacted on McDonald's and whole of the fast food industry. To sum it up, Spurlock ate McDonald's food for 30 days, he had to try every item in the menu at least once and accept any 'supersized' items. This had an effect on the filmmaker's health as he gained weight, experienced fat accumulation in his liver and began to feel depressed among other health-related issues. And how did the company react? Although McDonald's did not acknowledge the effect of *Super Size Me*, it changed the food menus, including more salads and fruits and it has eliminated the 'supersize' options. Consumers also became more aware about the repercussion of fast food on their health. More recently, a senior Vice President of McDonalds, Alistair Macrow, admitted the documentary had a serious impact on its consumer base. He stated that: 'We can't market our way out of this; it's about fundamental change' (Barnes 2014).

These two examples illustrated the power of the individual to change the way we behave in relation to environmental issues, as well as the impact individuals can make on corporations. In the same way, universities and business schools can have a major influence on the ability to create a more sustainable business future. Higher education institutions inform business practice and shape the leaders and managers of tomorrow who, in turn, will have an important role in the development of regulation and change in business (Tilbury and Ryan 2011).

The single most important driver of the sustainability agenda (business ethics, CSR, sustainability) at higher education institutions is the individual faculty member (Matten and Moon 2004). These individuals might have been someone with a research interest in ethics, CSR or sustainability. This finding emphasises the importance of the individual's initiative to drive sustainability education. After Matt and Moon published their research in 2004, sustainability became mainstream at Business Schools and Executive education centres. An important landmark for sustainable management education was the creation of the Principles for Responsible Management Education (PRME) initiative in 2007. PRME is supported by the United Nations and aims to raise the profile of sustainability in schools worldwide and to provide business students with the understanding and ability to deliver change in the future. PRME also aims to draws attention to the Sustainable Development Goals (SDGs) and brings into line academic institutions with the work of UN Global Compact. PRME is based on six principles: Purpose (develop the capabilities of students); Values (incorporate social responsibilities values in academic organisations); Methods (enable effective learning methods for responsible leadership); Research (encourage advances in the creation of social, environmental and economic value); Partnership (interaction with business corporations) and Dialogue (facilitate and support dialogue among educators, students, business, government and civil society).

Nowadays, Business Schools and executive centres provide students opportunities to build business skills but could also assist them to acknowledge the impact that business decisions can have on the environment and society, as well as the damage they may cause (Larrán Jorge et al. 2015). Incorporating ethics, CSR and sustainability into the programme is an important step to help students understand this balance (Kolodinsky et al. 2010) and provide them with tools to face these issues in the future. Ethics, CSR and sustainability are covered by the majority of the top 50 global MBA programmes, students seem to be very interested in these topics, especially in the top 10 school, and there is a tendency to teach the three topics together (Christensen et al. 2007). However, business ethics, CSR and sustainability courses are usually offered in only a limited number of postgraduate programmes, and are almost non-existent at undergraduate level (Fernández and Sanjuán 2010).

There are signs that teaching about sustainability has reached a reasonable level of maturity (Branco and Delgado 2016) and scholars agree that business schools play an important place in developing ethical behaviour and shaping the future behaviour of business professionals (Tormo-Carbó et al. 2016). The industry is looking for business graduates who are able to demonstrate an understanding of ethics, CSR and sustainability. It appears to be that business schools are aware of this demand and are providing students with the education they need to find future employment (Nicholls et al. 2013).

Individuals can have a positive impact on society through entrepreneurship, more specific, social entrepreneurship. Social entrepreneurship is defined as the process of employing business and entrepreneurship principles to alleviate social problems (Cochran 2007).

Social enterprises aim to make a positive social impact rather than to maximise shareholders profit.

Business people are incorporating their philanthropic agenda into their business, thus the new entrepreneurs are attempting to improve social and environmental issues through their enterprises. It is a new hybrid model that combines business with social organisations. Social entrepreneurs are tackling social issues at the same time as generating profits.

One example of a social entrepreneur is Blake Mycoskie, the founder of TOMS shoes. TOMS promised to donate one pair of shoes for everyone sold and by September 2018 has donated 70 million pairs of shoes for those in developing countries (TOMS 2018). The company donates shoes in 60 countries and works with 100 NGOs to distribute the donations. The company expanded their one-for-one model and embraced other causes such as providing safe water, restoring sight programmes and providing birth kits for expectant mothers. At the same time, the company showed that it is possible to reconcile social purpose with a successful business.

This book includes chapters that bring the focus back to the people who are driving change in contemporary corporate responsibility practice. In particular, we include contributions that expand current mainstream understanding of the role individuals have in shaping CSR theory, practice, policies and discourses. The chapters expand on conceptualizations of CSR and the role of individuals in charge of CSR practices in contributing to societal good. It provides contributions that extend current mainstream understanding of the role individuals have in shaping CSR theory, practice, policies and discourses. This book covers perspectives from Japan, Morocco, Germany, Sweden, Russia, Italy, Spain and the UK.

Responsible People—The Role of the Individual in CSR, Entrepreneurship and Management Education examines how people shape and influence CSR and investigates the role of the individual in promoting social change. The book consists of three parts that investigate the impact of people on CSR. Below we summarise each section.

1.1   People, Responsibility and Entrepreneurship

In the first section, Part 1: People, Responsibility and Entrepreneurship, we examine the rise of social entrepreneurs and explore the role they play in engaging in CSR practices. This section also focuses on CSR performance and practices in small and medium-size enterprises (SME) an area gaining increasing attention amongst scholars.

For example, in Chapter 2, Besrat Tesfaye and Anders Lundström discuss the economic and social impact of SME and highlight a growing emphasis on CSR engagement, practices and outcomes in SMEs. The authors investigate CSR Swedish SMEs, more specifically how successful migrant entrepreneurs (SuME) can be engaged in initiatives facilitating the labour market integration of new migrants. The CSR perceptions, motives and priorities of SuME in participating in initiatives that address broader social issues are explored.

In Chapter 3, Gianpaolo Tomaselli explores Corporate Family Responsibility (CFR), a company responsibility towards their employees, in the context of Italian SMEs. The chapter adopts a case study methodology and analyses five companies that have successfully implemented good CFR practices within their business strategy. Data were gathered through semi-structured interviews with companies' CEOs. Results demonstrated a growing attention by Italian SMEs towards the topics of CFR and work–life balance policies and linked this growth with a positive impact on companies' performance.

Kazue Haga (Chapter 4) offers a comparison of Japanese and German companies, where she investigates companies that made a positive contribution to aging and shrinking rural communities through business and entrepreneurship. Rural communities based on agriculture in developed countries suffer from aging and declining populations and structurally weak local economies, and require creative solutions to maintain the living standards and quality of life of the residents. Redefining and recreating local businesses are among these measures. Entrepreneurial leadership is a common feature of both companies. These companies engage in new combinations of local resources, including aging human capital, to stimulate residents to participate in their enterprises, and their efforts include business and social aspects.

Teresa Chahine and Yulia Fomina (Chapter 5) focus on social entrepreneurship in Russia, where it is still an emerging trend. Social entrepreneurship is a pathway for individuals and organizations to acknowledge responsibility for social and environmental outcomes. This chapter explores the factors influencing social entrepreneurship success and failure for nascent and mature entrepreneurs in the Omsk region of Russia where 58 social entrepreneurs were interviewed.

1.2   People, Practitioners and CSR Education

CSR poses a challenge for managerial education, as it is often approached somewhat instrumentally for its financial benefit and contribution to corporate value. The challenge is to integrate ethics, sustainability and responsibility in a more values-based CSR agenda. This challenge is developed and explored in the second part of the book, titled People, practitioners and CSR Education.

In Chapter 6, Irene Garnelo-Gomez and Anastasiya Saraeva explore effective ways of communicating CSR in MBA education. The authors address how the interplay between a messenger (i.e., a lecturer) and a message (i.e., module content) may influence MBA programme members' engagement with, and commitment to, CSR. The authors suggest that if there are high levels of identification with the lecturer and higher effectiveness of CSR messages (well-designed module content), MBA programme members would be more likely to commit to CSR issues. Hence, this chapter provides a theoretical framework which could shed light on how to effectively communicate CSR in MBA education with the purpose of not only transferring knowledge, but encouraging behavioural change. Finally, the authors discuss limitations of the proposed framework and highlight future research opportunities.

Maria Teresa Bosch Badia, Joan Montllor-Serrats, and Maria-Antonia Tarrazon-Rodon (Chapter 7) focus on how to develop the sensitivity of business students to sustainability through an analysis of literary fiction. This chapter analyses two plays: Shakespeare's *The Merchant of Venice* and Ibsen's *The Wild Duck*. *The Merchant of Venice* presents an interesting interweaving of financial and social sustainability. The authors identified in it an unregulated financial system in which lenders can freely decide the clauses of the contracts. Turning to the social side, the play shows a society dominated by the heterosexual male of a dominant social class. After class discussions, students should be able to answer questions like: which social consequences do the lack of a fair financial regulation foster? How do pride, hate, and revenge create a barrier to social progress? *The Wild Duck*, in turn, can be taken as a metaphor of how humans cannot live in conflict with nature. The environmental outrage that pervades the play and the tragedy that it creates are analyzed as the result of egotist management that puts aside environment and society. The Old Ekland's last sentence, *the forest has taken its revenge*, summarizes the failure of men going against nature.

Véronique Boulocher-Passet, Nadia Lonsdale, Wybe Popma and Francisca Farache (Chapter 8) discuss what being socially conscious means for marketers and draws on the experience of developing CSR and sustainability education at a UK business school, to gain deeper knowledge into the role universities can play to enhance future marketing managers' social consciousness and responsibility. Literature shows that socially conscious marketing practices are no longer just a 'perk' or selling point for PR purposes. From a business and profitability standpoint, as well as from a moral standpoint, being socially conscious should be a requirement. Marketing education has a role in helping students develop their consciousness of society. If marketing educators fail to integrate those dimensions into their teaching, they will fail to prepare students to be responsible members of the marketing community. A case study method was used to enhance discussion. Qualitative data were collected via interviews of different protagonists within the business school to capture how those incorporate CSR and sustainability issues into their marketing curriculum. Analysis shows that, beyond creating explicit student opportunities around CSR, universities can play an active role in embedding social consciousness and responsibility as part of their own strategic plan.

1.3   Citizens, Consumers, Stakeholders— Shaping the Future of CSR

CSR is context based and it is important not to overlook the impact of individual citizens, consumers and other stakeholders on ethical norms and values, notions of sustainability and CSR practices. The third part of the book explores a number of intriguing case studies from different CSR contexts, including the role of the individual in CSR education and management. This individual might be an entrepreneur, a senior manager or CEO, or a member of marketing or PR team with CSR responsibilities located at the heart of an organisation. The individual might also operate both within and outside, or at the very margins of an organisation. Here we can include a range of stakeholders, such as consultants, NGOs, union leaders, educators, politicians, buyers, suppliers, competitors and customers who each, in different ways, might play a critical role in driving change and upholding ethical standards.

It is also the case that groups and individuals typically dismissed as antithetical to the organisation's mission may, ultimately, be the most effective in holding an organisation to account for failures that threaten the wider community or environment. David McQueen (Chapter 9) explores this aspect of CSR with respect to the development of hydraulic fracturing (fracking) in the UK and considers how activists and protestors can play a central role in shifting public attitudes, changing the terms of debate, influencing political policy and shaping national legislation. Whilst such activity may, in the short term, damage corporate reputation, undermine the social licence to operate and ultimately cease specific operations, this can be seen as a driver of long-term progress towards a more sustainable and socially responsible energy sector.

Rick Molz, Gwyneth Edwards and Salma Msefer (Chapter 10) examine the activities of ten MNE Moroccan subsidiaries following the Arab Spring. Through onsite subsidiary interviews and site visits, along with analysis of public and corporate documents, the research explores how the MNE subsidiaries sought local legitimacy, through institutional work. The study finds that the subsidiaries strategically used CSR to respond proactively in their host environments during a period of institutional instability (the Arab Spring). These CSR actions ranged from the informal to the formal, from engagement with local actors to the introduction of new corporate CSR standards and practices. The findings suggest that CSR as a form of institutional work is an effective response to institutional change caused by social movements, benefiting not only the MNEs themselves, but also society in general.

Nizar Shbikat (Chapter 11) examines existing literature in order to identify the possible root causes that contribute to the contemporary labour exploitation practices in international supply chains. The causes were defined through a systematic literature review and then grouped based on multi-stakeholder analysis. Causes were then represented graphically by cause-and-effect analysis. The analysis illustrates the interdependencies of causes which supports the argument that the violation of labour rights in international businesses is a 'wicked problem' due to the complexity of global governance structures and conflicts of interests of different stakeholders. This chapter offers stakeholders an insight into the labor issues in their supply chains and helps them develop appropriate

Nobuyuki Chikudate (Chapter 12) investigates Japanese corporations involved in scandals that have poorly responded to public criticism and were subsequently dragged into various corporate crises. The managers in these corporations did not speak or behave in a responsible manner during the crises. In addition, they also offered negative views on CSR years before the crisis, disqualifying them from being considered responsible corporate citizens. By using a genealogical analysis, the author conducts an analysis of Toyota's recall crisis in 2010.

1.4   An Overview

Contemporary research suggests that CSR has become disconnected from the people (practitioners, consumers-citizens and other stakeholders) who make it happen or those who are most impacted by corporations. Companies are failing to walk the CSR talk, communicating their ethical stance in a way and behaving in another one. Thus, people are increasingly becoming sceptical of CSR as a result of greenwashing, corporate scandals and irresponsibility. Previous studies highlight the link between CSR and competitive advantage, reputation, communications, stakeholder groups or financial performance, but there is less emphasis on the role of individuals in charge of CSR practice in challenging corporate behaviour and contributing to societal good.

The book includes papers presented at the 'International Conference on Social Responsibility, Ethics and Sustainable Business' at HTW University, Berlin, in September 2017. This academic conference was held for the first time in Bucharest in 2012 and, since then, it has been hosted annually in different cities around Europe, attracting academics and practitioners from around the world. This book includes a selection of the best papers presented at the event. The theme of the conference in 2017 was 'People and Corporate Social Responsibility in a Globalized World' and included contributions on topics such as: social entrepreneurship, sustainability, CSR in SMEs, management education and human rights.

References

Barnes, R. 2014. McDonald's: 'We Knew We Couldn't Market Our Way Out of Super Size Me'. *Campaign*, May 21.

BBC. 2018. BBC Announces Major Initiative 'Plastics Watch' Following the Global Impact of Blue Planet II. Accessed July 17, 2018 https://www.bbc.co.uk/mediacentre/latestnews/2018/plastics-watch.

Branco, M.C., and C. Delgado. 2016. Corporate Social Responsibility Education and Research in Portuguese Business Schools. In *Social Responsibility Education Across Europe*, ed. Duygu Turker, Ceren Altuntas, and Samuel O. Idowu, 207–227. Cham: Springer.

Carroll, A.B. 2016. Carroll's Pyramid of CSR: Taking Another Look. *International Journal of Corporate Social Responsibility* 1 (1): 3.

Christensen, L.J., E. Peirce, L.P. Hartman, W.M. Hoffman, and J. Carrier. 2007. Ethics, CSR, and Sustainability Education in the Financial Times Top 50 Global Business Schools: Baseline Data and Future Research Directions. *Journal of Business Ethics* 73 (4): 347–368.

Cochran, P.L. 2007. The Evolution of Corporate Social Responsibility. *Business Horizons* 50: 449–454.

Fernández, F.J.L., and A.B. Sanjuán. 2010. The Presence of Business Ethics and CSR in the Higher Education Curricula for Executives: The Case of Spain. *Journal of Business Ethics Education* 7: 25–38.

Kolodinsky, R.W., T.M. Madden, D.S. Zisk, and E.T. Henkel. 2010. Attitudes About Corporate Social Responsibility: Business Student Predictors. *Journal of Business Ethics* 91 (2): 167–181.

Larrán Jorge, M., F.J. Andrades Pena, and M.J. Muriel de los Reyes. 2015. Factors Influencing the Presence of Ethics and CSR Stand-Alone Courses in the Accounting Masters Curriculum: An International Study. *Accounting Education* 24 (5): 361–382.

Matten, D., and J. Moon. 2004. Corporate Social Responsibility. *Journal of Business Ethics* 54 (4): 323–337.

Nicholls, J., J.F. Hair, Jr., C.B. Ragland, and K.E. Schimmel. 2013. Ethics, Corporate Social Responsibility, and Sustainability Education in AACSB Undergraduate and Graduate Marketing Curricula: A Benchmark Study. *Journal of Marketing Education* 35 (2): 129–140.

Tilbury, D., and A. Ryan. 2011. Today Becomes Tomorrow: Re-thinking Business Practice, Education and Learning in the Context of Sustainability. *Journal of Global Responsibility* 2 (2): 137–150.

TOMS. 2018. Improving Lives. Accessed September 26, 2018. https://www.toms.co.uk/improving-lives.

Tormo-Carbó, G., V. Oltra, E. Seguí-Mas, and K. Klimkiewicz. 2016. How Effective Are Business Ethics/CSR Courses in Higher Education? *Procedia-Social and Behavioral Sciences* 228: 567–574.

Part I

People, Responsibility and Entrepreneurship

2

Engaging Successful Migrant Entrepreneurs in Socially Responsible Causes: A Case from Sweden

Besrat Tesfaye and Anders Lundström

2.1   Introduction

Corporate Social Responsibility (CSR) has traditionally focused on ethical issues and practices in large corporations which is also reflected in mainstream research. In more recent years, however, there has been a growing demand for accountability for all business enterprises, irrespective of their size of operations, with regard to their impacts on society (Carroll 2000). This can be observed in the policies and practices aimed at improving the engagement and performance of CSR in SMEs (Zadek 2002; European Commission 2001) as well as a shift in research on CSR toward a more practice-oriented agenda (Garriga and Melé 2004; Aguinis and Glavas 2012). This development has drawn attention to the

B. Tesfaye (✉)
Department of Social Sciences, Södertörn University,
Stockholm, Sweden
e-mail: besrat.tesfaye@sh.se

A. Lundström
Institute of Innovative Entrepreneurship—IPREG, Stockholm, Sweden

© The Author(s) 2019   **15**
F. Farache et al. (eds.), *Responsible People*, Palgrave Studies in Governance,
Leadership and Responsibility, https://doi.org/10.1007/978-3-030-10740-6_2

significance of SMEs in socio-economic development and their contribution to the welfare of the wider society in which they are located. The demands are accentuated in challenging situations of national or local significance calling for social responsibility (Carroll 2000).

In 2014, 81,000 new migrants entered Sweden. In 2015, the number had increased to 163,000 individuals. The number of asylum seekers has been decreasing since then and had dropped to approximately 29,000 in 2016. Asylum seekers are not the only migrants hoping for a better future in Sweden. During this period, more than 9000 individuals outside the EU/EES had applied for a work permit in Sweden. Nevertheless, coupled with a labor market with high levels of unemployment among migrants, the recent inflow of new migrants, that is individuals who have been granted a permanent residence and work permit, is a major challenge for Swedish society. Currently, there is a general concern that the process of labor market integration of migrants may be too slow. Data on the labor market integration of migrants supports these views (Liebig 2007; Statistics Sweden 2017). The data on migrants who were granted a permanent residence and work permit in the year 2000 shows that only 43% of the men and 26% of the women had entered the labor market by 2005. By 2012 only 50% of the women in this group had employment. Apart from the humanitarian issues involved, a rapid entry is of greatest importance for achieving a wider societal integration. Barslund et al. (2017) show a link between a slow entry into the labor market and a slower economic and social integration of new migrants.

At present, much effort is made to facilitate a rapid entry of new migrants into the labor market through employment or self-employment. For individuals aspiring to start their own businesses, for example, the Swedish Public Employment Services Agency offers a variety of assistance programs including internship, business start-up courses, advisory services and mentor support, network services, and follow-up consultancy. An effective implementation of these programs calls for dialogue and collaboration among different actors and sectors in society. The business community as a source of entrepreneurial skills and social capital has a vital role in this process. Of particular importance are successful migrant entrepreneurs (SuMEs) with experiences of migrating and entrepreneurship.

Most migrant entrepreneurs operate small companies and share the informal and non-structured character of CSR practices in SMEs. There is some concern that the SMEs, for example, the SuMEs, may lack opportunities to engage in CSR activities that concern broader societal issues such as the integration of new migrants. The question is how to create opportunities for SMEs to engage in socially responsible activities. We summarize and analyze experiences from two interconnected projects that aimed at making it easier for SMEs to engage in the process of different forms of entry and integration of new migrants in the labor market. The term new migrant, which is the target of the project, refers to an individual who has received a residence and work permit in Sweden and is in the process of entering the labor market. SuMEs can play an important role in facilitating a rapid entry of newcomers into the labor market through entrepreneurship and self-employment because of their success as entrepreneurs and personal experiences as migrants. Successful entrepreneurs are perceived to be credible role models for nascent entrepreneurs (Shapero and Sokol 2000; Bosma et al. 2012). Nevertheless, empirical research is still lacking (Bosma et al. 2012). SuMEs can be credible role models that precipitate entrepreneurial activities among new migrants. Experiences from ethnic entrepreneurship further indicate that co-ethnic entrepreneurs play an important part in facilitating the rapid entry of new migrants in the labor market (Portes and Zhou 1996). Some migrants share the experiences of migrating and starting a new company and a new life in a new country. These experiences are best understood and communicated by those that have personally experienced a migration process. Migrant entrepreneurs with experiences of migrating and successful entrepreneurship can, therefore, be an important bridge to the labor market by sharing their personal experiences and knowledge of the culture and institutions of Swedish society as well as facilitating the access to social capital and networks. For established migrant entrepreneurs, the connection with newcomers may have advantages beyond social responsibility in that they may access unique skills which may not be available on the market or have access to entrepreneurial capital (Firkin 2001) of the newcomers to settle in their communities, and strengthen their unique images.

The remaining part of this chapter is organized as follows: First, there is a brief overview of the literature. This is followed by a short discussion of our methodology. The last section begins with a short description of the process of entry of new migrants into the labor market and the constraints faced by these individuals as a background to the appeal for CSR and the initiative to engage the SMEs in the integration of new migrants. The section is then devoted to an analysis and discussion of the lessons learned. In closing, our results are discussed with a view to the underlying research questions and future research.

2.2 Literature

Our study draws upon the theories of entrepreneurship and CSR in the context of migrants. In the literature, there is no consensus on the role of entrepreneurship in self-employment and the integration of migrants. Proportionally, a higher number of migrants start and operate their own business and are self-employed. At present, much policy effort is made to encourage and support new migrants to start businesses and create opportunities for self-employment. This makes entrepreneurship a useful framework to employ in exploring opportunities for intervention in the processes of entrepreneurial entry into the labor market.

CSR is useful in understanding the perceptions, motivations, and limitations of CSR practices among SMEs.

2.2.1 Entrepreneurship

There is little consensus with regard to the definition and measurements of the concept of entrepreneurship. Nevertheless, there is an extensive literature in entrepreneurship originating in different disciplinary traditions and definitions (Hérbert and Link 1989). A large proportion of this literature is devoted to what entrepreneurs are, what they do and how they differ from other economic actors (Schumpeter 1934; Kirzner 1997; McClelland 1962; Shane and Venkataraman 2000). In this view, entrepreneurs, whether individuals, groups, firms, etc., are specialized in identifying opportunities for profitably commercializing innovations. Opportunity recognition is commonly instantiated by a new venture, often a new company. Therefore, the entrepreneur is usually defined as the creator of a new company (Gartner 1988). It follows that the performance of the entrepreneur is defined by the performance of the company (venture). Entrepreneurs may initiate and continue to operate their businesses. The boundary between entrepreneurs and managers thus tends to be blurred. Moreover, entrepreneurial performance is not easily detached from that of the company (Sarasvathy et al. 2013).

In this study, we define entrepreneurs as those individuals who start-up and operate their own companies. Migrant entrepreneurs are individuals with foreign background (at least one of their parents or the entrepreneurs themselves are born outside Sweden) that have started up and operate a viable (successful) business. The concept of migrant entrepreneurship is complex and difficult to define. First, migrant and ethnic entrepreneurship are often used interchangeably. Second, migrants are a very heterogeneous group of individuals. They come from different political and socio-economic backgrounds and have diverging experiences of migration: some are refugees or asylum seekers, others are family members, yet others migrate for studies, job opportunities, and so on. Some are temporary residents, others intend to settle permanently in their host countries. Some are newcomers, others have been incorporated into society or were born in the host countries. Third, the official definitions of migrants and ethnic groups (minorities) vary widely among host countries.

Almost all migrant entrepreneurs (94%) that are included in our study were born outside Sweden. At some point in the years 2008–2013, these individuals participated in an annual Swedish competition for awards for "SuMEs" that is organized by IFS (International Entrepreneur Association in Sweden, see www.ifs.a.se). All participants in the competition have been appraised by professionals and considered to be successful. These companies were still operating in the market during 2016/2017.

Entrepreneurial processes are embedded in political, economic, and social contexts that may determine the structure of entrepreneurial opportunities in a society, how these emerge, how, when and by whom these opportunities are exploited and why some economic actors (and not others) exploit these opportunities (Welter 2011). Policy instruments are employed to encourage/discourage entrepreneurial activities in society (Lundström and Stevenson 2005). These interventions are often directed toward disadvantaged groups such as women and migrants. In Sweden, for instance, there is a wide range of policy tools, including tailored courses, internship, mentoring programs, and consultancy services in various languages that are intended to boost entrepreneurship and self-employment among new migrants (Kremel 2017). The small- and medium-size enterprises (SMEs) are a case in point in this context. In addition, SMEs are strongly embedded in the local communities in which they operate and can mediate social capital to new migrants. However, there is very little knowledge on how and to what extent SMEs engage in socially responsible activities such as the integration of new migrants. In this study, we present experiences from two interconnected projects employed in engaging SMEs in the integration of new migrants and discuss the lesson we learned with a view to future research and practice.

Migrant Entrepreneurship—Necessity or Opportunity?

The role of entrepreneurship in the economic and social integration of migrants has been widely discussed (Kremel 2017; Rath and Eurofound 2011; Hjerm 2004; Collins 2003; Saxenian 2001; Kloosterman 2010; Abbasian 2000; Najib 1999; Aldrich and Waldinger 1990). Some researchers suggest that entrepreneurship can be a "golden opportunity" for migrants (Ram and Barrett 2000). This view is commonly supported by the proportionately high number of migrant entrepreneurs in relation to the native-born as well as success stories such as Silicon Valley (Saxenian 2001). Sweden is no exception in this respect. Entrepreneurs with a foreign background stand for roughly 15% of all entrepreneurs (Swedish Agency for Economic and Regional Growth 2014). In total, these entrepreneurs employ over 200,000 individuals (Efendic et al. 2015). Nevertheless, some researchers argue that entrepreneurship is not an effective mechanism for integration. Light and Gold (2000), for example, state that migrants start their own businesses in spite of the multiplicity of constraints they face because of necessity and remain small and unprofitable. Furthermore, international research indicates failure rates among migrant firms to be higher than among the local-born. The vast majority of mainstream small businesses, that is migrant businesses, tend to remain small at the lower end of the market and may not generate enough income (Rath and Eurofound 2011). Yet, established migrant businesses are believed to be a seedbed for entrepreneurship among new migrants.

Research has identified a large number of constraints originating in the liabilities of newness (Stinchcombe 1965; Waldinger 1993). Migrants may circumvent these constraints by allying themselves to established migrants, for example starting their businesses in ethnic enclaves (Waldinger et al. 1990). The ethnic enclave theory suggests that new migrants may be able to capitalize on the resources, skills, social capital and networks of established migrant entrepreneurs. The research on entrepreneurship in ethnic enclaves (and ethnic entrepreneurship) is largely based on the experiences from large ethnic concentrations such as the Korean, Chinese and Cuban migrants.

In Sweden, there are large concentrations of multiethnic populations, in particular in the suburbs. But ethnic enclaves resembling those in the United States are very uncommon. Nevertheless, the experiences from ethnic enclaves imply that established migrants with their own experiences of migration and entrepreneurship can play an important role in facilitating the rapid entry of new migrants into entrepreneurship and the labor market. However, there is little knowledge about the experiences of interaction of migrant entrepreneurs with new migrants entering the labor market through entrepreneurship and self-employment. In general, the involvement of migrant entrepreneurs in socially responsible causes received very little attention. The idea underpinning our approach is that the smaller businesses can transmit their entrepreneurial skills and experiences to new migrants, for example through mentorship and counseling. SuME can be of particular importance because of their experiences of migration and entrepreneurship.

2.2.2 Corporate Social Responsibility and SMEs

There is a large body of literature on corporate social responsibility (Carroll 1994; Garriga and Melé 2004; Aguinis and Glavas 2012). Nevertheless, knowledge gaps in important areas still exist, in particular socially responsible practices of smaller business and CSR in the context of entrepreneurship (Kechiche and Soarnot 2012; Morsing and Perrini 2009; Perrini 2006; Azmat 2010). It is important to understand CSR practices in SMEs because these have a profound impact on societies. Approximately 99% of all businesses are SMEs. A study of European SMEs, for instance, indicates that more than 50% of them are involved in CSR activities (CERFE Group 2001; European Commission 2002). Some researchers posit that the experiences of CSR in the context of SMEs differ from that of large firms and thus theories derived from these experiences may not be adequate for studying SMEs (Kechiche and Soparnot 2012).

Santos (2011), for instance, observes that SMEs prioritize CSR activities that are simple, cheap, visible, and commonly located in the local communities. Furthermore, the study indicated SMEs' view of CSR to be instrumental with a strong focus on benefits and gains such as higher status in the local community. Spence and Rutherford (2003) found the personal perceptions of the entrepreneurs (managers), social capital, and their networks to be important drivers of CSR in SMEs. However, their priorities and practices are not very well understood (Morsing and Perrini 2009).

Table 2.1 Data collection

Sources of data	Data collection	Comments
Successful migrant entrepreneurs	Telephone interviews	Total population: 165 Contacted: 109 No of respondents: 88 Response rate: 52% Non-responses: (a) refusals, unable: 21 and (b) 59 could not be contacted
Entrepreneurs in focus-groups	Notes from focus-group interviews (workshops and group discussions)	Participants: 25 successful entrepreneurs in 4 cities
Entrepreneurs and new migrants	Protocols and feedback from participants	414 matching meetings in three cities

2.3 Methodology

The data underlying the case presentation is based on documents, telephone interviews, focus-group seminars and matching events. The sources of data, the data collection method, and the outcome are summarized in Table 2.1. First, a research group set out to map and analyze SuMEs across Sweden. This is a challenge because there is no ethnic register in Sweden. Therefore, it is difficult to identify migrant entrepreneurs or access data on their performance. Against this background, we primarily focus on a population of migrant entrepreneurs that have previously been recognized as successful entrepreneurs, either as candidates or winners of a regional and national competition for The Pioneer of the Year or The New Entrepreneur of the Year awards.

The Pioneer of the Year award is given to a migrant entrepreneur that has started up a high-impact company that introduces innovative ideas to the market and contributes to national growth and has been running for at least five years. The Entrepreneur of the Year is an entrepreneur that has been running a company less than five years and has managed to start-up a new viable business operation. Both these categories of entrepreneurs have strong social capital and broad networks. They are well grounded in the institutional and cultural contexts of entrepreneurship. These are highly relevant qualities of existing migrant entrepreneurs that can be valuable resources for new migrants in establishing themselves as entrepreneurs in the labor market.

2.3.1 Telephone Interviews

During this phase, we had a joint project with IFS, an organization which has been assisting entrepreneurs with foreign backgrounds for many years and which is responsible for the award competition. We were able to access a register of migrant entrepreneurs that over the years have participated in the annual competition for the Pioneer Entrepreneur of the Year and/or the New Entrepreneur of the Year. Both projects are operated by IFS. SuMEs across Sweden could therefore be identified and contacted. We started the first project in early 2016 with the purpose of investigating and analyzing the involvement and/or interest of SuMEs in participating in activities to support the integration of new migrants. We formed a research group together with researchers from Linköping University and contacted a professional telecommunication market company to help us with the telephone-based survey.

During the spring of 2016, telephone interviews with 88 SuMEs were conducted (Fig. 2.2). 15 attempts to contact each entrepreneur were made before it was considered impossible to interview that entrepreneur. If we were able to reach them, then the most common answer from them was that we should try to reach them again later on. Twenty-one entrepreneurs were unwilling to participate in the project. In a couple of cases, it was not possible to talk to the entrepreneurs because of illness. Questions were asked concerning various aspects of the entrepreneurs and their companies including background, connections to their countries of origin, their entrepreneurial experiences, the state of their firms in figures and demography such as age, size, sector, and gender.

Focus-Group Interviews

Following the telephone interviews, a focus-group study was conducted. The focus-group interviews were conducted as seminars, small workshops and concluding group discussions. The main points from each part were documented as notes. These seminars took place in four cities. On average, 10–15 entrepreneurs participated in each city. The main idea was to get a deeper understanding of their role in the different local communities and their potential interest in playing an active role in the integration process of new migrants. Each focus-group interview was documented and analyzed.

Matching Events

The outcomes of these interviews were used when constructing a second project concerning so-called winning match events. This project was carried out during the fall of 2016 and the early spring of 2017. In brief, it was about creating matching events in three different cities. In each event, we matched a SuME with a new migrant for a meeting lasting 30 minutes. In total, there were 415 such meetings in the project. The summaries from each meeting provide an overview of the main result of the meeting. The meeting schedule was constructed with the help of a data program taking into account aspects such as gender, education, the main interests of the entrepreneurs as well as the new migrants, and the competencies of new migrants. In the following section, we present a short overview of the process of the entry of migrants into the labor market as a background for the initiative to develop a CSR interactive platform for SMEs. Following this, we summarize our experiences in developing the platform.

2.4 The Process of Entry of Migrants into the Labor Market

The initial phase of the integration process is important because it has an impact on when, how and where the migrants enter the labor market and integrate in Swedish society. Research has indicated that the variation in the capacity of the host nations to rapidly integrate new migrants into the labor market is associated with the level of economic

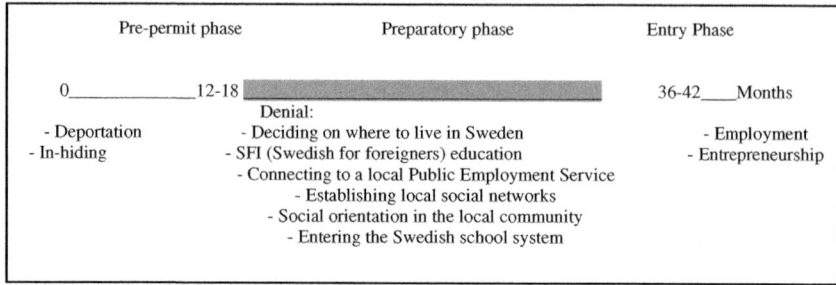

Fig. 2.1 Labor market entry process in Sweden

and social integration of migrants (Barslund et al. 2017). The experiences of the integration process also have an impact on migrants' opportunities, skills, and motivations for self-employment and entrepreneurship of the migrants. The process of labor market integration can be divided into three phases: pre-permit, preparatory, and entry (Fig. 2.1).

2.4.1 Pre-permit Phase

This phase begins when a migrant arrives in Sweden and continues until the asylum application has been approved. The processing of such an application can, on average, take 12–18 months. This, in itself, is a big problem since individuals cannot formally start learning Swedish or apply for a job or start a company with very few exceptions during this pending period. During this phase, the Swedish Migration Agency is responsible for the migrants. The Agency decides, for example, on the placement of the new migrants in different communities and housing arrangements.

2.4.2 Preparatory Phase

Once the Migration Agency reaches a decision to grant the application, the responsibility for the individual is transferred to a local Public Employment Services Agency. New migrants constitute the red part on the integration timeline in Fig. 2.1. New migrants who are granted approval of their applications are allowed to follow SFI courses (Swedish for new migrants). During this phase, the new migrant is expected to learn the Swedish language, develop her skill and networks required for entry into the labor market through employment or self-employment/entrepreneurship. There are, of course, many people who will learn and speak Swedish during their first part of the process whereas other individuals will have difficulties in learning the language even after completed courses. Learning the Swedish language is an important step, but entry into the labor market will still be difficult.

New migrants need to settle in their new or their present local community. Although some constraints exist, new migrants can decide to settle in the same local communities where they have been placed by the Immigration Agency or move to other communities or cities in Sweden.

2.4.3 Entry Phase

Many efforts are made by the Public Employment Services Agency and other actors such as the authorities for SFI education to facilitate the integration of new migrants. The mission of the establishment program offered by the Public Employment Service Agency is mainly to rapidly integrate new migrants into the Swedish labor market and/or into the school system. Each new migrant is registered in the program for two years. Nevertheless, the success rate has not been encouraging. Only one out of three participants in the program is likely to be established on the Swedish labor market 90 days after the completion of the two-year program. On the other hand, many young new migrants have been integrated in the Swedish school system. Another major effort involves projects, including business start-up courses, which are intended to facilitate entrepreneurship among new migrants. The ambition of the projects has been to establish a platform for interaction between successful entrepreneurs and new migrants during the preparatory phase in order for the relationships to develop into possible entry into the labor market.

2.5   Engaging the SuMEs in Creating Interactive Platforms for CSR Activities

As indicated in prior research, SMEs' engagement in CSR activities is determined by the entrepreneurs' perceptions, views and values as well as the capacity of their businesses (Spence and Rutherfoord 2003). An overview of the SuMEs in the study and their companies is presented in Sect. 2.4.1.

2.5.1 The Successful Migrant Entrepreneurs and Their Companies

The average age of the entrepreneurs that participated in the telephone interviews is 44 years. On average, the entrepreneurs have lived more than 20 years in Sweden, normally in the communities where they operate their present businesses. About 60% had some kind of post-secondary schooling. 96% responded that they were personally involved in the start-up of their present business, 50% of whom as sole entrepreneurs. 60% had started more than one business. The longer the migrant entrepreneur has lived in Sweden, the more likely it is that s/he will start multiple businesses. They have been operating their existing companies for 10 years on average.

Most of the companies operated by the entrepreneurs are found in the service sector. 90% of the companies were started after the turn of the millennium. The average annual turnover of the companies was approximately 2.5 million euros. 17% had more than 20 employees. Approximately 10% reported that they had employees in other countries. The companies are locally embedded with limited export. They primarily serve their local markets. 40% reported that they import from other countries, 50% of the entrepreneurs operating the businesses had connections with enterprises in their country of origin.

The entrepreneurs largely perceive themselves as active community members. A large proportion of these entrepreneurs said that they were involved in mentoring activities, including informal mentoring of new migrants. Many had previous experiences of trainees and/or some kind of short-term placement employees. The entrepreneurs indicated that they were positive and interested in CSR. Roughly nine out of ten entrepreneurs were prepared to act as a mentor to new migrants and offer these some sort of temporary employment such as trainee posts. Second, two out of three entrepreneurs responded that the local environment was of great importance measured by a four alternative ordinal scale procedure summarizing the two positive alternatives. The successful entrepreneurs also perceived that they had a great influence in their local community. We became convinced from the results of the focus-group seminars that the interest was indeed high among the SuMEs. At the same time, the entrepreneurs emphasized the importance of win-win collaborations whereby their companies and the new migrants benefit.

2.5.2 Developing the Interactive Platform

The first task in the process of developing an interactive platform was to identify and establish contacts with the group of SMEs targeted in the project. The second step was to form the interactive platform followed by matching events whereby the SMEs hold personal meetings with individual new migrants. Finally, the experiences are summarized for input for future course of action (Fig. 2.2). An important task in building the platform has been the telephone interviews in combination with

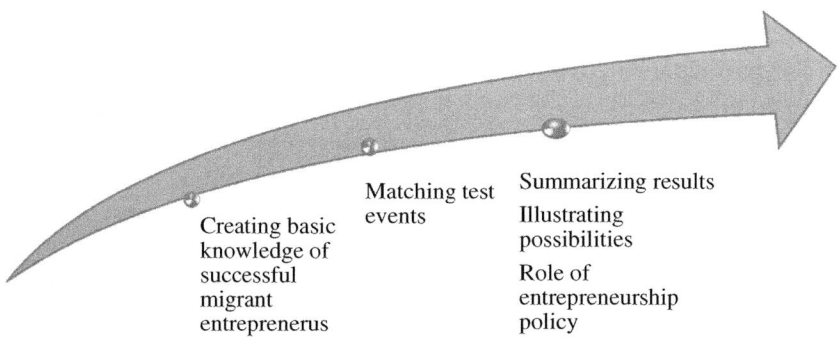

Fig. 2.2 Phases of platform development activities

the focus-group study generated knowledge about the specific profile of the SuMEs, their views and involvement in supporting new migrants, and the type of resources that may become available through their collaboration. In particular, the focus-group study revealed the fears and expectations of the migrant entrepreneurs in future collaboration. For example, the entrepreneurs emphasized the need for matching platforms facilitating intensive meetings with the new migrants, a platform which did not exist at the time.

The Matching Events

Based on the results from the interviews and focus-group studies, the researchers forwarded a number of proposals on how SuMEs could be involved in a CSR process with new migrants. During these interviews, the entrepreneurs had emphasized the importance of well-planned and intensive matching meetings on an individual level which they thought did not exist today. This led to the conclusion that a new type of platform for interaction between entrepreneurs and new migrants was required. Acting on the proposals of the researchers and the migrant entrepreneurs, a matching platform was initiated in three different Swedish cities.

Based on the insights from our research, a computer-based system with several variables for a matching program was created in collaboration with IFS. Each meeting between an entrepreneur and a new migrant was planned to last approximately 30 minutes. We developed a specific computer-based matching system to meet the requirements of the participants. In total, 414 meetings were carried out during the three matching test events which were conducted. Of the more than 200 participants in the meetings, roughly 25% were entrepreneurs. Furthermore, 40% of the new migrants were women.

The number of new migrants participating in these activities was three times the number of entrepreneurs. This will be mirrored in the number of possible meetings. Each new migrant was supposed to have at least three meetings, meaning that each entrepreneur had roughly three times that number of meetings. In the end, this means that the number of possible choices was much higher for entrepreneurs. One could argue that there ought to be as many entrepreneurs as new migrants. This was not a practical solution since the areas from which we could get interested entrepreneurs are limited while the number of possible new migrants is always much higher. Therefore, it would be interesting for the future to also involve entrepreneurs born in Sweden, meaning that a huge part of the local private sector should be involved.

We are aware that an initial meeting is only the start of a process of creating collaboration between two individuals who have not met before. One expected positive outcome of the matching events is an agreement between the matching individuals for a second meeting. This was the outcome in two out of three meetings. More than one out of every ten meetings resulted in a concrete collaboration between the two participants which was more than we expected. It is to be noted that the new migrants are slightly more positive concerning the outcomes of the meetings than the entrepreneurs. New migrants should be more active in the follow-up process than the entrepreneurs. On the other hand, it is to be remembered, which is mentioned above, that, on average, each entrepreneur had more meetings than each new migrant, so the entrepreneurs have more cases to consider and choose from.

2.6   Summary and Discussion

2.6.1 Summary

The entrepreneurs in the study have a positive attitude toward socially responsible practices and are willing to engage in initiatives that contribute to the welfare of society in broad terms. As a rule, they tend to engage in socially responsible activities initiated in the communities in which they operate. They perceive their role as successful entrepreneurs in local communities as important, for example, as drivers of CSR issues. Their motives to engage in socially responsible activities in the local community include social priorities, self-interest, and business (subsistence) motives. First, they perceive their engagement as an act of good citizenship. Second, they hope that their CSR activities will strengthen their social standing in their local communities. Third, they perceive their engagement as an opportunity for accessing scarce or unique skills. In terms of commitment to the public CSR initiatives, they emphasize instrumental motives. The entrepreneurs put much emphasis on a "win-win" collaboration in CSR initiatives which implies that they expect tangible returns on their efforts, for example, in terms of cost-effective recruitment or compensation for extraordinary input in time and effort to support new migrants.

The high turnout in support of the matching projects for labor market integration of new migrants may be linked to the social status as nominees for the Pioneers/Entrepreneur of the year. Affinity for the new migrant may not be the only explanation. For example, the immediate positive outcomes of the matching events suggest that interactive platforms can be a useful arena for effective collaboration with socially responsible entrepreneurs operating SMEs. The outcome from the first matching event was that approximately 80% of the cases had decided to take their collaboration to the next level. This promises a high rate of success (compared to our expectation). Perhaps more importantly, in conducting the interviews, engaging the entrepreneurs in discussions about the challenges of integration and their own significance in the integration process is an effective way of raising CSR awareness and sense of responsibility. The focus-group discussions, for example, initially focused on various challenges in participating in public CSR initiatives, such as institutional constraints, their expectations, and the effectiveness of the projects but tended to increasingly focus on social responsibility and the need for engagement of business organizations in the labor market integration of new migrants. In this sense, we can draw a tentative conclusion that the initiative was successful in engaging about 100 SMEs in the issues of social responsibility.

The initiative aimed at engaging SMEs in social responsibility has indicated promising results as is illustrated by the positive response of the entrepreneurs invited. The strong response to the appeal implied in the initiative suggests that there is a need to support SMEs' engagement in CSR activities, in particular in broader societal issues. Initiatives emanating from local communities are more likely to appeal to SMEs than national-level projects. How these interactions, mentorship or opportunities for practices in the SMEs impact the entrepreneurial intentions and labor market integration of new migrants is an important issue for future research.

2.6.2 Discussion

Our study draws upon experiences gained from engaging migrant entrepreneurs in the SMEs' sector in CSR projects addressing integration issues. The focus is on successful entrepreneurs with a foreign background in the SMEs' sector. Furthermore, the study considers engagement of entrepreneurs only in external CSRs projects. Despite these limitations, our study contributes to research issues that need to be addressed by future research as well as policy. In this section, we briefly discuss the lessons we learned and the implication this may have for research on CSR in SMEs.

A cursory review of prior research reveals that only a small proportion of the existing literature on CSR addresses the context of SMEs (Aquinis and Glawas 2012; Kechiche and Soparnot 2012; Morsing and Perrini 2009; Perrini 2006). Much less research has been done on the micromechanisms of CSR in SMEs. Our study contributes to this discussion by bringing to the forefront the issue of the microfoundations of CSR in SMEs. For example, our focus on migrant entrepreneurs raises the issue of entrepreneurial linkage between background variables and CSR priorities, i.e., do entrepreneurs with migrant experiences prioritize social issues addressing migrants/integration? Or, do women entrepreneurs tend to prioritize social issues relating to women? One argument for engaging SuMEs in labor market integration issues, particularly through entrepreneurship, is their potential as credible role models for new migrants. Credible role models are believed to be an important influence on entrepreneurial intentions (Shapero and Sokol 2000; Bosma et al. 2012). However, there is very little empirical research on this subject (Bosma et al. 2012). The high turnout among successful migrant entrepreneurs to the matching events and their willingness to continue with further engagement observed in our study might suggest a link between background and choice of CSR issues to pursue. A comparison to a population of local-born entrepreneurs in the SMEs sector is needed in order to answer this question.

A second lesson of relevance for CSR studies in the SME sector relates to the issue of policy/public initiatives to raise awareness and engagement in businesses. There is a wide range of cause-based initiatives aimed at CSR in SMEs at all levels of society (Nejati and Amran 2009; European Commission 2001). The multiplicity of initiatives indicates that there is a need to support CSR activities in SMEs. Our study indicates that public initiatives can positively impact on the engagement of SMEs in CSR activities. Nevertheless, these initiatives seldom address the heterogeneity of SMEs. By focusing on a population of entrepreneurs with similar backgrounds and social positions, our study attempted to mitigate some of the problems (methodological, practical) of heterogeneity. Against this background, standardized initiatives aimed at CSR in SMEs that are common may not be very effective. Input from further research is highly needed.

A third issue that the study raises is that of measurement of the output of CSR initiatives. Our attempt to provide an overview of the outcome from the projects in a short-term perspective generates some indicators, for example, the number of participants, resources such as number of hours, events, and further engagements. The lack of measurements impacts on the commitment to CSR engagements because of the difficulty in evaluating outcomes.

In conclusion, our study illustrates the centrality of the individual entrepreneur in CSR in SMEs. The emphasis on multiple outcomes of CRS activities, i.e., good citizenship, entrepreneurial leadership (in the local community), and good management practice (subsistence of the business) observed in the study locates CSR in SME at the nexus of social responsibility, entrepreneurship, and management in SMEs. These concepts are intertwined and inseparable.

References

Abbasian, Saeid. 2000. Residential Patterns, Entrepreneurship and Integration (in Swedish). Unit for Human Geography, University of Gothenburg.

Aguinis, Herman, and Ante A. Glavas. 2012. What We Know and Don't Know About Corporate Social Responsibility: A Review and Research Agenda. *Journal of Management* 38: 932–968.

Aldrich, Howard, and Roger Waldinger. 1990. Ethnicity and Entrepreneurship. *Annual Review of Sociology* 15: 111–135.

Azmat, Fara. 2010. Exploring Social Responsibility of Immigrant Entrepreneurs: Do Home Country Contextual Factors Play a Role? *European Management Journal* 28: 377–386.

Barslund, Mikkel, Matthias Busse, Karolien Lenaerts, Lars Ludolph, and Renman Vilde. 2017. Labor Market Integration of Refugees: A Comparative Survey of Bosnians in Five EU Countries. *Mercator Dialogue on Asylum and Migration*.

Bosma, Niels, Jolanda Hessels, Veronique Schutjens, Mirjam Van Praag, and Ingrid Verheul. 2012. Entrepreneurship and Role Models. *Journal of Economic Psychology* 33 (2): 410–424.

Carroll, Archie B. 1994. Social Issues in Management Research. *Business and Society* 33: 5–29.

Carroll, Archie B. 2000. Ethical Challenges for Business in the New Millennium: Corporate Social Responsibility and Models of Management Morality. *Business Ethics Quarterly* 10 (1): 33–42.

CERFE Group. 2001. Action Research in Corporate Citizenship Among European Small and Medium Enterprises. CERFE Laboratory, Rome, Italy.

Collins, Jock. 2003. Cultural Diversity and Entrepreneurship: Policy Responses to Immigrant Entrepreneurs in Australia. *Entrepreneurship and Regional Development* 15 (2): 137–149.

Efendic, Nadim, Fredrik C. Andersson, and Karl Wennberg. 2015. Growth in First and Second Generation Immigrant Firms in Sweden. *International Small Business Journal* 34: 1028–1052.

European Commission. 2001. *Green Paper: Promoting a European Framework for Corporate Social Responsibility*. Brussels: European Commission.

European Commission. 2002. *European SMEs and Social and Environmental Responsibility*. Belgium: Enterprise Publications.

Firkin, Patrick. 2001. Entrepreneurial Capital: A Resource-Based Conceptualization of the Entrepreneurial Process. Working Paper No. 1, Labor Market Dynamics Research Program.

Garriga, Elizabeth, and Doménec Melé. 2004. Corporate Social Responsibility Theories: Mapping the Territory. *Journal of Business Ethics* 55: 51–71.

Gartner, William. 1988. Who Is an Entrepreneur? Is the Wrong Question. *Entrepreneurship Theory and Practice*. University of Baltimore, Educational Foundation.

Hérbert, Robert F., and Albert N. Link. 1989. In Search of the Meaning of Entrepreneurship. *Small Business Economics* 1: 39–49.

Hjerm, M. 2004. Immigrant Entrepreneurship in the Swedish Welfare. *Sociology* 38 (4): 739–756.

Kechiche, Amina, and Richard Soparnot. 2012. CSR Within SMEs: Literature Review. *International Business Research* 5 (7): 97.

Kirzner, Israel. 1997. Entrepreneurial Discovery and the Competitive Market Process: An Austrian Approach. *Journal of Economic Literature* 35: 60–85.

Kloosterman, Robert C. 2010. Matching Opportunities with Resources: A Framework for Analyzing Migrant Entrepreneurship from a Mixed Embeddedness Perspective. *Entrepreneurship and Regional Development* 22: 25–45.

Kremel, Anna. 2017. Heterogeneity in the Level and Handling of the Liability of Newness. Female and Immigrant Entrepreneurs Need for and Use of Business Advisory Service. PhD diss., School of Business, Society and Engineering, Mälardalen University, Sweden.

Liebig, Thomas. 2007. The Labor Market Integration of Immigrants in Denmark. OECD Social, Employment and Migration. Working Papers No. 50.

Light, Ivan, and Steven J. Gold. 2000. *Ethnic Economies*. San Diego: Academic Press.

Lundström, Anders, and Lois Stevenson. 2005. *Entrepreneurship Policy: Theory and Practice, International Studies in Entrepreneurship*. New York: Springer.

McClelland, David. 1962. *The Achieving Society*. Princeton, NJ: Van Nostrand Co.

Morsing, Mette, and Francesco Perrini. 2009. CSR in SMEs: Do SMEs Matter for the CSR Agenda. *Business Ethics: A European Review* 18 (1): 1–6.

Najib, B. Ali. 1999. Immigrant Business—Some Basic Facts (in Swedish). *SOU 1999:49*.

Nejati, Mehran, and Azlan Amran. 2009. Corporate Social Responsibility and SMEs: Exploratory Study on Motivations from a Malaysian Perspective. *Business Strategy Series* 10 (5): 259–265.

Perrini, Francesco. 2006. SMEs and CSR Theory: Evidence and Implications from an Italian Perspective. *Journal of Business Ethics* 67: 305–316.

Portes, Alejandro, and Min Zhou. 1996. Self-Employment and the Earnings of Immigrants. *American Sociological Review* 61 (2): 219–230.

Ram, Monder, and George A. Barrett. 2000. Ethnicity and Enterprise. In *Enterprise and Small Business: Principles, Practice and Policy*, ed. Sara Carter and Dylan Jones-Evans. Harlow: Pearson Education Limited.

Rath, Jan, and Eurofound. 2011. *Promoting Ethnic Entrepreneurship in European Cities*. Luxembourg: Publications Office of the European Union.

Santos, Maria. 2011. CSR in SMEs: Strategies, Practices, Motivations and Obstacles. *Social Responsibility Journal* 7 (3): 490–508.

Sarasvathy, Sara, Anil R. Menon, and Graciela Kuechle. 2013. Failing Firms and Successful Entrepreneurs: Serial Entrepreneurship as a Temporal Portfolio. *Small Business Economics* 40 (2): 417–434.

Saxenian, AnnaLee. 2001. The Role of Immigrant Entrepreneurs in New Venture Creation. In *The Entrepreneurship Dynamic*, ed. Claudia B. Schoonhoven and Elaline Romanelli. Stanford: Stanford University Press.

Schumpeter, Joseph. 1934. *Theory of Economic Development: An Inquiry into Profits, Capital, Credit, Interest and the Business Cycle*. New Brunswick, NJ: Transaction Publisher.

Shane, Scott, and Sankaran M. Venkataraman. 2000. The Promise of Entrepreneurship as a Field of Research. *Academy of Management Review* 25 (1): 217–226.

Shapero, Albert, and Lisa Sokol. 2000. The Social Dimension of Entrepreneurship. In *Encyclopedia of Entrepreneurship*, ed. C.A. Sexton Kent and Karl Vesper. Englewood Cliffs, NJ: Prentice Hall.

Spence, Laura, and Robert Rutherfoord. 2003. Small Business and Empirical Perspectives in Business Ethics. *Journal of Business Ethics* 47 (1): 1–5.

Statistics Sweden. 2017. Refugees Entry into the Swedish Labor Market (in Swedish). *Välfärd 2017:3*.

Stinchcombe, L. Arthur. 1965. Social Structures and Organizations. In *Handbook of Organizations*, ed. James G. March. Chicago: Rand McNally.

Waldinger, Roger. 1993. The Two Sides of Ethnic Entrepreneurship. *The International Migration Review* 27 (3): 692–701.

Waldinger, Roger, Robin Ward, and Howard E. Aldrich. 1990. *Ethnic Entrepreneurs: Migrant Business in Industrial Societies*. Newbury Park, CA: Sage.

Welter, Friederike. 2011. Contextualizing Entrepreneurship—Conceptual Challenges and Ways Forward. *Entrepreneurship Theory and Practice* 35 (1): 39–55.

Zadek, Simon. 2002. *Mapping Instruments for Corporate Social Responsibility, Directorate General for Employment and Social Affairs.* Brussels: European Commission.

3

Corporate Family Responsibility as a Driver for Entrepreneurial Success

Gianpaolo Tomaselli

3.1 Introduction

Corporate Social Responsibility (CSR) has been a subject of interest in both political and academic debates for more than a century (from the beginnings of the twentieth century up to present). As a result, CSR is a concept that has many different meanings, interpretations and definitions. In an effort at summarizing the different meanings of CSR, the European Commission defined it as "The responsibility of enterprises for their impacts on society" (European Commission 2011, p. 6). However, CSR concerns a wide range of issues including (among others): the environment; sustainability; human dignity and rights; economic development; the alleviation of global poverty; disease prevention and eradication; and community involvement (Rindova et al. 2005; Pirsch et al. 2007; Kesavan et al. 2013; Tomaselli and Melia 2014). Within these issues, there is one dimension of CSR that is particularly important for companies and it concerns the responsibility

G. Tomaselli (✉)
Marco Vigorelli Foundation, Milan, Italy

© The Author(s) 2019
F. Farache et al. (eds.), *Responsible People*, Palgrave Studies in Governance, Leadership and Responsibility, https://doi.org/10.1007/978-3-030-10740-6_3

towards their human capital. In this respect, one of the most interesting developments of internal CSR is represented by the concept of Corporate Family Responsibility (CFR) which focuses on employees' well-being, Work–Life Balance (WLB) and family-friendly policies (Faldetta 2008).

In the last decade, there has been growing attention by Italian governments to the different ways of rethinking welfare policies, particularly those concerning the promotion and support of families (Chinchilla et al. 2010; Koubova and Buchko 2013). In this respect, the employee's family has been considered a potential stakeholder for companies of all types and across all sectors since it is an important variable for enhancing employee well-being and increasing their productivity and increasing a company's competitive advantage (Osoian et al. 2009). Moreover, these topics are even more crucial in the current social and political context, characterized by economic crisis, scarcity of resources, social needs, globalization, stalling female labour participation and the transformation of the traditional family structure. These changes also involve a growing attention by companies towards employees' (and their families) needs in order to increase—on the one hand—stakeholder value, sales and productivity with a positive impact on return-on-investment (ROI) and cost-reduction (Meyer et al. 2001; Gray 2002; Dex and Smith 2002; Bloom et al. 2011; Yamamoto and Matsuura 2012); while, on the other hand, allowing companies to recruit and retain talents and improve employees' engagement and morale, with positive effects on their performance (Beauregard and Henry 2009; Sirota et al. 2005; Grover and Crooker 1995; Lockwood 2003; Allen 2001; Baughman et al. 2003; Boushey and Glynn 2012; Chinchilla and León Llorente 2011). Moreover, WLB and family-friendly policies are helpful to reduce individual stress and absenteeism in the company (Beauregard and Henry 2009; Sirota et al. 2005). Thus, CFR is a key factor for both large companies and Small and Medium Sized Enterprises (SMEs) since it has a significant impact on a company's performance, improving efficiency and worker productivity, and the revenues generated are higher than the costs of carrying out its implementation (Meyer et al. 2001). In this respect, the concept of CFR is interrelated with the topic concerning the role of people in CSR. Thus, this chapter is relevant to the theme of the book "Responsible People: the Role of the Individual in CSR, Entrepreneurship and Management Education".

This chapter aims to: (i) analyse practical application of CFR in the context of Italian SMEs; and (ii) identify good practice among companies that have successfully implemented CFR policies in their business strategy. The analysis is conducted on SMEs for two main reasons. First, in Italy SMEs represent 95% of the economic system and employ over 81% of workers in the private sector. Second, nowadays SMEs are becoming more interested in providing and sustaining employees' well-being and corporate welfare along with specific policies and measures (including CFR, WLB and family-friendly policies).

The focus is on two main research questions: (i) how can the employee's family (present and future) be considered as a potential stakeholder for the company?; and (ii) what are the motivations that guide companies to implement CFR, WLB and family-friendly policies?

The work is structured as follows: first, the theoretical framework is provided based on key contributions in CFR research. The following sections outline the research design. Then the empirical findings are presented and discussed. The chapter concludes with a discussion of the implications and main limitations of the study.

3.2 Theoretical Framework

The theoretical framework—upon which the research conducted in the chapter is based—is focused on the topics of CFR and WLB as drivers for both employees' well-being and entrepreneurial success. First, a narrative literature review of the main theoretical contributions of CFR and WLB research is provided; second, an analysis of how CFR can be implemented into business strategy is presented, providing some practical examples according to current welfare plans and regulations; finally, practitioner and managerial perspectives of CFR are identified according to available literature.

CFR represents the internal, nuclear dimension of CSR. It is a term coined by the International Center for Work and Family (ICWF) of

IESE Business School (University of Navarra, Spain) which indicates that a company counts on the leaders, culture and policies of flexibility that foster the integration of work, family and personal life. CSR scholarship suggests that CFR is a strategic asset to business management which pays attention to employees' (and their families) well-being and WLF (Faldetta 2008). In this respect, building on Greenhaus et al. (2003) and Clark (2001), CFR and WLB are the extent to which employees are involved in both work and family life and succeed in balancing their professional and personal life with positive effects on their performances.

CFR (as well as CSR) is a driver of social innovation aimed at the sustainability of the company and the stakeholder network in which it is integrated (Perrini and Tencati 2011); moreover, it allows higher female labour participation and helps to increase competitiveness of companies. CFR is based on the relationship between two fundamental pillars of society: work and family. In this view, family is intended as a social and economic resource since family itself is a "company" that produces stability, support, motivation for engagement, and can be a potential driver for both economic and sustainable development (Annoni 2009).

Thus, the existing literature on CFR has been focusing mainly on the balance between work and family life. The existing theory on WLB is divided into two strands: (i) the boundary theory, and (ii) the enrichment theory. According to the boundary theory, the lack of balance is due to an overlap between the two spheres (work and family life) causing a negative impact on employees' quality of life (Chen et al. 2009; Barnett and Gareis 2006). According to the enrichment theory, the balance between work and family-duties produces positive externalities affecting the employee's overall well-being (Rothbard 2001; Grzywacz and Marks 2000; Grzywacz and Bass 2003; Sumer and Knight 2001; Ruderman et al. 2003; Wayne et al. 2004). However, both strands of literature recognize the fact that two spheres (work and family life) are interconnected with each other.

CFR and WLB literature focus on the human capital role for companies. Human capital can be seen either as a resource for production or as a set of single individuals with their own needs, or as an entity of a larger system (the social system) that considers the employees and their relationships inside and outside the company. Specifically, if the perspective is resources-based, the company needs to find the way in which the depletion of resources will be reduced while maintaining a certain level of productivity (for example more flexible working hours to increase productivity). If the perspective is individual-based, the company cares about employees' well-being which impacts on their productivity, engagement and trust. In this case, the implementation of policies assumes not only an instrumental value (more profit and less cost) but also an intrinsic value for the company itself. Finally, if the company assumes a social-network based or relational-based perspective (Donati 2006), it will consider itself and the human capital as entities in connection with each other and the whole stakeholder network (including other people, family, society, the environment and future generations). In this perspective, the company will need to look not only for its profit or the well-being of the single employees, but the broad network of interests in order to increase profit, reduce costs and increase innovative behaviour (with both monetary and non-monetary returns, as well as tangible and intangible ones).

In the research for this chapter, the focus remained on the aforementioned relational approach (Donati 2006; Donati and Prandini 2006; Macchioni 2012) based on the hypothesis that CFR and WLB policies produce positive effects from both the employees' perspective (higher levels of happiness and serenity and less stress) and the employer's perspective (low turnover levels and increased productivity). Specifically, the study design was influenced by Macchioni's (2012) questionnaire that was used in her empirical surveys on WLB application in Italy. However, the questionnaire was integrated with some questions of original elaboration, in order to better understand the origins of companies' commitment to CFR and WLB, as well as the factors and reasons that influence them to carry out these policies.

Literature regarding CFR theories and models has thus been explored, but how can companies practically implement CFR in their business strategy? CFR good practice includes family-friendly and WLF policies aimed at promoting the necessary balance between work and personal/family life (Molteni et al. 2007; Pedrini and Petri 2009).

Companies have different ways and tools to implement CFR in their business practices, according to family welfare plans implemented by governments.

Practical application of CFR include inbound and outbound flexibility policies, flexible working hours (flexitime), part-time, smart working, home working, job sharing, family leave programmes, facilities for mothers, company nurseries, financial and informational support for childcare and eldercare (Walsh 2005; Beauregard and Henry 2009). Table 3.1 lists the main CFR and WLF policies and summarizes their features according to national welfare programmes (this work refers to Italian regulations, however, these measures may be different and vary among countries).

To sum up, CFR allows companies to create flexible and equal opportunity among employees, fosters their commitment to work and their increased satisfaction with a positive effect on companies' competitiveness and sustainability.

The CFR level is determined according to three dimensions: (i) policies; (ii) supervisor support; and (iii) the organizational culture. These aspects affect the ability of employees to reconcile their professional, personal and family life and contribute to enhancing the environment in which the employee works (Duffin et al. 2017). CFR affords employees better physical health, lower absenteeism, higher job performance and availability (van Steenbergen et al. 2007), job satisfaction and higher organizational commitment (Beutell and Witting-Berman 2008). Moreover, this approach also produces economic and profit results: employees are less stressed; they work better and are more productive. Thus, CFR may be considered as a potential driver for entrepreneurial success.

From a practitioner point of view, the services that increase flexibility, without loss of generality, can identify and summarize the practice of WLB according to (i) Care; (ii) Cash; and (iii) Time. From a management point of view, a company with CFR has managers that: (i) make sure every decision made takes people into account; (ii) create flexible and equal opportunity policies and practices; (iii) foster workers' commitment and satisfaction; and (iv) increase the competitiveness and sustainability of the company.

Table 3.1 CFR and WLB policies

Tool	Features
Flexibility policies	Concern both inbound and outbound flexibility policies to the labour market. Inbound flexibility regards entry into the labour market; outbound flexibility refers to those regulations related to dismissal or staff reductions due to a corporate crisis and provides support and help for employees' replacement
Flexible working hours	Allow employees a better organization of both personal and professional life. These policies include the possibility to work without specific time constraints, part-time, smart working, home working, etc.
Part-time	Refers to a reduced amount of hours per day and/or week, month, year. For instance, one employee is allowed to work five days a week 50% of regular working hours, or a few days a week with regular working hours
Smart working/ home working	Is a new approach to corporate organization, in which the individual needs of the employees coexist, in a complementary way, with those of the enterprise. It concerns different aspects regarding flexibility of working hours or spatial-type work, up to corporate welfare programmes in order to facilitate parents' work or engaging in parental assistance
Job sharing	Allows two or more subordinate employees to share the same job position. Both of them take on responsibility for a single job performance
Family leave programmes	Allow employees to make use of particular opportunities for balancing work and family life. These policies are particularly used for supporting family care i.e. working mothers and fathers with young children and/or for eldercare needs of employees While in Italy paternity leaves are allowed in a few specific situations (i.e. mother's death or infirmity, exclusive custody of the child to the father), in other countries (i.e. Sweden) both parents can share subsidized leaves per child as they wish
Paternity leave for mothers/ fathers	Allow working mothers and/or fathers to benefit from maternity/paternity leaves in order to take care of their family and newborn needs for a fixed period of time (as by specific laws which vary among countries—see above)
Company nurseries	Some companies have nurseries inside their buildings which allow working mothers to have their children at their workplace with onsite childcare assistance
Economic support to families	Allows employees to benefit from a series of economic measures to support their families (i.e. economic support for children's education, mobility support, etc.)

3.3   Methodology

This work is based on a qualitative research methodology in which the case study method (Yin 2002) is combined with netnography method (Kozinets 2015). The project has a multi-sectoral approach (companies have different businesses) and the survey is conducted across different regions of Italy (with a prevalence from central and northern Italy). CFR indicators and reports published in Italy (such as Welfareindex PMI, Welfarenet, etc.) were consulted while selecting the five SMEs included in this study.

3.3.1   Data Collection

Research activity was carried out between September 2016 and February 2017. Data were collected in three phases. In the first phase (secondary data collection and research strategy design), a sample of companies to be contacted was identified through non-participant observation of web sources (websites, social media, publications, reports, welfare indexes, etc.). This phase—netnography analysis— was aimed at identifying potential good practices of CFR and WLB in Italy. Subsequently, a database containing 50 Italian companies (SMEs) and their related CFR/WLB policies (collated during early web-based research) was created. This first phase also included defining the interview questions and design (for the second phase). In the second phase (primary data collection), companies included in the database were contacted and those who were interested to participate in this project were interviewed. Data were collected through semi-structured and guided interviews with the companies' CEOs. In the third phase, interviews— which were previously tape-recorded—were transcribed verbatim, translated in English and directly verified by the CEOs involved. Participants expressed their willingness to participate in this study through written agreements via e-mail.

Data were collected through semi-structured interviews with CEOs of the analysed SMEs. During the phase of formulation of questions, the questionnaire produced by Macchioni (2012) was taken as a reference and was integrated with some newly elaborated questions. Although most of the survey questions were based on the aforementioned source, it was decided to implement them with a few other questions in order to better understand; (i) when and how companies started to implement CFR and WLB policies in their business strategies?; (ii) which were the factors and stimulus that convinced them to take advantage of these issues?; and (iii) which were their aims at implementing CFR?

3.3.2 Data Analysis

Data were analysed using a mixed netnography (Kozinetz 2015) and case study methodology (Yin 2002). The netnography approach is particularly suitable for investigating and collecting data from the web and without involving any direct influence of researchers (Kozinetz 2015). The case study method (Yin 2002) seeks to get data from the business sector. It allows collecting qualitative data for one or more contexts and to analyse in-depth any features related to policies implemented, outcomes and measurement of results. Although this approach presents some limitations—such as generalizability of results and scientific rigour (since it is not based on quantitative analysis and/or statistical techniques)—it allows the exhaustive description of business contexts and the ability to distinguish their related facts, opinions and comments (Mari 1994). Moreover, this approach is particularly useful for those studies that are, at the same time, explanatory, explorative and descriptive, as is the case in this work. The combined case study and netnography method strengthens the trustworthiness of the research by allowing the availability of information with differing levels of depth. In this perspective, netnography completes case-based analysis.

The analysed variables include: (i) the meaning of CSR for the surveyed companies; (ii) their attention to employees' well-being, WLB and family-friendly policies; (iii) the CFR policies implemented; and (iv) outcomes and results. The analysis was based on the "relational theory" by Donati (2006) and Donati and Prandini (2006) and empirical research conducted by Macchioni (2012) on WLB and family-friendly policies among Italian companies. This research was based on the hypothesis that these policies produce positive effects on both employees' perspective (for example increasing their happiness and serenity and reducing stress levels) and entrepreneurial perspective (for example low turnover levels and higher productivity).

The relational approach was used since it considers CFR and WLB roles in both managerial, entrepreneurial and employees' perspectives and identifies the positive effects of these variables in increasing workers' well-being, performance and productivity. In this view, the organization does not only look at its profit margin, or the well-being of the single employees, but it considers the broad sphere of interests (increasing profits, reducing costs, increasing innovative behaviours, etc.) and the entire stakeholder network (employees, families, community, environment, etc.), as it emerged from the interviews conducted for this study.

3.4   Case Studies

The five SMEs surveyed in this chapter are Amyko, Berto S.r.l., C.A.T. Progetti, ErgonixART and Tribe Communication. This section provides a brief summary and description of the case studies, including companies' overviews, missions, values and features (with a specific focus on summarizing their CFR practices).

3.4.1 Amyko

Founded in October 2013 by Riccardo Zanini (entrepreneur, today Amyko's COO) and Filippo Scorza (bio-engineer and industrial designer, today Amyko's CEO). Its main business concerns a product/service (a bracelet with passive technology) whose aim is to connect people and institutions operating in the health sector. Today, the company is located in Genoa and Milan, where the staff meet twice a week

Table 3.2 Main features of Amyko

Company	Amyko
Website	www.amyko.it
Business	Health informatics apps
CFR policies	Smart working
	Social security and insurance measures
	Training programmes
Outcomes	Work autonomy and higher productivity
Employees	22
Person interviewed	Riccardo Zanini—COO & Co-Founder

and the other four days employees are free to work from home, without fixed timetables but with the responsibility to meet deadlines. Table 3.2 shows Amyko's main features.

3.4.2 Berto S.r.l.

It is a purely commercial company and is currently based in Tombolo (Padua). It was born in the first post-war period in Cittadella (Padua), founded by Giuseppe Berto and today carried out by Giuseppe Boschiero. The company has ten employees. The aim is to sell products mainly to mechanical engineering companies; their customers are machine makers, and maintenance is one of their core businesses. Their reference market is divided into maintenance and first assembly. Table 3.3 shows Berto S.r.l. main features.

Table 3.3 Main features of Berto S.r.l.

Company	Berto S.r.l.
Website	www.bertosrl.com
Business	Sale of equipment and tools for machine manufacturers
	Maintenance and monitoring
CFR policies	"One-to-one" meetings to set personalized objectives
	Economic and production awards
	Shopping vouchers
Outcomes	Happiness and serenity of employees
Employees	11
Person interviewed	Giuseppe Boschiero—CEO

Table 3.4 Main features of C.A.T. Progetti

Company	C.A.T. Progetti
Website	www.catprogetti.it
Business	Wiring and design
CFR policies	Flexible working hours and part-time (with a particular attention to working mothers)
Outcomes	Higher productivity and low conflict
Employees	25
Person interviewed	Paolo Bertuzzi—Vice President

3.4.3 C.A.T. Progetti

It is a company composed of four members and twenty-one employees working together from about 35 years. The turnover is practically non-existent and they are implementing family-friendly and WLB policies (such as flexibility, part-time). Working hours are 8.00–8.30 a.m./17.00 p.m. with one hour break for lunch; tasks include cabling and computer design. The company was established in 1984 as a spin-off of the holding, whose activity was that of research and prototypes design. In 2000 they left the group and became independent. C.A.T. Progetti deals with 85% of sub-furniture and automatic machines and 15% of electrophilic/electro-medical. Table 3.4 shows C.A.T. Progetti main features.

3.4.4 ErgonixART

Born in 2004 as a technology start-up, their mission is to develop bio-medical devices to be marketed together with consulting around innovative technologies, to be resold to third-party manufacturers in order to develop devices for people affected by disabilities. Their business model is to patent a product and then sell it or launch it directly into the market (maybe without their name but always with at least their brand). It is a company which does not assemble its products directly but carries out R&D at an earlier stage in their office or at research centres (for this reason, employees are mainly researchers), and in a second

Table 3.5 Main features of ErgonixART

Company	ErgonixART
Website	www.ergonixart.it
Business	Informatics and development of devices for disabled
CFR policies	Flexible working hours and smart working
•	Company nursery
•	Insurance (for employees' children)
Outcomes	Low turnover levels, higher availability, interest and commitment from employees
Employees	4
Person interviewed	Paolo Mondini—Chairman and founder

phase at third-party companies which own the necessary production equipment. Table 3.5 shows ErgonixART main features.

3.4.5 Tribe Communication

Established in 2005 with the aim of creating a communications agency that, in addition to being focused on business, was primarily dedicated to people and their needs as human beings, Tribe Communication creates communication strategies and practices to be translated into technological solutions. Two are the areas of development: one for digital products (such as sites, digital promo, CRM) and the other deals with television spots, social channels, communication, packaging or rebranding. Table 3.6 shows Tribe Communication's main features.

Table 3.6 Main features of Tribe Communication

Company	Tribe Communication
Website	www.tribecommunication.it
Business	Strategic consulting and communication
CFR policies	Economic support for family needs; recreational and cultural activities; home-work mobility (tickets for public transport)
Outcomes	Flexibility, higher availability and best results from a qualitative point of view
Employees	25
Person interviewed	Alessandro Fellegara—CEO

3.5   Findings

Results of the qualitative survey conducted in this chapter can be summarized in four main categories: (i) the meaning of CSR for the surveyed companies; (ii) the importance of employees' well-being, WLB and family-friendly policies; (iii) the CFR policies implemented by the surveyed companies; and (iv) the outcomes of implemented CFR policies (concerning both employees and entrepreneurial perspectives).

Each company surveyed in this study recognized the importance of CSR and its particular importance for both the internal dimensions—concerning employees' (and their families) well-being and WLB—and the external dimension, concerning the society at all and the environment in which they operate.

> First, CSR means the responsibility of our company towards our employees and their families. Second, CSR is the responsibility towards the environment in which we operate because if I guarantee security to my employees, they will bring home the necessary incomes that will be livelihood for themselves and even for the territory. (…) Thus CSR means, in essence, to share the well-being generated by the company with employees and outside the company. Giuseppe Boschiero—CEO of Berto S.r.l.

> The meaning of CSR applies both to the people who founded the company and to the employees who work for us. It is important for us to develop a sense of what is happening in the world today and an attention to the community in which we live and operate. Recognizing social responsibility for the work we do is natural because communication itself has a social impact both from the ethical and behavioural point of view. Alessandro Fellegara—CEO of Tribe Communication

While Berto S.r.l. and Tribe Communication stressed both internal and external dimensions of CSR highlighting their commitment towards the society/community in which they operate, C.A.T. Progetti's focus was mainly on the internal dimension—and thus on the importance of WLB and family-friendly policies as part of the company's CSR strategy and social impact.

CSR for us means ensuring conditions that allow WLB and work family balance for employees by implementing family-friendly policies such as flexible time schedules, part-time, and facilitations for working mothers. Paolo Bertuzzi—Vice President of C.A.T. Progetti

To this extent, the importance of employees' (and their families) well-being was commonly agreed by the majority of companies involved in this study. Interviewees recognized human capital's value as stakeholder for the company and potential driver for entrepreneurial success. Human resources are considered as an investment for the company and their happiness and satisfaction has a positive impact on performance.

If employees are happy the will definitely work better, they will make less problems and fewer mistakes. Paolo Bertuzzi (C.A.T. Progetti)

Companies with a higher level of human capital (such as ErgonixART) tend to valorise both the professional skills and personal attitudes of their human resources. It is such an investment, our group works well and there is no sense in cutting personnel (except for economic reasons). Paolo Mondini—Chairman and founder of ErgonixART

About CFR and WLB policies implemented by the investigated companies, these include: flexible working hours, smart working, facilities for working mothers, company nurseries, economic benefits, insurance and social security, personalized meeting times for employees.

As specific activities we left free choice for our employees, so those who had family needs were supported on that front, both at recreational and cultural level. We have also helped many of our employees regarding mobility, with home-to-work tickets for public transport, or financial support for using their own car. Alessandro Fellegara (Tribe Communication)

We have scheduled personalized meetings. To manage the ordinary work there are regular meetings that take place between the company's sectors: a manager in every sector has the "obligation" to bring together other employees, at least once a month, but this is to organize practical work. Every six months, I meet every employ of the company because each one of them has his/her own schedule with personal goals to achieve in order to improve their professionalism. These goals are measured together, talking about and setting objectives for the next semester. Based on this process, at the end of the year some of the resources generated by the company are subdivided as extra, as an award for employees based on the goals they have achieved. In the same way we have, for example, the voucher of €250, which is totally tax deductible and the gifts associated with the main festivities (i.e. Christmas festivities). Giuseppe Boschiero (Berto S.r.l.)

While Tribe communication focused on the economic support for families, recreational/cultural activities and mobility, Berto S.r.l. stressed the importance of personalized meetings for employees. Other companies (such as ErgonixART and Amyko) are experimenting with smart working and flexible working hours which allow employees to work from home through the use of new Information Technologies.

Basically, we have flexible hours. Of course there is a total amount of hours per week as by law contracts. We do not invent things on our own, but we try to practice flexibility as best as we can: people are equipped with communication tools provided by the company (PC, phone, connectivity and so on) so they can often work from home rather than bring their children to work. We also have insurance for our employees' children. Among our employees there are fixed-time employees, usually younger with younger kids, where flexibility is more important, and others with older children, where it is less. Paolo Mondini (ErgonixART)

We are currently working on the possibility of smart working, but we are also thinking about social security schemes, in order to find insurance solutions for our employees both during the working period and even at the end. And of course we do not forget about training: our staff members, at least once a month, attend training courses (specific for their fields), which will make them grow personally first and then at company level. Riccardo Zanini—COO & Co-Founder of Amyko

Outcomes and results of CFR and WLB policies implementation in companies' strategies include: employees' happiness and well-being, higher work autonomy and productivity, low turnover levels, higher levels of availability, interest and commitment from employees, flexibility and best qualitative results.

> For sure the main result is reduced, or almost non-existent, conflict. Paolo Bertuzzi (C.A.T. Progetti)

> In my opinion, the main advantage is the serenity in the relationships between people inside the company. Each positive economic result comes from the work of a close and cohesive team. Giuseppe Boschiero (Berto S.r.l.)

While C.A.T. Progetti and Berto S.r.l. highlighted serenity levels and absence of conflicts as the main outcomes of CFR policies, Tribe Communication, Amyko and ErgonixART also focused on outcomes in terms of increased commitment and productivity of employees with consequent higher quality of results.

> The main benefits are flexibility, availability and motivation from our employees; moreover, we also have the best results from a qualitative point of view. Alessandro Fellegara (Tribe Communication)

> We have more than 20 collaborators employed under smart working conditions. Work autonomy is a boost to productivity and brings added value compared to traditional work from the office. Moreover, another result is the equally positive counterpart for the company in terms of cost-effective flexibility. Riccardo Zanini (Amyko)

> People – apart those who had to leave for cash issues – have always remained and continue to do so, demonstrating both availability and interest for the company. What we got is a higher commitment from our employees. Paolo Mondini (ErgonixART)

Thus, all companies involved in this study agreed about the positive impact of implementing CFR policies within their CSR strategy. CFR enabled these companies to maximize employees' motivation and commitment to work (and, as a consequence, to increase productivity and performance), minimize conflicts and turnover levels and reduce costs.

3.6   Discussion

CFR is a key issue of concern for today's companies that aim at improving their competitive advantage and reaching entrepreneurial success though placing value on their human resources. Taking care of employees' (and their families') needs and expectations allows companies to obtain higher performances and better qualitative results.

As emerged from the interviews reported in this chapter, the importance of CSR—in both its internal and external dimensions—is largely recognized by companies and they tend to consider employees' needs and expectations in their business practices. Regarding the internal dimension of CSR (namely CFR), each company agreed about the key importance of employees' (and their families') well-being and recognized their value as stakeholders for the company and drivers for long-term entrepreneurial success. In this way, family itself can be considered as a stakeholder for the company as well as a driver for social innovation since it produces stability, support, motivation for engagement, higher levels of female labour participation, and can be a potential driver for both economic and sustainable development in today's societies (Annoni 2009).

Regarding the main policies adopted: Berto S.r.l. focuses on "one-to-one" meetings with employees, personalized schedules for each employee and the evaluation of achieved results. Personalized schedules aim at setting and measuring personalized goals and improving workers' professionalism and performances. C.A.T. Progetti focuses on flexibility, part-time, flexi-hours and facilities for working mothers to ensure employees have adequate work and family-life balance levels. Tribe Communication implements several initiatives for the economic support of families, as well as offering recreational and cultural activities and mobility. This, in order to approach supports employees in both their personal and family life and, enhances their flexibility, availability and motivation to work. Finally, Amyko and ErgonixART are successfully implementing smart working approaches which allow employees higher levels of work autonomy than traditional office-based work with a positive impact on their commitment, performance and productivity as well as in terms of cost-effective flexibility of the company.

Table 3.7 CFR policies across analysed companies

SMEs	CFR Policies	Outcomes
Amyko	Social security and insurance measures Training programmes Higher productivity	Smart working Work autonomy
Berto S.r.l.	"One-to-one" meetings Economic and production awards' Shopping vouchers	Happiness Serenity
C.A.T. Progetti	Flexible working hours Part-time Particular attention to working mothers	Higher productivity Low conflict
ErgonixART	Flexible working hours and smart working Company nursery Insurance (for employees' children)	Low turnover levels Higher availability, interest and commitment from employees
Tribe Communication	Economic support to family needs Recreational and cultural activities Home-work mobility	Flexibility Higher availability Best qualitative results

Table 3.7 illustrates and compares similarities and differences of CFR policies among the companies under analysis. It also compares outcomes of the implemented CFR policies according to CEOs' perception.

The implementation of these policies has led to several outcomes for these companies including employees' happiness and well-being, higher levels of work autonomy and productivity, low turnover levels, higher availability, interest and commitment from employees, flexibility and better qualitative results. Both similarities and differences emerged from these interviews. However, they all have a common element: the awareness that taking care of employees' (and families) needs—and giving the right attention to the issues of CFR and WLB—allows companies to improve both personal and professional serenity levels of employees and reduce stress factors with positive impacts on their performance. Thus, initial results presented in this chapter confirm the relevance of CFR with the theme of this book, regarding the role of people in CSR.

However, there are limitations in this study that suggest opportunities for further research directions. First, the results presented in this project do not include data from any failure in the implementation of CFR and WLB policies as well as any detailed evaluation programme from the implemented policies. This is because Italian welfare measures do not involve specific programmes for evaluating these variables within internal CFR strategies. Therefore, this chapter suggests some inputs for future research on these topics, which are intended to analyse and deepen the above-mentioned aspects and expand the sample of surveyed companies.

A second limitation concerns the use of case study methodology which lacks—as is known—scientific rigour, generalizability of results and data precision (Yin 2002; Mari 1994). These gaps can be strengthened i.e. using mixed qualitative-quantitative research methods in future research.

3.7 Implications

It is largely agreed that the best qualitative results to work come from a series of features which include, particularly, the levels of employees' well-being and a job environment that meets their needs, values and expectations (Green 2006; Drafke and Kossen 1998; Tanim 2016), Moreover, the levels of employees well-being are even higher if companies take care of their related family's needs and expectations as stakeholders of the company. To this extent, WLB and work family balance are key factors for job satisfaction and the good functioning of work practices (Clark 2001).

Thus, from a managerial perspective CFR encourages better physical and psychological health, lower absenteeism, higher job performance (van Steenbergen et al. 2007), wider availability and deeper organizational commitment from employees (Beutell and Witting-Berman 2008). Furthermore, from an entrepreneurial point of view, this approach also produces economic and profit results: employees are less stressed; they work better and are more productive. In this respect, CFR may be considered as a potential driver for entrepreneurial success.

From a research perspective, this work attempted to contribute to the scientific debate on CFR and WLB by offering some theoretical and practical insights in the field as well as some inputs of further research.

On the family side, the organization commitment to CFR returns several advantages. First, a competitive advantage at community level: the higher the awareness of local family issues the more likely the company is to be the recipient of funds on behalf of social investors, banks and so forth. Furthermore, the delivery of family-oriented services within a context of increasing private–public sector partnership may have a positive impact on a company's image and can be a potential feature to attract and maintain talent.

Second, the organization investing in family-friendly initiatives, may encourage family members to join the workforce; it could increase the number of dual-earners in a family, enabling more people to work (with positive effects on GDP and production); it might even increase fertility rates and ensure higher disposal of intergenerational human capital. Clearly, however, the evidence suggests it is very likely to increase entrepreneurial activities.

Acknowledgements This work was conducted within the framework of the pilot research project "Good practices of Corporate Family Responsibility and Work-Life Balance", carried out by the Marco Vigorelli Foundation (FMV) in Milan (Italy). Details of FMV projects and activities are available at: http://www.marcovigorelli.org/good-practices-conciliazione-lavoro-famiglia-welfare-aziendale/.

The author would like to thank the members of the Scientific Committee within FMV for their feedback, as well as the coordinating and research team for the support provided during the making of this first step of the project.

References

Allen, Tammy D. 2001. Family-Supportive Work Environments: The Role of Organizational Perceptions. *Journal of Vocational Behavior* 58: 414–435.

Annoni, Sara. 2009. *Famiglia e lavoro in Lombardia. L'esperienza del progetto e premio famiglia lavoro, prima edizione*. Milano: Educatt.

Barnett, Rosalind C., and Karen C. Gareis. 2006. Role Theory Perspectives on Work and Family. In *The Work and Family Handbook: Multi-disciplinary Perspectives and Approaches*, 209–221. Mahwah, NJ: Lawrence Erlbaum Associates.

Baughman, Reagan, Daniela DiNardi, and Douglas Holtz-Eakin. 2003. Productivity and Wage Effects of "Family-Friendly" Fringe Benefits. *International Journal of Manpower* 24 (3): 247–259.

Beauregard, T. Alexandra, and Lesley C. Henry. 2009. Making the Link Between Work-Life Balance Practices and Organizational Performance. *Human Resource Management Review* 19 (1): 9–22.

Beutell, Nicholas J., and Ursula Wittig-Berman. 2008. Work-Family Conflict and Work-Family Synergy for Generation X, Baby Boomers, and Matures: Generational Differences, Predictors, and Satisfaction Outcomes. *Journal of Managerial Psychology* 23 (5): 507–523.

Bloom, Nick, Tobias Kretschmer, and John Van Reenen. 2011. Are Family-Friendly Workplace Practices a Valuable Firm Resource? *Strategic Management Journal* 32 (4): 343–367.

Boushey, Heather, and Sara J. Glynn. 2012. There Are Significant Business Costs to Replacing Employees. http://cdn.americanprogress.org/wp-content/uploads/2012/11/CostofTurnover.pdf.

Chen, Zheng, Gary N. Powell, and Jeffrey H. Greenhaus. 2009. Work-to-Family Conflict, Positive Spillover, and Boundary Management: A Person-Environment Fit Approach. *Journal of Vocational Behavior* 74 (1): 82–93.

Chinchilla Albiol, N., and Consuelo León Llorente. 2011. *Diez años de conciliación en España (1999–2009)*. Madrid: Editorial Grupo 5.

Chinchilla, Albiol, Mireia Las Heras, Alin D. Masuda, and Laurel A. McNall. 2010. *Balancing Work and Family: A Practical Guide to Help Organizations Meet the Global Workforce Challenge*. Amherst, MA: HRD Press.

Clark, Sue Campbell. 2001. Work Cultures and Work/Family Balance. *Journal of Vocational Behavior* 58 (3): 348–365.

Dex, Shirley, and Colin Smith. 2002. *The Nature and Pattern of Family-Friendly Employment Policies in Britain*. Bristol: Policy Press.

Donati, Pierpaolo. 2006. *Manuale di sociologia della famiglia*. Roma-Bari: Laterza.

Donati, Pierpaolo, and Riccardo Prandini. 2006. *Buone pratiche e servizi innovativi per la famiglia*. Milano: Franco Angeli.

Drafke, M.W., and Stan Kossen. 1998. *The Human Side of Organisations*. Harlow: Addison-Wesley.

Duffin, J.S., Laura Carlson, and Livia Sz. Oláh. 2017. *The Contribution of Civil Society: Good Practices*. IFFD: The International Federation for Family Development.

European Commission. 2011. A Renewed EU Strategy 2011–14 for Corporate Social Responsibility. http://eur-lex.europa.eu/legal-content/EN/TXT/?uri=CELEX:52011DC0681.

Faldetta, Guglielmo. 2008. *Corporate Family Responsibility e Work-Life Balance.* Milano: Franco Angeli.

Gray, Helen. 2002. *Family-Friendly Working: What a Performance! An Analysis of the Relationship Between the Availability of Family-Friendly Policies and Establishment Performance.* London: Centre for Economic Performance, London School of Economics and Political Science.

Green, Francis. 2006. *Demanding Work: The Paradox of Job Quality in the Affluent Economy.* Princeton: Princeton University Press.

Greenhaus, Jeffrey H., Karen M. Collins, and Jason D. Shaw. 2003. The Relation Between Work–Family Balance and Quality of Life. *Journal of Vocational Behavior* 63 (3): 510–531.

Grover, Steven L., and Karen J. Crooker. 1995. Who Appreciates Family-Responsive Human Resource Policies: The Impact of Family-Friendly Policies on the Organizational Attachment of Parents and Non-Parents. *Personnel Psychology* 48 (2): 271–288.

Grzywacz, Joseph G., and Brenda L. Bass. 2003. Work, Family, and Mental Health: Testing Different Models of Work-Family Fit. *Journal of Marriage and Family* 65 (1): 248–261.

Grzywacz, Joseph G., and Nadine F. Marks. 2000. Reconceptualizing the Work–Family Interface: An Ecological Perspective on the Correlates of Positive and Negative Spillover Between Work and Family. *Journal of Occupational Health Psychology* 5 (1): 111.

Kesavan, Ram, Michael D. Bernacchi, and Oswald A.J. Mascarenhas. 2013. Word of Mouse: CSR Communication and the Social Media. *International Management Review* 9 (1): 58.

Koubova, Veronika, and Aaron A. Buchko. 2013. Life-Work Balance: Emotional Intelligence as a Crucial Component of Achieving Both Personal Life and Work Performance. *Management Research Review* 36 (7): 700–719.

Kozinets, Robert V. 2015. *Netnography.* Hoboken: Wiley.

Lockwood, Nancy R. 2003. Work/Life Balance: Challenges and Solutions. *Benefits Quarterly* 19 (4): 94.

Macchioni, Elena. 2012. Welfare aziendale. Buone pratiche di conciliazione famiglia lavoro. http://www.politichefamiglia.it/media/81502/elenamacchioni.pdf.

Mari, Carlo. 1994. *Metodi qualitativi di ricerca I. casi aziendali.* Torino: Giappichelli.

Meyer, Christine Siegwarth, Swati Mukerjee, and Ann Sestero. 2001. Work-Family Benefits: Which Ones Maximize Profits? *Journal of Managerial Issues* 13 (1): 28–44.

Molteni, Mario, Stefania Bertolini, and Matteo Pedrini. 2007. Il mestiere di CSR manager. Milano. *Il Sole 24 ore.*

Osoian, Codruta, Lucretia Lazar, and Patricia Ratiu. 2009. The Benefits of Implementing and Supporting Work-Life Balance Policies in Organizations. Managerial Challenges of the Contemporary Society. Proceedings: 333.

Pedrini, M., and Carlotta Petri. 2009. Politiche e misure di conciliazione nelle aziende socialmente responsabili. In *Famiglia e Lavoro in Lombardia. L'esperienza del Progetto e Premio FamigliaLavoro*, ed. Sara Annoni. Milano: Altis. http://altis.unicatt.it/altis-2009_quaderno.pdf.

Perrini, Francesco, and Antonio Tencati. 2011. La responsabilità sociale d'impresa: strategia per l'impresa relazionale e innovazione per la sostenibilità. Sinergie Italiane. *Journal of Management* 77: 23–43.

Pirsch, Julie, Shruti Gupta, and Stacy Landreth Grau. 2007. A Framework for Understanding Corporate Social Responsibility Programs as a Continuum: An Exploratory Study. *Journal of Business Ethics* 70 (2): 125–140.

Rindova, Violina P., Ian O. Williamson, Antoaneta P. Petkova, and Joy M. Sever. 2005. Being Good or Being Known: An Empirical Examination of the Dimensions, Antecedents, and Consequences of Organizational Reputation. *Academy of Management Journal* 48 (6): 1033–1049.

Rothbard, Nancy P. 2001. Enriching or Depleting? The Dynamics of Engagement in Work and Family Roles. *Administrative Science Quarterly* 46 (4): 655–684.

Ruderman, Neil B., Asish K. Saha, and Edward W. Kraegen. 2003. Minireview: Malonyl CoA, AMP-Activated Protein Kinase, and Adiposity. *Endocrinology* 144 (12): 5166–5171.

Sirota, David, Louis A. Mischkind, and Michael Irwin Meltzer. 2005. *The Enthusiastic Employee*. Philadelphia, PA: Wharton School Publishing.

Sumer, H. Canan, and Patrick A. Knight. 2001. How do People with Different Attachment Styles Balance Work and Family? A Personality Perspective on Work–Family Linkage. *Journal of Applied Psychology* 86 (4): 653.

Tanim, Tasnim Rezoana. 2016. Work-Life Balance and Employee Job Satisfaction: A Case of UK Call Centre. *World Review of Business Research* 6 (2): 66–79.

Tomaselli, Gianpaolo, and Monia Melia. 2014. The Role of Interactive Technologies for CSR Communication. *Journal of International Scientific Publication* 8: 324–340.

van Steenbergen, Elianne F., Naomi Ellemers, and Ab Mooijaart. 2007. How Work and Family Can Facilitate Each Other: Distinct Types of Work-Family Facilitation and Outcomes for Women and Men. *Journal of Occupational Health Psychology* 12 (3): 279.

Yamamoto, Isamu, and Toshiyuki Matsuura. 2012. Effect of Work-Life Balance Practices on Firm Productivity. Working Paper.

Yin, Robert. 2002. *Case Study Research: Design and Methods*. London: Sage.

Walsh, Janet. 2005. Work-Life Balance: Challenging the Overwork Culture. In *Managing Human Resources: Personnel Management in Transition*, 148–77. Oxford: Blackwell.

Wayne, Julie Holliday, Nicholas Musisca, and William Fleeson. 2004. Considering the Role of Personality in the Work–Family Experience: Relationships of the Big Five to Work–Family Conflict and Facilitation. *Journal of Vocational Behavior* 64 (1): 108–130.

4

Entrepreneurial Functions and Approaches for Sustainable Maintenance of Aging and Shrinking Rural Communities

Kazue Haga

4.1 Introduction and Research Questions

Rural communities in developed countries such as Japan and Germany face declining and aging populations and structural problems in their regional economies (Small and Medium Enterprise Agency 2014; Bundesministerium für Ernährung und Landwirtschaft 2017). They face challenges to the maintenance of municipal functions and thus to their sustainability, including aspects such as infrastructure and residents' well-being and networks (Ishikawa 2013, p. 57). Remodeling their local economies is one essential task for rural communities to ensure their sustainability. Discussions on sustainable development of rural communities cover a wide range of aspects (Ishikawa 2013, pp. 57–58). Modernization and diversification of agricultural business are commonly recommended as an expected contribution from the economic side (Ministry of Agriculture, Forestry and Fisheries 2017;

K. Haga (✉)
Bunkyo Gakuin University, Tokyo, Japan
e-mail: khaga@bgu.ac.jp

© The Author(s) 2019
F. Farache et al. (eds.), *Responsible People*, Palgrave Studies in Governance, Leadership and Responsibility, https://doi.org/10.1007/978-3-030-10740-6_4

Bundesministerium für Ernährung und Landwirtschaft 2016). If firms can contribute to maintaining the community in which they are located, through modernized and diversified business, such companies realize their responsibility to society. This kind of contribution by companies can be considered a variety of social entrepreneurship.

This chapter explores functions and approaches of entrepreneurial leadership to remodeling local economies in rural agriculture-based communities in developed countries, focusing on approaches in which the residents stay in their shrinking and aging rural communities.[1] It examines the performance of companies in modernizing and stimulating local economies as part of measures taken by residents for the sustainable maintenance of their communities. Among such enterprises, in which many residents participate, there is a wide variety of fields of business and organization management. A case from Japan is compared with a case from Germany to discuss what the approaches have in common and how they differ.

4.2 Challenges in Rural Communities in Developed Countries and Measures to Deal with Them

The challenges faced by rural communities are structural, linked with economic change. Japan is a typical example. Along with industrialization, rural districts, particularly agricultural ones, have increasingly functioned as providers of labor for industries in urban districts (Odagiri 2014, pp. 16–17). This and the deregulation of prices of

---

[1]Rational solutions for regional management of demographic change, such as the "compact city" strategy are not discussed here. The term "compact city" approach was first coined in 1973 by George Dantzig and Thomas L. Saatyaims. It aims at more efficient use of resources. In relation to demographic change, it is often associated with reconstruction of a city with an efficient transportation system and concentration of municipal services to reduce local government costs (Matsumoto 2011). The monetary advantages gained through the concentration of municipal functions, such as the maintenance of municipal infrastructure, are traded off against a decline in the physical and mental condition of elderly people who change their place of residence despite wishing to remain in their hometown.

agricultural products such as mandarins from the developed countries in the 1980s reduced the price competitiveness of agriculture in rural mountainous villages (Tashiro 2001, p. 127) and led to the migration of young residents to urban industrial regions, aging populations, and economic decline (Odagiri 2014, pp. 16–18). Rural agricultural communities risk being unable to maintain their independence as municipalities. Papers by Masuda in 2013 and 2014, together called the Masuda Report (Odagiri 2014, pp. 2–4), estimated that 869 Japanese municipalities would not be able to survive long-term (Masuda 2014, pp. 29–31).

Stimulation of the local economy through modernization of agricultural business is an important measure that is required for rural communities facing aging and shrinking populations. Nakamura stresses two points for sustainable vigorous economies in rural agricultural communities far from industrial areas: creating new business utilizing the key competencies of the community, and obtaining money from other regions through business (Nakamura 2014, pp. 76–78; 2016). It is important that a business which brings gains from other regions stimulates other local businesses in the community and has a multiplier effect in the economic circulation of the community (Schumpeter 2010, p. 154) (Fig. 4.1). To maintain the regional economy, the sales profits from the market of the community alone are an insufficient function of the small market volume of rural communities (Nakamura 2014, pp. 74–76).

Projects to stimulate local economies and improve the sustainability of rural communities, based on concepts of innovation and entrepreneurship as change makers, are undertaken in developed countries. For example, in Japan the government has promoted "the sixth industry" approach since 2010 with the promulgation of the Act for Sixth Industry and Local Production for Local Consumption (Japanese: Rokujikasangyō chisanchishō hō) (Ministry of Agriculture, Forestry and Fisheries, n.d.; Yoshida 2010, p. 3). According to Araki (2012), "The notion of a 'sixth industry' is reached by multiplying industrial sectors—primary × secondary × tertiary (i.e., $1 \times 2 \times 3 = 6$)." The concept has been recommended by Naraomi Imamura since the mid-1990s (Yoshida 2010, p. 2). It was expected that rural regions would

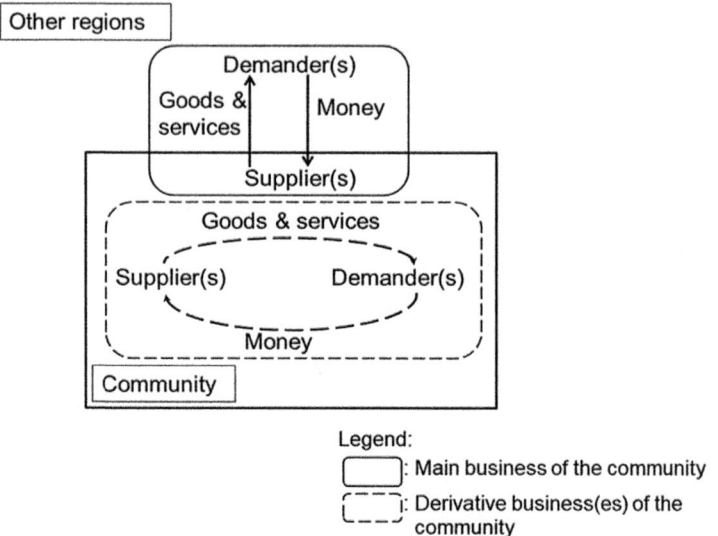

Fig. 4.1 Circulation of goods, services, and money for a sustainable regional economy in rural areas (*Source* Based on Nakamura [2016])

create new added value synergistically through the effective use of agricultural, forestry, and fishery products, as well as land, water, and other assets in farming, mountain, and fishing villages (primary sector), by integrating elements of industry, such as processing (secondary sector), and services (tertiary sector), such as restaurants.

Effective projects are undertaken by policymakers and actors in business in direct and indirect cooperation (Vanebo and Murdock 2012, p. 143). To bring about radical structural change, municipalities have to act innovatively (Vanebo and Murdock 2012, p. 143). Policymakers prepare appropriate conditions for reforms, considering promotion of innovation and entrepreneurship. Entrepreneurship policy "consists of measures taken to stimulate more entrepreneurial behavior in *a region*" (Lundström and Stevenson 2001, p. 19, emphasis added) and has a broad focus.

Business people and companies undertake innovative business as change makers. Actors in business (business people and companies) in various fields contribute to the better maintenance of communities through economic effects. To maintain communities in rural agricultural regions, various problems have to be solved (Ishikawa 2013, p. 57). The local economy has to function well, networks between residents have to work well in daily life, residents have to be able to enjoy a high quality of life, and the infrastructure for daily life has to be well maintained (Ishikawa 2013, pp. 57–58). Older people have to be able to stay independent longer and the younger population has to increase (Fig. 4.2). Companies of all kinds and in every business field have a lot of potential to contribute to solving problems through their businesses.

The preferred business content undertaken to improve the local economy of rural aging and shrinking communities differs in each country. In Japan, the participation of older people in the workforce is considered important in solving the challenges faced by such communities (Ministry of Agriculture, Forestry and Fisheries 2016), as illustrated by Irodori (see Sect. 4.4.1). Opportunities for older residents to participate in the regional economy can help them to become healthier, better-off, and better connected to the community. This can help to maintain municipal functions and reduce costs, for example, health

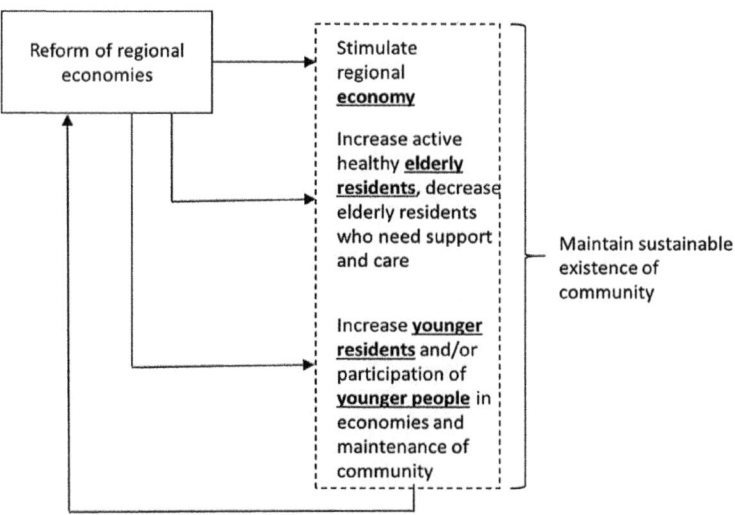

Fig. 4.2 Positive interaction between economies, older residents, and younger generations

care expenditure (Ministry of Agriculture, Forestry and Fisheries 2016). Moreover, developing projects which promote younger people from outside the community moving to the community as new residents or repeated visitors and developing friendly relationships with older residents is helpful in counteracting the decline in the whole population of the community and the resulting problems (Ministry of Agriculture, Forestry and Fisheries 2017). Germany has a different focus in stimulating rural regions: renewable energy businesses are involved as an approach to improve the challenging situation of rural communities (Bundesministerium für Ernährung und Landwirtschaft 2016, pp. 38–52), as the case of Agrokraft shows (see Sect. 4.4.2).

Whatever the type of business, it is important that the company makes a profit and benefits residents through its business, beyond its own gain and business success, and helps to resolve the challenges that the community faces. The companies achieve this kind of social contribution by creating new business (Haga 2013, pp. 620–621). Entrepreneurial behavior accompanied by innovativeness is an important trait of business people in terms of stimulating the local economy (Aßmann 2003, p. 48), as well as in terms of social contribution. This chapter investigates the functions and approaches of companies that contribute to better maintenance of communities, with a focus on their entrepreneurial behavior.

4.3   Functions of Entrepreneurship

4.3.1   Schumpeter's Entrepreneurship Approach and Subsequent Theoretical Developments

Entrepreneurship is a relatively old topic. Hébert and Link give an excellent overview of the history of research on entrepreneurship and its broad variety of definitions (Hébert and Link 1988). There are three main perspectives from economics: "the German Tradition, based on von Thuenen and Schumpeter, the Chicago Tradition, based on Knight and Schultz, and the Austrian Tradition, based on von Mises, Kirzner and Shackle" (Audretsch 2003, p. 2). The Schumpeterian approach seems to be most relevant for our topic in this chapter, because of its emphasis on entrepreneurs being "change makers." Schumpeter ([1912] 2006, 2010) combines entrepreneurship and economic development. A Schumpeterian entrepreneur is a person who creates innovation as the starting point for the creation of a new path in the economy (Schumpeter [1912] 2006, p. 131). Schumpeter ([1912] 2006, p. 529) considered personalities an important element of entrepreneurship research: "The entrepreneur uses his personality and nothing but his personality."

The Schumpeterian definition remains a valid description of the core features of entrepreneurship. Stevenson and Jarillo (1990, p. 18) emphasize the three research questions, "*what* happens when entrepreneurs act: *why* they act; and *how* they act" (emphasis in original). Entrepreneurial traits remain one of the most interesting research topics in economics, business administration, and psychology (Rauch and Frese 2007, p. 18; Zhao et al. 2010, pp. 382–383; Fuller and Marler 2009, pp. 329–345; Röpke 2002, pp. 59–127). Besides Schumpeter's heroic image of entrepreneurs, research on entrepreneurship after Schumpeter also shed light on non-heroic people who succeed in creating innovation and success in new businesses (Collins and Hansen 2011). In a further development of Schumpeter's theory, innovation in low technology that is embedded in the region has also been investigated in terms of the regional economy. In this kind of innovation, moderate leadership is observed (Aßmann 2003, p. 48).

In a further development of entrepreneurship research, the field has split into diverse disciplines. According to Stevenson and Jarillo (1990, p. 21), economics focuses on what entrepreneurs contribute; psychology and sociology investigate the motivation of entrepreneurs; and business management studies the approaches of entrepreneurs. Psychology and business management have accepted traditional concepts of the entrepreneur,[2] but each discipline develops research on entrepreneurship in a specific way. This diversification of entrepreneurship research helps to

---

[2]See, for example, Robinson et al. (1991, pp. 13–31), Brandstätter (1997, pp. 157–177), Rauch and Frese (2007), and Shane et al. (2003, pp. 257–279).

reduce the complexities of research topics[3]; however, on the other hand, economics fails to integrate insights from other disciplines.

4.3.2 Social Entrepreneurship Approach

The focus of this chapter is on entrepreneurship that is able to activate the potential of residents, including those in higher age groups, to remodel the local economy and to increase the community's sustainability. Such enterprises work on social challenges in rural communities. Therefore research on social entrepreneurship is examined next.

Social entrepreneurship is a new approach in the discipline of business administration, focusing on social aspects of firms, business people, and businesses. Social consciousness and business thinking have come closer together in the last decades: efficiency in economic aspects has become important for public organizations working on social problems (Achleitner et al. 2007, p. 4; Kraus et al. 2014, p. 276; Schneiders 2017, p. 364); and interest in the social responsibility and performance of companies has also increased. The number of studies on social entrepreneurship has grown rapidly in the last two decades (Dey 2006, p. 121; Short et al. 2009, p. 162; Kraus et al. 2014, p. 276). Social entrepreneurship research has focused on the investigation of activities and players who work to find solutions to social problems, such as violence, corruption, poor education, and environmental issues (Achleitner et al. 2007, p. 4). Without the term and corresponding emphasis, these aspects would be rather less researched, as Achleitner et al. (2007, pp. 5–6) argue. Discussions on social entrepreneurship shed light on blind spots of earlier research.

The dominant definition is one recommended by Dees (1998, pp. 54–68; 2001), based on Say, Schumpeter, and Drucker (Kraus et al. 2014, p. 278): social entrepreneurship "combines the passion of a social mission with an image of business-like discipline, innovation, and determination commonly associated with, for instance, the high-tech

---

[3]For reduction of complexities by creating subsystems, see, for example, Luhmann (1998).

pioneers of Silicon Valley" (Dees 2001). Most definitions of social entrepreneurship share an image of entrepreneurs as heroic individuals who change the world, as argued by Bornstein (2004, pp. 2, 233). Entrepreneurship remains the essential feature. Similar to the research on conventional entrepreneurship (see Sect. 4.3.1), the integration of insights and research methods from other disciplines (Short et al. 2009, pp. 184–185), such as psychology, sociology, and political science, is considered helpful for research development by researchers.

Research on social entrepreneurship covers a broad variety of research topics, which is good for the development of multifaceted discussions on social entrepreneurship. There are also diverse definitions of social entrepreneurship (Martin and Osberg 2007, p. 30; Achleitner et al. 2007, p. 6; Dacin et al. 2011, pp. 1204–1205). A distinction between entrepreneurship and social entrepreneurship which many researchers support lies in the creation of social value (Martin and Osberg 2007, pp. 34–35; Yunus 2010, p. 1). John proposes a distinction between types of enterprise and argues that drawing a clear border between social enterprises and "normal" ones is difficult, because the social entrepreneurship approach intentionally understands the word "social" in a broader sense (John 2015).

Despite the theoretical ambiguity,[4] this broad inclusion of types of entrepreneurs in terms of enterprises and organizational forms raises a useful point for the case studies in this chapter. It suggests that not only specifically social enterprises, but also conventional organizational forms can act for social purposes. Glöckner et al. (2012, pp. 1133–1134) emphasize the necessity for organizations to innovate to sustain entrepreneurship and to maintain their effectiveness.[5] The idea that conventional organizations can also contribute to society is plausible, if we consider Schumpeter's idea that entrepreneurship is a function, that everyone can be an entrepreneur, and that he or she is only then an

---

[4]Along with increased interest in social entrepreneurship, researchers face challenges (Short et al. 2009, p. 161). Many researchers see a problem precisely in the diversity of interpretations of the word "social" (Cho 2006, p. 35; Achleitner et al. 2007, pp. 6–7).

[5]Glöckner et al. (2012) compare new organizational forms for social purposes with cooperatives as conventional self-help organizational forms in Germany.

entrepreneur so long he or she undertakes that function (Schumpeter [1912] 2006, pp. 174–175).

4.4 Case Studies from Japan and Germany

The cases from Germany and Japan examined here have well organized participation of residents and respect for the social life and well-being of the residents as common features.

4.4.1 Kamikatsu, Japan

Kamikatsu is a typical small village located in a mountainous area on Shikoku, Japan's fourth main island, approximately 40 km from Tokushima City, the prefectural capital, 135 km from Osaka, 180 km from Kyoto, and 530 km from Tokyo. Kamikatsu is relatively inconveniently located for access to these big cities and to important industrial districts such as the Hanshin area (around Osaka and Kobe). Kamikatsu faces typical challenges for rural small municipalities: a declining and aging population and a weak regional economy. The population fell from 4000 in 1970 to 1699 in 2016 (as of January 2016. Municipality of Kamikatsu 2016). The proportion of residents aged 65 years and older was 51.3% (Municipality of Kamikatsu 2016), the highest proportion in Tokushima Prefecture.

Kamikatsu is well known as a successful example of a creative solution to the challenges explored here through the establishment of a unique local enterprise, Irodori. Tomoji Yokoishi, from Tokushima City, is the key person responsible for establishing and developing the enterprise. He started in 1979 as a technical adviser at the Agricultural Cooperative of Kamikatsu. In 1987 he started the Irodori project as part of this post and developed it in cooperation with the local Agricultural Cooperative, the municipality, and local farmers in a loose relationship. Working for Irodori as independent farmers without being employed is convenient for them and helps to motivate them to participate. 197 farmers work for Irodori, approximately 10% of

Kamikatsu's population. Their average age is 70 and 90% are women (Kasamatsu and Sato 2008, p. 53). The project created a market for decorative leaves (Japanese: tsumamono) to garnish traditional Japanese cuisine and created the Irodori brand. Irodori offers 320 types of decorative leaves and the brand has 70% share of the national market. The total sales volume of the market for decorative leaves amounts to 1000 million yen (9.6 million dollars) annually.[6]

The important outcomes for the purposes of this chapter are the profits and benefits for Kamikatsu, in particular, for elderly female farmers. Farmers who work for Irodori get income besides their pensions. The top farmers there earn 10 million yen (around 10,000 dollars) per year (Yokoishi 2007, p. 152). The municipality gets tax from them. Through participation in Irodori, elderly female farmers have gained a social role and a feeling of independence (Haga 2015, p. 135). Besides the economic effects, the health effects of working for Irodori are interesting. Health expenditure has reduced dramatically. Medical expenditure on people aged 65 or older in Kamikatsu amounts to 732,000 yen (7027 dollars) per capita, while the Japanese average for this age group is about 833,000 yen (7997 dollars) per capita (Kasamatsu and Sato 2008, p. 57). In 2000, although Kamikatsu had the third highest population of people aged over 65 in Tokushima Prefecture (44.3%), its medical expenses ranked 32nd of its 48 municipalities (Yoshida 2007, p. 21).

Irodori farmers have relatively few diseases, but the causality—whether the lower rates of self-reported disease are the consequence of working for Irodori or good health is a precondition for working for Irodori—is not clear (Inaba 2013, p. 465). An interesting finding is a positive relationship between physical and psychological health among Irodori farmers. Another interesting finding is that the subjective well-being of Irodori farmers is high (Yamaguchi et al. 2012, p. 65). In contrast, according to a statistical survey by Yamaguchi, Kondo, and Shibata, unlike Irodori farmers, working farmers in Kamikatsu who

---

[6]In a broader sense, the market for tsumamono is much bigger, and the total sales volume in Japan amounts to 10,000 million yen (around 96 million dollars). This is still a small market. For example, the market volume of the Japanese automobile industry amounts to 50 trillion yen (around 480 million dollars) annually (Japan Automobile Manufacturers Association, n.d.).

are engaged in other tasks show no statistical correlation between their occupation and well-being (Yamaguchi et al. 2012, p. 65).

4.4.2 Großbardorf, Germany

Großbardorf is a small village in the Rhön-Grabfeld district in northern Bavaria in Germany, close to the former border with East Germany (German Democratic Republic). As a border district, it had not been promoted for regional development. The main economy in Rhön-Grabfeld is agriculture. However, this district is disadvantaged in geographical conditions for agriculture compared to, for example, the Allgäu in southern Bavaria (Murata 2013, p. 51). Only 318 households, that is, 21.7% of all the farming households, in Rhön-Grabfeld are full-time farmers. The other farmers earn also from other sources (Murata 2013, p. 50). The municipalities in Rhön-Grabfeld are small-sized: Großbardorf had 895 residents in 2014 (Bayerisches Landesamt für Statistik 2018a, p. 6), and the district capital, Bad Neustadt, had 15,053 residents in 2014 (Bayerisches Landesamt für Statistik 2018b, p. 6).

Rural districts in Germany face similar challenges to those in Japan: low numbers of residents, problems in maintaining the functions of the municipality and infrastructure, and structurally weak regional economies. Rhön-Grabfeld has succeeded in developing a model for start-up projects as residents' enterprises for the communities. The limited company Agrokraft GmbH plays a key role, and Großbardorf is the first and most successful municipality in renewable energy projects developed by Agrokraft (Kaphengst and Velten 2014).

The renewable energy movement was recognized by residents of Rhön-Grabfeld as a chance to establish an effective business for sustainable development of the region. In Rhön-Grabfeld it is windy and sunny, and there are rich forests: good conditions for wind, solar, and biomass energy (Murata 2013, p. 51). Aware that large-scale electric power supply companies were interested in developing wind power plants in the district, two local agricultural cooperatives, Bayerischer Bauernverband (Bavarian Farmers' Association) Rhön-Grabfeld branch and Maschinenringe Rhön-Grabfeld (Agricultural machinery syndicate), took action to protect the interests of residents (Neumann 2013, p. 124). Development by large-scale companies from outside Rhön-Grabfeld would eliminate the opportunity to gain income from local business tax (German: Gewerbesteuer) for the municipalities in the region (Diestel, presentation on November 2, 2016). Companies from outside the region also place lower priority on local job creation and sustainable development of the region, and have less respect for the wishes and requirements of residents (Diestel, presentation on November 2, 2016). The best solution for the community is self-development of renewable energy businesses. With this aim, Bayerischer Bauernverband Rhön-Grabfeld and Maschinenringe Rhön-Grabfeld established a company, Agrokraft, in 2006 (Neumann 2013, p. 124).

Agrokraft decided on a two-layer organizational structure to realize projects through the participation of residents. Agrokraft chose the organizational form of a GmbH, a limited company, to be able to make a profit, and because professional management is required in the long run. Agrokraft concentrates on the coordination function to find: (1) residents who have project ideas, (2) residents as investors for the projects, and (3) residents who engage in the realization process of the projects, and to bring them together in project teams and support them in the sustainable and successful development of the project process (Diestel, interviewed by author on September 5, 2017). For the project organizations, cooperatives are chosen. People can join and leave a cooperative whenever they want, and every cooperative member has an equal vote so that a flat organization structure is realized. These features help to improve the participation of residents in projects (Diestel, interviewed by author on September 5, 2017). Agrokraft's strategy is to create a cooperative for each project. If one cooperative is responsible for one project, the project's purpose and motivation remain clear; residents can decide the project content in the most satisfying way and undertake it, and they can participate in selected projects in which they are interested (Diestel, presentation on November 2, 2016).

Großbardorf has been the first of the municipalities in Rhön-Grabfeld to undertake such enterprises. Five projects have been undertaken by cooperatives (see Table 4.1).

Table 4.1 Overview of projects in Großbardorf

Project	Year built	Investment (million euros)	Number of members involved
Photovoltaic power plant	2007	7.60 (8.58)	154
Grandstand with solar panels for the football stadium	2010	0.49 (0.55)	38
Photovoltaic roof system for a storehouse	2010	0.04 (0.04)	8
Biogas plant	2011	3.70 (4.18)	–
Heating network for part of the village	2012	3.00 (3.39)	113

Note The numbers in brackets in the row "Investment" are converted into dollars (in millions)
Sources Murata (2013, pp. 54–61); Diestel, presentation on November 2, 2016

These projects have positive economic and emotional effects for Großbardorf. The municipality gets local business tax from the enterprises, and the cooperative members get cooperative dividends and profits from the sale of surplus electric power. The municipality gets a local business tax of 60,000 euros (around 67,000 dollars) per year; orders for the local firms for the building of the energy plants amount to 4 million euros (around 4.5 million dollars); and amortization of the energy plants amounts to 2 million euros (around 2.3 million dollars) per year (Murata 2013, pp. 60–61). The strategic coordination of cooperatives leads to the development of projects which meet just the needs of residents. The biogas plants were built only in the districts in which the produced heat is consumed through the year (Neumann 2013, p. 124), in order to avoid wasting the heat. Cooperatives of residents can develop projects flexibly: an energy cooperative in Großbardorf undertook a project installing photovoltaic panels on the roof of a new local football stadium, by leasing the roof in advance from the local football teams to provide finance for them to build the roof (Neumann 2013, p. 124). Participation in cooperatives that one likes and to the extent one wishes results in harmonized cooperation between participants without upsetting each other because of envy (Diz Agrarmagazin 2015, p. 90). Residents who engage in the projects feel more tied to the village (Diestel, interviewed by author on September 5, 2017), and through engaged cooperation in the projects between cooperatives and municipalities, both feel tied together and responsible for the community (Neumann 2013, p. 126).

4.4.3 Discussion

The two cases from Japan and Germany have some features in common. First, improvement of the well-being of residents and satisfaction of their requirements are considered an important aim. Second, to achieve this aim, approaches involving residents' participation are undertaken. Third, efforts with entrepreneurial behavior in the cases examined have effects beyond the participants directly, for the communities as a whole. Fourth, organizations which work for a collective purpose in the community have been involved in starting up the enterprises. In Kamikatsu and Großbardorf, the local branches of the agricultural cooperatives, which support farmers and introduce them to technologies and approaches to improve agriculture and agricultural business, have been the main initiators. The creation of Irodori and Agrokraft is effective compared with cases in which the municipality and/or agricultural cooperative supports each farmer's business individually (Haga 2018, p. 108).

Both Irodori and Agrokraft are active initiators, encouraging residents by giving them opportunities to express their wishes. Neither company acts in the heroic manner illustrated by Schumpeter, but their moderate leadership is welcomed by residents and successful in getting them together in the creation of new businesses which bring more profit for the communities. Both companies concentrate on the coordination of business projects and providing an information service for business projects. The success of both companies is owed to the leaders, who have an entrepreneurial spirit. The president of Irodori, Tomoji Yokoishi, and the director of Agrokraft, Michael Diestel, believe in the potential of residents to undertake projects effectively to cope with the challenges due to declining populations, such as workforce shortages, and they talk to residents repeatedly in friendly and sincere ways to gradually encourage them to cooperate in the business projects.

Irodori in Kamikatsu concentrates on local, elderly farmers and created the agricultural business with them as co-workers. In contrast, Agrokraft in Großbardorf targets village residents of all age groups as members of enterprise projects. Furthermore, Agrokraft undertakes enterprises in diverse branches of business, whereas Irodori concentrates on one business.

4.5 Conclusions: Insights and the Need for Further Research

The rural regional economy is not a new research topic. However, with an increased research interest in the social aspects of economics and business, a certain interest in the rural regional economy combined with sustainability can be observed in recent years, as implied by a research focus on local enterprises such as the cases examined in this chapter. Such locally embedded enterprises seek economic efficiency and try to cope with social challenges in the community as well.

Irodori and Agrokraft are similar in terms of the intentions of the entrepreneurs, the people for whom they act with social responsibility, who should benefit from the enterprise, and how they benefit. Both companies act for profit and for the benefit of residents of the communities. Both have designed their enterprises so that the participation of local residents is stimulated. The relationship between work and well-being (see the case of Irodori in Sect. 4.4.1) is observed. Irodori and Agrokraft started from ideas or projects of the local agricultural cooperatives, which endeavor to improve agriculture and farmers' quality of life. Having a background at or with, the agricultural cooperative suggests that entrepreneurs' decisions can be influenced by their circumstances. What decision-makers regularly see, hear, and think about influences their cognition and viewpoints. Entrepreneurs who have effects in the communities in rural regions undergoing demographic change work on diverse challenges in the community. This suggests that the communities face a wide variety of challenges and that there is not a single effective solution: different challenges need to be solved by different specific approaches.

Evaluation of the orientation of social consciousness of an enterprise should be undertaken on two levels, based on the cognition of the entrepreneurs and of the researchers (observers of the enterprises).

Entrepreneurs are not necessarily aware of the features of their contributions: for example, Diestel, the director of Agrokraft, does not consider it to be public benefit oriented. Therefore, the questions of how the entrepreneurs themselves evaluate their businesses and what type of entrepreneur they consider themselves to be need to be re-evaluated by researchers as third persons. This kind of comparative research approach will be helpful in coping with the unclear distinction between social enterprises and less socially conscious ones and in investigating the entrepreneurial functions and features of companies that initiate businesses that contribute to communities' sustainability.

An interesting question for further research is under what kind of conditions individuals act as entrepreneurs. It seems reasonable to apply both the discussions on entrepreneurship in traditional ways based on the Schumpeterian approach and those on social entrepreneurship to this issue. This research topic has both aspects, and neither the conventional discussions nor social entrepreneurship alone covers it fully. It would be safe to argue that the research focus and discussions from both research streams can complement each other. Integration of research in psychology on the personality and the cognition processes of entrepreneurs are certainly helpful to develop the research on "social" entrepreneurship in rural communities undergoing a demographic change in developed countries.

References

Aßmann, Jörg. 2003. *Innovationslogik und regionales Wirtschaftswachstum: Theorie und Empirie autopoietischer Innovationsdynamik* [Logic of Innovation and Economic Growth of Regions. Theoretical Reflection on Autopoietic Innovation Dynamics and Its Empirical Observation]. Marburg: Mafex (BOD).

Achleitner, Ann-Kristin, Peter Heister, and Erwin Stahl. 2007. Social entrepreneurship — ein Überblick [Social Entrepreneurship—An Overview]. In *Finanzierung von Sozialunternehmern: Konzepte zur finanziellen Unterstützung von Social Entrepreneurs* [Financing of Social Entrepreneurs: Concepts for

Finance Support for Social Entrepreneurs], ed. Ann-Katrin Achleitner, Peter Heister, and Erwin Stahl, 3–25. Stuttgart: Schäffer Poeschel.

Araki, Laura. 2012. Japanese Agricultural Reform and the Trans-Pacific Partnership. An Interview with Aurelia George Mulgan. The National Bureau of Asian Research. Accessed September 15, 2017. http://www.nbr. org/research/activity.aspx?id=257.

Audretsch, David B. 2003. *Entrepreneurship: A Survey of the Literature.* Enterprises Papers No. 14. Luxembourg: Office for Official Publications of the European Communities.

Bayerisches Landesamt für Statistik. 2018a. *Statistik kommunal 2017. Stadt Bad Neustadt a. d. Saale 09 673 114. Eine Auswahl wichtiger statistischer Daten* [Communal Statistics City of Bad Neustadt a. d. Saale 09 673 1214. A Selection of Important Statistical Data]. Fürth: Bayerisches Landesamt für Statistik.

Bayerisches Landesamt für Statistik. 2018b. *Statistik kommunal 2017. Gemeinde Großbardorf 09 673 126. Eine Auswahl wichtiger statistischer Daten* [Communal Statistics Municipality Großbardorf 09 673 126. A Selection of Important Statistical Data]. Fürth: Bayerisches Landesamt für Statistik.

Bornstein, David. 2004. *How to Change the World: Social Entrepreneurs and the Power of New Ideas.* Oxford and New York: Oxford University Press.

Brandstätter, Hermann. 1997. Becoming an Entrepreneur—A Question of Personality Structure? *Journal of Economic Psychology* 18 (2): 157–177.

Bundesministerium für Ernährung und Landwirtschaft. 2016. *Bericht der Bundesregierung zur Entwicklung der ländlichen Räume 2016* [Report of the Federal Government on the Development of Rural Areas 2016]. Berlin: Bundesministerium für Ernährung und Landwirtschaft.

Bundesministerium für Ernährung und Landwirtschaft. 2017. Ländliche Regionen verstehen — Fakten und Hintergründe [Understanding Rural Regions—Facts and Background]. Accessed June 30, 2018. https://www.bundesregierung.de/Content/Infomaterial/BMELV/LR-verstehen_5814332.html.

Cho, Albert Hyunbae. 2006. Politics, Values and Social Entrepreneurship: A Critical Appraisal. In *Social Entrepreneurship*, ed. Johanna Mair, Jeffrey Robinson, and Kai Hockerts, 34–56. London: Palgrave Macmillan.

Collins, Jim, and Morten T. Hansen. 2011. *Great by Choice.* New York: Harper.

Dacin, M. Tina, Peter A. Dacin, and Paul Tracey. 2011. Social Entrepreneurship: A Critique and Future Directions. *Organization Science* 22 (5): 1203–1213.

Dees, J. Gregory. 1998. Enterprising Nonprofits. *Harvard Business Review* 76: 54–69.

Dees, J. Gregory. 2001. The Meaning of "Social Entrepreneurship". Accessed September 15, 2017. https://centers.fuqua.duke.edu/case/wp-content/uploads/sites/7/2015/03/Article_Dees_MeaningofSocialEntrepreneurship_2001.pdf.

Dey, Pascal. 2006. The Rhetoric of Social Entrepreneurship: Paralogy and New Language Games in Academic Discourse. In *Entrepreneurship*, ed. Chris Steyaert and Daniel Hjorth, 121–144. Cheltenham: Edward Elgar.

Diz Agrarmagazin. 2015. Gemeinsam statt einsam [Together Instead of Alone]. *Diz Agrarmagazin*, July: 90–93.

Fuller, J.R. Bryan, and Laura E. Marler. 2009. Change Driven by Nature: A Meta-Analytic Review of the Proactive Personality Literature. *Journal of Vocational Behavior* 75 (3): 329–345.

Glöckner, Rick, Kornelia Ehrlich, and Thilo Lang. 2012. Genossenschaften in der Neuen Sozialen Ökonomie — Ergebnisse einer Vorstudie aus Deutschland und Forschungsperspektiven [Cooperatives in the New Social Economy—Results of a Preliminary Study from Germany and Research Perspectives]. In *Genossenschaften im Fokus einer neuen Wirtschaftspolitik* [Cooperatives in the Focus of a New Economic Policy], ed. Johann Brazda, Markus Dellinger, and Dietmer Rößl, 1127–1138. Vienna: Lit.

Haga, Kazue. 2013. *Innovations- und Evolutionsdynamik in demographisch alternden Gesellschaften* [Innovation and Evolutionary Dynamics in Demographically Aging Societies]. Marburg: Metropolis.

Haga, Kazue. 2015. Innovation and Entrepreneurship in Aging Societies: Theoretical Reflection and a Case Study from Kamikatsu, Japan. *Journal of Innovation Economics & Management* 18: 119–141. Accessed June 8, 2018. https://doi.org/10.3917/jie.018.0119.

Haga, Kazue. 2018. Innovation in Rural Japan: Entrepreneurs and Residents Meeting the Challenges of Aging and Shrinking Agricultural Communities. *Journal of Innovation Economics & Management* 25: 87–117. Accessed June 8, 2018. https://doi.org/10.3917/jie.pr1.0023.

Hébert, Robert F., and Albert N. Link. 1988. *The Entrepreneur: Mainstream Views & Radical Critiques*. New York: Praeger Publishers.

Inaba, Yoji. 2013. Kōreisha no shakai sanka de iryōhi teigen. Tokushima-ken Kamikatsu-chō no kēsu [Decrease in Medical Expenses of Elderly People Through Social Participation. The Case of Kamikatsu]. *The Japanese Journal for Public Health Nurse* 69 (6): 462–466.

Ishikawa, Kimihiko. 2013. Keizai shakai o sōzōsuru 'machizukuri no ronri' [An "Approach for Building Communities" to Create a Society in Which the Economy Works Well]. *Hitotsubashi Business Review* 61 (2): 56–71.

John, Rob. 2015. Venture Philanthropy: The Evolution of High Engagement Philanthropy in Europe. Last Modified October 23, 2015. http://eureka.sbs.ox.ac.uk/745/.

Kaphengst, Timom, and Eike Karola Velten. 2014. Energy Transition and Behavioural Change in Rural Areas. WWW for Europe Working Paper 60. Accessed June 30, 2018. http://hdl.handle.net/10419/125718.

Kasamatsu, Kazuichi, and Yumi Sato. 2008. *Jizokukanō-na machi wa chiisaku utsukushii* [Sustainable Communities Are Small and Beautiful]. Kyoto: Gakugei shuppansha.

Kraus, Sascha, Matthias Filser, Michele O'Dwyer, and Eleanor Shaw. 2014. Social Entrepreneurship: An Exploratory Citation Analysis. *Review of Managerial Science* 8 (2): 275–292.

Luhmann, Niklas. 1998. *Die Gesellschaft der Gesellschaft* [Society of the Society]. Frankfurt am Main: Suhrkamp.

Lundström, Anders, and Lois Stevenson. 2001. *Entrepreneurship Policy for the Future*. Stockholm: Swedish Foundation for Small Business Research (Forum för småföretagsforskning).

Martin, Roger L., and Sally Osberg. 2007. Social Entrepreneurship: The Case for Definition. *Stanford Social Innovation Review* 5 (2): 28–39.

Masuda, Hiroya. 2014. *Chihō shōmetsu* [Disappearance of Rural Communities]. Tokyo: Chuokoronsha.

Matsumoto, Tadashi. 2011. Compact City Policies: Comparative Assessment. Paper presented at 47th ISOCARP Congress Wuhan, China, October 24–28.

Ministry of Agriculture, Forestry and Fisheries. 2016. Heisei27nendo shokuryō, nōgyō, nōson hakusho [White Paper on Food, Agriculture, and Agricultural Communities 2015]. Accessed June 30, 2018. http://www.maff.go.jp/j/wpaper/w_maff/h27/h27_h/trend/part1/chap3/c3_0_00.html.

Ministry of Agriculture, Forestry and Fisheries. 2017. Heisei28nendo shokuryō, nōgyō, nōson hakusho [White Paper on Food, Agriculture and

Agricultural Communities 2016]. Accessed June 30, 2018. http://www.maff.go.jp/j/wpaper/w_maff/h28/h28_h/trend/part1/chap3/c3_1_00.html.

Ministry of Agriculture, Forestry and Fisheries. n.d. Chiiki shigen o katsuyō shita nōringyōtō ni yoru shinjigyō no sōshutsutō oyobi nōrinsuisanbutsu no riyōsokushin ni kansuru hōritsu (rokujisangyōka chisanchi shōhō) ni tsuite [On the Act for Promotion of Creation of New Business by Farmers, Foresters, and Fishermen Applying Local Resources as Well as for Promotion of Application of Local Products in Agriculture, Forestry, and Fisheries (Act for the Sixth Industry and Local Production for Local Consumption)]. Accessed September 15, 2017. http://www.maff.go.jp/j/shokusan/sanki/6jika/houritu/index.html.

Municipality of Kamikatsu. 2016. Nenreibetsu jinkōjōkyō [Population According to Age Group]. Accessed August 24, 2017. http://www.kamikatsu.jp/docs/2011012800173/.

Murata, Takeshi. 2013. *Doitsu nōgyō to "enerugii tenkan"* [Agriculture and Energy Transition in Germany]. Tokyo: Tsukuba Shobo.

Nakamura, Ryōhei. 2014. *Machizukuri kōzō kaikaku. Chiiki keizai kozō o dezain suru* [Restructuring of Communities. Designing for the Economic Structure of Rural Regions]. Tokyo: Nihon Kajoshuppan.

Nakamura, Ryōhei. 2016. Chihō o genki ni suru chihō sōsei no arikata [Strategy for Regional Revitalization]. Research Institute of Economy, Trade and Industry (RIETI). Accessed June 3, 2018. https://www.rieti.go.jp/jp/papers/contribution/nakamura/14.html.

Neumann, Heinrich. 2013. Genossenschaften beleben eine ganze Region [Cooperatives Stimulate an Entire Region]. *top agrar* 8: 124–129.

Odagiri, Tokumi. 2014. *Nōsanson wa shōmetsu shinai* [Rural Agricultural Communities Will Not Be Eliminated]. Tokyo: Iwanami Shoten.

Rauch, Andreas, and Michael Frese. 2007. Let's Put the Person Back into Entrepreneurship Research: A Meta-Analysis on the Relationship Between Business Owners' Personality Traits, Business Creation, and Success. *European Journal of Work and Organizational Psychology* 16 (4): 353–385.

Robinson, Peter B., David V. Stimpson, Jonathan C. Huefner, and H. Keith Hunt. 1991. An Attitude Approach to the Prediction of Entrepreneurship. *Entrepreneurship Theory and Practice* 15 (4): 13–31.

Röpke, Jochen. 2002. *Der lernende Unternehmer* [The Learning Entrepreneur]. Norderstadt: BOD.

Schneiders, Katrin. 2017. Social Entrepreneurship als neues Leitbild der Sozialpolitik? In *Gegenwart und Zukunft des Sozialmanagements und der*

Sozialwirtschaft, ed. Waltraud Grillitsch, Paul Brandl, and Stephanie Schuller, 363–376. Wiesbaden: Springer VS.

Schumpeter, Joseph A. [1912] 2006. *Theorie der wirtschaftlichen Entwicklung* [Theory of Economic Development], 1st ed. Berlin: Duncker & Humblot.

Schumpeter, Joseph A. 2010. *Konjunkturzyklen* [Business Cycles: A Theoretical, Historical, and Statistical Analysis of the Capitalist Process]. Göttingen: Vandenhoeck & Ruprecht.

Shane, Scott, Edwin A. Locke, and Christopher J. Collins. 2003. Entrepreneurial Motivation. *Human Resource Management Review* 13 (2): 257–279.

Short, Jeremy C., Todd W. Moss, and G.T. Lumpkin. 2009. Research in Social Entrepreneurship: Past Contributions and Future Opportunities. *Strategic Entrepreneurship Journal* 3 (2): 161–194.

Small and Medium Enterprise Agency. 2014. 2014 White Paper on Small and Medium Enterprises in Japan. Fight Song for Micro Businesses. Accessed June 30, 2018. http://www.chusho.meti.go.jp/pamflet/hakusyo/H26/download/2014hakusho_eng.pdf.

Stevenson, Howard H., and J. Carlos Jarillo. 1990. A Paradigm of Entrepreneurship: Entrepreneurial Management. *Strategic Management Journal* 11: 17–27.

Tashiro, Yoichi. 2001. *Nihon ni nōgyō wa ikinokoreru ka* [Can Japanese Agriculture Survive?]. Tokyo: Otsuki Shoten.

Vanebo, Jan Ole, and Alex Murdock. 2012. Innovation and Creative Leadership in Local Government. In *Foundations of the Knowledge Economy*, ed. Knut Ingar, 139–157. Cheltenham and Northampton: Edward Elgar.

Yamaguchi, Shizue, Hiroshi Kondo, and Hiroshi Shibata. 2012. Nōson chiiki no jiritsu kōreisha ni okeru productive activities ga shukanteki kōfukukan ni oyobosu eikyō [Relationships of Productive Activities to Subjective Well-Being in the Elderly Living Independently at Home in a Rural Area]. *Applied Gerontology* 6 (1): 59–69.

Yokoishi, Tomoji. 2007. *Sōda happa o urō! Kaso no machi, donzoko kara no saisei* [Oh, Let's Sell Leaves! Revitalization of a Community Suffering from Population Decline]. Tokyo: SoftbankCreative.

Yoshida, Toshiyuki. 2007. Kōreishanōgyō no kanōsei to sono shakaiteki igi — Chūkōnensō de no shinkishūnō, shūnō no tsuyomari [The Possibility and Social Senses of Farming by Elderly People (Aged 65 and Over): The Increased Trend for New Farming and Self-Employed Agriculture Among

Middle-Aged and Older People]. *Regional Policy Research of Takasaki City University* 9 (2&3): 17–33.

Yoshida, Shigeo. 2010. Nōgyō no rokujisangōka no sentan kara mieru mono—inobēshon, nettowāku, kōdinētā [Insights from the Forefront of the Sixth Industry Approach—Innovation, Networks and Coordinators]. *JA Sōken Repōto* 16 (Winter): 2–6.

Yunus, Muhammad. 2010. *Building Social Business: The New Kind of Capitalism That Serves Humanity's Most Pressing Needs.* New York: Public Affairs.

Zhao, Hao, Scott E. Seibert, and G. Thomas Lumpkin. 2010. The Relationship of Personality to Entrepreneurial Intentions and Performance: A Meta-Analytic Review. *Journal of Management* 36 (2): 381–404.

5

Social Entrepreneurship Factors of Success and Failure in the Omsk Region of Russia

Yulia Fomina and Teresa Chahine

5.1 Introduction

The new social, ecological, and economic challenges of our globalized world have led to a pressing need for effective and sustainable solutions. Engaging individuals and institutions across sectors in designing and implementing these solutions is the only chance to ensure that we reach the internationally agreed UN Sustainable Development Goals (SDGs). Sustainable development is defined as "development that meets the needs of the present without compromising the ability of future generations to meet their own needs" (WCED 1987, p. 43). There are numerous pathways to sustainable development; social entrepreneurship is just one of them.

Y. Fomina
Omsk State University, Omsk, Russia

T. Chahine (✉)
Yale School of Management, Yale University, New Haven, CT, USA
e-mail: teresa.chahine@yale.edu

© The Author(s) 2019
F. Farache et al. (eds.), *Responsible People*, Palgrave Studies in Governance,
Leadership and Responsibility, https://doi.org/10.1007/978-3-030-10740-6_5

Social entrepreneurship is a hybrid form of entrepreneurship that pursues a social mission and, at the same time, "uses market-based approaches to earn commercial income to accomplish its mission" (Alter 2003, p. 2). Some have also considered it to be part of corporate social responsibility (CSR) when practiced within existing institutions (Austin et al. 2004). In our research we consider social entrepreneurship as a broad path to implement individual as well as corporate responsibility "to improve the conditions, livelihoods, and standards of living of populations and ecosystems" (Chahine 2016, p. 5).

Social entrepreneurship has become a very popular phenomenon over the last two decades. The social economy of the EU27 (2010) has provided paid employment for about 6.5% of the working population—about 14.1 million people, including about 2.5 million in Germany, 2.3 million in France, and 2.2 million in Italy. Paid employment in the social economy in Europe increased by about 27% between 2002 and 2010, and, at the same time, the number of volunteers in the EU27 (2011) participating in the activities of nonprofit organizations was about 102 million people (Monzon and Chaves 2012). The nonprofit sector in the United States employed 11.4 million people in 2012, compared to 10.5 million in 2007 (U.S. Bureau of Labor Statistics 2014). In comparison, the social economy is relatively small in the Russian Federation. Social entrepreneurship started to develop as a mass phenomenon in the Russian Federation beginning in the early 2000s. Paid employment in the social economy was about 1.4% of the working population (990,000 of 68.5 million paid workers) in 2015, compared to 0.9% in 2009.

In the Russian Federation social entrepreneurship is an emerging trend, growing in popularity in recent years. The number of volunteers in Russia increased from 0.33 million in 2009 to 1.435 million people in 2016 (Labour and Employment in Russia 2017, p. 99; Krutikov 2013, pp. 62–63). From our point of view, social entrepreneurship is much needed in Russia, especially in low-income regions with a budget deficit, such as the Omsk region.

The Omsk region is located in Siberia and specializes in petrochemical refining in urban areas and grain growing in rural areas, and exporting oil products and grain to other Russian regions and abroad. Despite these industries the Omsk region is not considered high income due to a historical shift whereby its main plants and factories had to change their legal address from Omsk to Moscow or St. Petersburg in the 1990s and early 2000s and pay most of their taxes there. Per capita income in the Omsk region has been decreasing from 2013 and was about US$5,000 per year in 2017, but 13–14% of the region's population had an average income under US$1,500 per year in 2017 (Territorial Body of the Federal State Statistics Service in the Omsk Region 2018). The main challenges of the Omsk region include air and water pollution; increasing rates of cancer, allergic, and respiratory diseases; and poor road quality and housing infrastructure (Atmospheric Air and Public Health 2010; Fomina and Fomin 2014). While the regional government and businesses have attempted to solve these problems, they have faced limited resources and competing priorities.

Social entrepreneurship may help catalyze civil society and engage citizens in creating a better future for the region. As of the beginning of 2018, there were 2593 non-commercial organizations in the Omsk region employing about 28,000 people and involving about 47,000 volunteers (Non-commercial Organizations of the Omsk Region 2018).

This study explores what factors can lead to the success or failure of social entrepreneurship in the Omsk region of Russia. Drawing on existing literature, it seeks to determine whether nascent and mature entrepreneurs consider the factors related to the success or failure of social entrepreneurship similarly or differently in the Omsk region of Russia.

We begin our study with existing definitions of social entrepreneurship to outline the framework for our research. Our research relies on the concepts of social entrepreneurship provided by Leadbeater (1997), Dees (1998), Austin et al. (2006), and Dacin et al. (2010). We also explore recent studies of social entrepreneurship success and failure, which provide a reliable foundation for further research in this field (Sharir and Lerner 2006; Dacin et al. 2010; Newth and Woods 2014; Roy et al. 2014; Zhang and Swanson 2014).

Our research questions were raised from the research gaps identified by Dacin et al. (2010) and Newth and Woods (2014), which allowed us to formulate the aim of our research as follows: to understand differences and similarities in perceptions of social entrepreneurship success and failure factors across nascent and mature entrepreneurs in the Omsk region of Russia.

To reach our aim, we used a qualitative approach, namely the phenomenological approach (Germak and Robinson 2014). We held five in-depth interviews with social entrepreneurs in the autumn of 2016. The interviews allowed us to develop a semi-structured questionnaire. Our qualitative survey was conducted in online and offline forms in the Omsk region of Russia in the spring of 2017. Our final data contains answers from 58 respondents from social entrepreneurs of the Omsk region.

5.2 Theoretical Background and Research Questions

There are many definitions of social entrepreneurship, but two main aspects can be found in almost every definition: the entrepreneurial and the social (Leadbeater 1997; Dees 1998; Austin et al. 2006). From one side, social entrepreneurs can be described as Schumpeterian entrepreneurs—they mobilize inventions, they innovate, carry out new combinations, and bring creativity. In this regard, social entrepreneurship "is not a distinct type of entrepreneurship" (Dacin et al. 2010, p. 53). From another side, social entrepreneurs aim at a social mission, so in this sense social entrepreneurship differs from commercial entrepreneurship in such aspects as different motivation, the way they pursue opportunities, the outcomes they aim for (Mair and Noboa 2006), and success metrics. Russian scholars have defined social entrepreneurship as an economic activity characterized by the following: a social purpose, an entrepreneurial innovation, and an aspiration to self-sufficiency (Makarevich and Sazonova 2012).

In our research, we have followed a definition given by Austin et al. (2006, p. 2): "We define social entrepreneurship as innovative, social value creating activity that can occur within or across the nonprofit, business, or government sectors." In other words, we consider social entrepreneurship as an innovative activity that pursues a social mission.

While the nonprofit sector is usually considered as the main sector for social entrepreneurship (Stecker 2014), the business and public sectors are often involved as well (McMullen 2011; Keohane 2013).

The success of social entrepreneurship is also a complex phenomenon and discussed in recent literature from different points of view. Dees (2012) considered social entrepreneurship as an intersection of two cultures: a culture of charity and a culture of entrepreneurial problem solving, while the success of social entrepreneurship requires values integrated from both cultures. Social entrepreneurship success may be defined as being the generation of "social goods" (Cukier et al. 2011) or measured according to three success criteria: the achievement of declared goals; the ability to ensure sustainable current activities including obtaining resources; and the ability to find resources for further growth and development (Sharir and Lerner 2006). Roy et al. (2014) discussed the criteria proposed by the Ashoka Foundation (i.e. demonstration of a new idea; creativity; entrepreneurial quality; social impact of the idea; ethical fiber) and the Schwab Foundation (i.e. transformative social change; organizational sustainability; proven social and/or environmental impact; reach and scope; scalability) to select social entrepreneurs that have been successful over long periods of time and separated these criteria from antecedents of social entrepreneurship success.

The factors influencing success in social entrepreneurship have been studied by many scholars. Social networking and the creation of social capital are broadly discussed as some of the most important factors of social entrepreneurship success by Leadbeater (1997), Dufays and Huybrechts (2014), and Zhang and Swanson (2014). Lehner (2014) analyzed the transformation of social capital into economic capital and claimed that the success of social ventures is based upon the social capital of the entrepreneurial team. Zhang and Swanson (2014) divided factors that can enhance the success of social enterprise on internal factors (including leadership committed to social cause; resource endowment; network embedding) and external factors (a supportive government policy environment; a dynamic social environment; a poor economic environment) and outlined the processes of successful social entrepreneurship (a social entrepreneurship orientation; continuous mission adaptation; and effectuation capabilities). According to Newth and Woods (2014), social entrepreneurship opportunities are the constructed outcomes of entrepreneurial alertness and motivation, and the organizational, societal, institutional, and market contexts in which the entrepreneur is embedded. These contextual forces are considered as barriers (Robinson 2006) and factors of resistance (Newth and Woods 2014) to social entrepreneurship, but they also provide success in social innovation. Sharir and Lerner (2006) identified eight variables that contribute to the success of social ventures: (1) the entrepreneur's social network; (2) total dedication to the venture's success; (3) the capital base at the establishment stage; (4) the acceptance of the venture idea in the public discourse; (5) the composition of the venturing team, including the ratio of volunteers to salaried employees; (6) ensuring cooperation in the public and nonprofit sectors in the long term; (7) the ability of the service to stand the market test; and (8) the entrepreneurs' previous managerial experience.

Although social entrepreneurship success and its factors are discussed widely in recent literature, the failures of social enterprises have attracted less attention. According to Dacin et al. (2010), social entrepreneurship researchers and practitioners could benefit from a stronger dialogue and understanding of entrepreneurial failure; entrepreneurial failure is just as crucial to understanding the potential sustainability of social enterprises. Cukier et al. (2011) also point out the need to do more empirical research to evaluate successes and failures and ultimately to harness the best practices of social entrepreneurship. Newth and Woods (2014) propose the exploration of factors of resistance and how the context shapes social innovation for further understanding of social entrepreneurship and a greater appreciation for the ways in which innovations can succeed because of resistance, not in spite of it.

Social entrepreneurship in the Russian Federation has been studied in the context of its business models, trends, and main features (Batalina et al. 2008; Moskovskaya 2011; Aray et al. 2014; Zhokhova 2015); however, the factors of success and failure in Russia have yet to be investigated. Germak and Robinson (2014), in their study of the motivation of nascent social entrepreneurs, proposed for further research the comparison of the motivation of nascent and mature social entrepreneurs.

This led us to our study design which compares the perception of factors of success and failure by nascent and mature social entrepreneurs.

Our research questions are as follows:

- What are the main factors that lead to the success or failure of social entrepreneurial ventures across the Omsk region of Russia?
- What are the differences and similarities in the factors of success or failure among nascent and mature social entrepreneurs in the Omsk region of Russia?

5.3 Research Methods

We followed a qualitative approach to address our research questions regarding factors of social entrepreneurial success and failure. Phenomenological methodology was practiced by different researchers such as Germak and Robinson (2014), and Sharir and Lerner (2006) in their qualitative studies in social entrepreneurship.

The data frame for this study includes respondents in the Omsk region of Russia who participated in our research in 2016 and 2017. We conducted our research using the following two steps: first, the five in-depth interviews with social entrepreneurs; second, a qualitative survey among nascent and mature entrepreneurs that aimed to understand the factors that may underlie social entrepreneurial success or failure. We defined the mature entrepreneurs as those with more than three years entrepreneurial experience and the nascent entrepreneurs as those with less than three years entrepreneurial experience.

Step 1. The first in-depth interviews were held in the autumn of 2016 with five participants who ran social entrepreneurial ventures. The respondents for the in-depth interviews were randomly chosen from the participants of the Presidential Management Training Program in the Omsk region. All participants of this Program have more than three years' executive experience and may be classified as mature entrepreneurs. Some of them run social ventures and agreed to participate in the interview. For the purposes of this study a social venture is defined as any social initiative working toward positive social and environmental change, including an organization or a project (Chahine 2016, p. 7).

The average length of each interview was about one and a half hours. These interviews allowed us to develop a semi-structured questionnaire for the next step of our study. The interviews, as well as the semi-structured questionnaire, included only open questions concerning the factors that led to a venture's success or failure. According to the phenomenological approach there were no prepared answers to choose from. We wanted our respondents to express their own opinion, which would allow us to understand deeper the phenomenon of social entrepreneurial success and failure.

Step 2. In the spring of 2017, we asked the alumni of the Presidential Management Training Program via email and phone calls to participate in the online semi-structured questionnaire. We obtained 27 respondents out of 42 in this online survey, the response rate being about 64%.

At the same time, in the spring of 2017, we also conducted a semi-structured survey with 31 nascent social entrepreneurs who had developed and implemented social ventures in the Omsk region of Russia. All of them were the leaders of social ventures and had less than three years' experience in social entrepreneurship. These nascent social entrepreneurs were participants of the training courses in Social Entrepreneurship at Dostoevsky Omsk State University and agreed to participate in the survey. We asked them to fill in the semi-structured questionnaire and answer the open-ended survey questions offline.

Our final sample contains 58 individuals: among them 31 were nascent and 27 were mature entrepreneurs at the time of participation in the survey. Our sample also includes information about gender: we have 17 male and 41 female participants. All our respondents have been trained in Social Entrepreneurship and Project Management.

The content of the survey included questions about social venture aims; current phase of venture; motives to run a social venture; achieved results; a social innovation that was implemented; the team, beneficiaries, and other participants; plans for the future; success factors; barriers and obstacles; personal satisfaction with venture success; etc.

For the aim of the research, the social ventures were divided into successful and failed. To classify the social ventures as successful or not we used the following criteria:

1. The implementation of the venture in practice and the ability to ensure sustainable current activities (Witt 2004; Sharir and Lerner 2006). Ventures that couldn't proceed from the planning phase to execution and sustainable performance, and those that were rejected and closed without implementation were considered as failed. We asked the leaders of start-up social ventures to identify the current phase of their venture (the phase they were in at the time of the survey) and about funding and other resources they had attracted. The long-term ventures were considered as already proceeding to the performance phase;

2. The subjective evaluation of social entrepreneurial success by the social venture leader or participant (Witt 2004) and the achievement of the social goals (Cukier et al. 2011; Sharir and Lerner 2006). We asked our respondents to describe the main aim and results of their social ventures. Then we asked: "Do you think that your social venture was a successful one?" The possible answers were "yes," "no," or "maybe." If the social venture was assessed as being successful, we asked our respondents to explain how.

We considered a venture as successful if we had positive answers for both criteria. If, for the second criteria question, we had the answer "maybe," but there was a clear description of results and an explanation of how the venture had been successful, the venture also was considered as successful.

The questionnaire included the following open-ended questions: "What were the main factors that led to the success of your social venture?," "What were the main obstacles or barriers for your social venture?" The content of the survey was manually codified and analyzed. Step-by-step the coded phrases were related to particular factors of success or failure and combined in groups. This iteration process allowed us to clarify the factors of social entrepreneurial success and failure. Finally, the results were compared to understand differences and similarities in factors affecting the success and failure of social ventures across nascent and mature entrepreneurs in the Omsk region of Russia.

5.4   Findings

Our findings are presented below. All interviewers from the first step participated in the survey as well, so the results below are given without double counting. Factors of success were identified by the leaders of successful ventures, factors of failure by the leaders of failed ventures. The names and age of our respondents, as well as the names of their ventures are real. Permission was obtained from the venture leaders to include their names and the names of their ventures.

5.4.1 Evaluation of Nascent Social Entrepreneurs in the Omsk Region About Factors of Success and Failure

The age of our nascent social entrepreneurs was between 19 and 24, including six male and 25 female respondents. The ventures were classified by sector: twelve educational, ten ecological, five charity, and four sports ventures.

Nascent entrepreneurs, the leaders of 28 successful ventures in the Omsk region, described the following factors of success:

1. Social Networking

The most important factor of success identified by nascent entrepreneurs was networking. Respondents talked about networking sponsors, volunteers, or beneficiaries. They noticed the importance of using existing personal connections and building new contacts. Networking helps to build the trust of friends, relatives, and other participants. The phrase "personal connections" was mentioned by 15 respondents as a factor that leads to success.

Christina, aged 22, the leader of the venture "Happy Wardrobe" that aims to help low-income customers obtain clothing free of charge or at low prices noted: "Using social nets helps us to succeed. We work with the target audience using existing social groups on the Internet."

Victoria, aged 22, the leader of the venture "Help a Friend!" that aims to help homeless dogs and other pets discussed the factors of success by saying: "Active involvement of beneficiaries. Positive connections with project sponsors."

2. Motivated Leader and Team

The respondents said that the enthusiasm of the team and its members has strong implications toward the success of the venture. The phrase "team cohesion" was mentioned by ten respondents as a factor that leads to success. In addition to team cohesion, the teams' dedication and drive toward addressing social challenge emerged from the data, illustrating team motivation.

Catherine, aged 20, the leader of "Ecological Lessons," an initiative that aims to promote ecological knowledge among children and teenagers by means of lessons and ecological events explained that team cohesion for the project aim was crucial for the project's success. The team believed that the new generation may change the ecological situation in the region, fueling team motivation.

Alexandra, aged 24, one of the leaders of the venture "Sunday Up!," a nonprofit school of personal growth, noted the shared motivation: "The team was interested in the project. We are the young leaders and we want to help children to develop their managerial skills."

3. Previous Experience of the Team Members and Team Leader

Both the experience and knowledge of the team members were considered as important factors of success. For example, respondents talked about their experience in public relations, working with children, public speaking, sports, and event management.

Alexander, aged 20, the leader of the venture "The world without AIDS" that aims to inform youth about infection using creative active learning methods noted: "The team members have experience in event management and knowledge about HIV/AIDS. Many of us had participated already in volunteer work organized by medical centers. We had lessons about HIV/AIDS and we want to share our knowledge with the youth to warn them about the danger." Thus, in addition to the shared goal which motivates team members, they are driven by their desire to apply their skills and previous experience to solving social problems.

4. Ability to find Resources and Financial and Organizational Support

Catherine, aged 23, the leader of the venture "Healthy" that aims to promote a healthy style of life by means of mass sport events noted: "The ability to find sponsors that were interested to organize sport events for citizens was one of the most important factors that led to the project's success because the main participants of the project were families from low-income districts including children and pensioners." Mobilizing stakeholders outside their ventures to support a cause and channel resources to support it was a cross-cutting success factor for social entrepreneurs.

Nascent entrepreneurs who led failed ventures identified only social networking and the motivation of the leader and team as potential factors of success, but we didn't include their answers in our findings because their ventures failed.

Nascent entrepreneurs who led three failed ventures described the following obstacles and barriers that they couldn't overcome:

1. Lack of Team Motivation and Cohesion

The most important factor of failure was lack of motivation and cohesion. For instance, a woman, aged 22, the leader of the venture "Book turnover" that targeted the idea of book sharing in coffee shops observed that "the idea turned out to be not so interesting for the team as it seemed at the beginning. We started the project and then understood that it's very time consuming and we don't have any desire to spend our free time to develop this project." In this case, the venture was formed around an idea rather than a problem and did not share the same source of motivation that fueled teams who successfully tackled social challenges and remained dedicated to iterating potential solutions to these challenges.

2. Poor Networking

Some of the nascent entrepreneurs considered networking as a stumbling block for their project. Lack of skills for networking as well as the wrong target group for networking led to the project's failure.

Maria, aged 23, the leader of the venture "Battery" that aimed to prevent the dumping of batteries and accumulators: "We started from a very narrow target group. We didn't build communication channels with citizens and were not able to inform them about our project." Such cases reflect the importance of stakeholder mobilization described above, illustrating the failed outcomes which are more likely to occur when resources are not channeled to support the cause. It also links to the importance of previous experience and skills; and existing social networks.

3. Organizational Context

The structure of the parent organization and its internal institutions have a strong influence on the project. If there is a contradiction between the organizational rules and a new project, either a project fails or develops beyond the parent organization.

Anastasia, aged 20, the leader of the educational venture: "Bureaucracy of the parent organization didn't allow us to reach all the aims of the project." In this case the parent organization blocked some activities of the project that led to the project's failure. This observation is specific to intrapreneurship—innovating within existing organizations—which can have the advantages of existing structures and resources to support a new venture, while it may inflict the disadvantage of having to maneuver within these existing structures which are not always conducive to trying new approaches.

5.4.2 Evaluation of Mature Social Entrepreneurs in the Omsk Region About Factors of Success and Failure

The age of the mature social entrepreneurs was between 28 and 49 years, including 11 male and 16 female respondents. The following types of ventures were identified: eight medical, five educational, four cultural, three sport, two ecological, and five other ventures (agricultural, political, industrial, science, transport).

Mature entrepreneurs, the leaders of 13 successful ventures in the Omsk region, described the following factors of success:

1. Institutional and Market Context

The most important factor of success identified by mature social entrepreneurs was the institutional and market context. In these cases, entrepreneurs were able to successful navigate existing structures and innovate within existing institutions.

Tatyana, aged 49, the leader of the sport and wellness venture "Siberian school of health" that aims to build playgrounds and sports grounds in public parks noted: "The project matched the priority areas of government policy." This alignment of goals between the nascent venture and the existing institution prevented the bureaucracy and blocking seen in the failed ventures above.

Vitaly, aged 39, the leader of an ecological and industrial venture that aims to construct a water purification plant explained the project's success by saying: "Changes in environmental legislation. If the legislation hadn't been changed, the power plant wouldn't have invested in a new water purification plant." Thus, external factors including policy, law, and environmental prioritization paved the path for innovation.

A man aged 45, the leader of a high-tech science venture noted that "the government policy of import substitution provided the project success." The sanctions against Russia motivated the Russian government to support research and development to reduce imports. Again, here the timing and alignment with both internal and external priorities and agenda created a fertile ground to build new ventures.

Similarly, Eugene, aged 41, the leader of a venture that aims at the development and implementation of distance learning courses in the nonprofit sector of education claimed that "demand for short-term online courses in the market was a key factor of success."

2. Ability to Find Resources and Financial and Organizational Support

The second most important factor for success was the ability to garner support, both financial and non-financial. While revenue is seen as a means to an end in social ventures rather than the end goal, without financial sustainability long-term impact is impossible.

Anna, aged 39, the leader of the venture "Call Center for Diagnostic Clinic" explained that "sustainable financial position of the company and organizational support of the company administration were the bases for success."

Marina, aged 46, the leader of the venture "Multifunctional Youth Center" noted that "the project received a subsidy from the federal budget." Thus, social entrepreneurs have benefited from a range of revenue streams, both private and public. These were important at several stages of the social ventures, including seed funding and growth.

3. Motivated Leader and Team

The people behind the idea were viewed as equally important if not more important than the idea itself. Having a dedicated chief executive and core team to see the social venture through its early stages and growth was expressed as being critical to its survival and success.

The mature entrepreneurs assigned a very important role to the motivation of the project leader and project team on their way to success.

Anna, aged 35, the leader of the cross-cultural social venture "United Creative Area" explained that her "personal motivation was a main factor of the project's success."

Anna, aged 39, the venture "Call Center for Diagnostic Clinic" also linked the project success with motivated project manager.

Olga, aged 36, the leader of a venture that aimed to open a dental orthopedic cabinet with free of charge services underlined that they desired the development of the organization. Strong desire and dedication to the medicine led this team to the successful implementation of the project idea on practice.

4. Previous Experience of the Team Members and Leader

Motivation and dedication however are not enough if not backed by tangible skills. Respondents viewed the previous experience of the team members and leader as being critical to the success of a venture.

Galina, aged 39, the leader of a venture that aims to promote the standards of "Ready for Work and Defense" (renovation of former Soviet Union standards) in the Omsk region noted that building an interdisciplinary team was crucial for the project's success. The team included people from sport, the army, public administration, marketing, and project management, also the project leader had experience in the implementation of similar projects.

Natalia, aged 43, the leader of a venture that aims to implement electronic textbooks—the "ABC System"—in the educational system of the Omsk region among the other factors that led to success named her "experience of working with this product." Thus, having subject matter knowledge on technical aspects and product development was viewed as important alongside diversity in people and management skills.

5. Organizational Context

Beyond the people, the health of the organization itself as an entity was considered important. These factors of success are linked to the internal structure of the organization and its institutions.

Elena, aged 39, the leader of a medical venture that aims to organize day care centers in hospitals noted that "the need to change the organizational structure of the parent organization was a driver of the project's success."

Vitaly, aged 39, (the venture of a new water purification plant) noted that "exhaustion of the resource of existing equipment led to the need of the new water purification plant that brought the change of the organizational structure of the power plant." In both these cases, demonstrating agility and adaptability was critical to survival and success.

6. Social Networking

Beyond the organization, the social network surrounding the team and structure provide the support needed to penetrate the market.

Natalia, aged 43, (a venture for the implementation of electronic textbooks "ABC System") explained that "building good relationships with suppliers of electronic textbooks and consumers (schools and parents) are the most important for the project's success."

A man aged 45, the leader of the high-tech science venture, noticed that they developed "an effective scheme of interaction between the project stakeholders." Effective interaction was considered as an important factor of success. Mature entrepreneurs, the leaders of failed ventures, identified only the institutional and market context and organizational context as potential factors of success. Eight of them didn't identify any factors of success, probably because they were disappointed by the project failure.

Mature leaders of 14 failed ventures described the following obstacles and barriers that they couldn't overcome:

1. Lack of Team Motivation and Cohesion

It was the most important factor of failure for mature social entrepreneurs, the same as for nascent entrepreneurs.

Tatyana, aged 47, the leader of the venture "Boarding house for temporary stay for elderly people" noted that "the project's failure was connected to lack of motivation and shortage of time." She argued that the project would require all her free time, but she can't leave her job, so she lost her passion for the project.

Anna, aged 44, the leader of a venture that aimed for the development of a rehabilitation center to help sick and disabled people at home claimed that she lost her dedication to the project because she doesn't have enough time for this project. She has already helped sick and disabled people but she understood that these days it can't be her main activity.

2. Lack of Funding

Alexey, aged 34, the leader of a venture that aimed for tourism development in the Tara district of the Omsk region (a remote area to the north of the region) complained about the lack of any funding.

3. Institutional and Market Context

Elena, aged 37, the leader of "Board of young artists" that aimed cooperation of the young leaders from the state cultural organizations blamed "the system of regional government for the failure of the venture. Nowadays many state and municipal cultural organizations of the Omsk region have an unbalanced age structure, especially in their management that leads to a lack of creativity and competitiveness." The informal institutions of the regional government contradicted the project idea and led to the project's failure.

Andrey, aged 46, the leader of the agricultural venture "Dutch cooperative" complained that "project participants in the countryside do not have the required skills." The institutions of the Soviet Union are still very strong in Russian society, especially in the countryside. These institutions wouldn't allow for the cooperation required for the Dutch cooperative.

5.5   Conclusions

This study analyzes the factors of success and failure of social entrepreneurship among nascent and mature entrepreneurs in the Omsk region of Russia. To understand the phenomenon of social entrepreneurial success and failure more deeply we conducted a qualitative research with social entrepreneurs. In this study, the total sample included 58 respondents who ran social ventures.

The main contribution of our paper is that it shows that the factors of success and failure are related to each other inside each group of respondents, while nascent and mature social entrepreneurs have different perceptions of the factors leading to social entrepreneurship success or failure.

Using a phenomenological approach to understand the factors of social entrepreneurship success and failure, we found that social entrepreneurs across the Omsk region (Russia) identified the following factors of success: social networking; motivated leader and team; previous experience of the team members and leader; ability to find resources and financial and organizational support; institutional and market context;

organizational context. These factors of success were previously discussed by Dufays and Huybrechts (2014), Leadbeater (1997), Lehner (2014), Newth and Woods (2014), Sharir and Lerner (2006), and Zhang and Swanson (2014), but our findings show the particular perceptions of Russian social entrepreneurs.

Institutional and market context was the most important factor of success for mature entrepreneurs, while networking was the most important for nascent social entrepreneurs. Mature entrepreneurs identified all the factors of success that were mentioned above. Nascent entrepreneurs didn't identify institutional, market, or organizational context as factors of success.

The factors of failure for the Omsk region were the following: lack of team motivation and cohesion; poor networking; organizational context; lack of funding; institutional, and market context. The most important factor of failure for both groups of respondents was lack of motivation; it was the only factor that was identified in both groups of respondents. While the factors of motivation and organizational, institutional, and market context were considered already as barriers by Robinson (2006), and factors of resistance by Newth and Woods (2014), our findings show that poor networking and lack of funding may also become barriers that social entrepreneurs cannot overcome.

It was noticed that the factors of failure are related to the factors of success inside each group. The most important factors of success and failure for nascent entrepreneurs are the following: level of motivation; networking skills. The most important factors of success and failure for mature entrepreneurs are the positive and negative influence of the institutional and market context on the venture; the ability to find resources and lack of funding; and level of motivation.

This study has limitations that provide directions for future research. Firstly, our study is focused on a particular region of the Russian Federation, precisely the Omsk region is an industrial region in Siberia. Further research could compare different regions of Russia as well as different regions of the world. It would definitely require enlarging the number of respondents.

Secondly, our data includes information about the gender of respondents. The large majority of nascent entrepreneurs were women, while this proportion was reduced among mature entrepreneurs, which may show that social entrepreneurship is more attractive for female nascent entrepreneurs, but this fact should be tested in further studies. Applying a gender lens to future studies on factors for success and failure will help to better understand gender differences.

Finally, we discussed only factors of success identified by successful entrepreneurs and barriers identified by failed entrepreneurs. We did not discuss the barriers that were identified by successful entrepreneurs. According to Newth and Woods (2014), some of the factors of resistance may lead to the success of social innovation. To prove this hypothesis, we would suggest asking social entrepreneurs to identify separately those barriers that were overcome and what was learnt from the experience.

In summary, this study provides a starting point in understanding factors related to the success and failure of social entrepreneurs in a unique region in the Russian Federation. If the practice of social entrepreneurship grows in various regions of the Russian Federation, as seems likely, so too will the ecosystem surrounding it, including stakeholders such as funders and other supporters, and most importantly the communities served. Building on this preliminary research by creating larger datasets and including a larger number of social entrepreneurs and other stakeholders in the ecosystem will allow for a more multi-dimensional perspective to be added to the entrepreneurs' perspective, which can be used to inform the design, financing, implementation, and growth of social ventures in the future.

References

Alter, Sutia K. 2003. Social Enterprise: A Typology of the Field Contextualized in Latin America. Working Paper, Washington, DC.

Aray, Yulia N., and Tatyana A. Burmistrova. 2014. Specificity of Business Models in Social Entrepreneurship. *Russian Management Journal* 12 (4): 55–78.

Austin, James E., Dutch Leonard, Ezequiel Reficco, and Jane Wei-Skillern. 2004. Corporate Social Entrepreneurship: A New Vision of CSR. Working Paper No. 05-021, Harvard Business School, Boston.

Austin, James, Howard Stevenson, and Jane Wei-Skillern. 2006. Social and Commercial Entrepreneurship: Same, Different, or Both? *Entrepreneurship Theory and Practice* 30 (1): 1–22.

Batalina, Marina, Alexandra Moskovskaya, and Larisa Taradina. 2008. The Overview of Experience and Concepts of Social Entrepreneurship: Taking into Account the Possibilities of its Application in Modern Russia. Preprint, WP1 (02). Higher School of Economics, Moscow.

Chahine, Teresa. 2016. *Introduction to Social Entrepreneurship*. Boca Raton: CRC Press.

Cukier, Wendy, Susan Trenholm, Dale Carl, and George Gekas. 2011. Social Entrepreneurship: A Content Analysis. *Journal of Strategic Innovation and Sustainability* 7 (1): 99–119.

Dacin, Peter A., M. Tina Dacin, and Margaret Matear. 2010. Social Entrepreneurship: Why We Don't Need a New Theory and How We Move Forward from Here. *Academy of Management Perspectives* 24 (3): 37–53.

Dees, J. Gregory. 1998. The Meaning of Social Entrepreneurship. Original draft, Revised 2001. Accessed August 8, 2017. https://entrepreneurship.duke.edu/news-item/the-meaning-of-social-entrepreneurship/.

Dees, J. Gregory. 2012. A Tale of Two Cultures: Charity, Problem Solving, and the Future of Social Entrepreneurship. *Journal of Business Ethics* 111 (3): 321–334.

Dufays, Frédéric, and Benjamin Huybrechts. 2014. Connecting the Dots for Social Value: A Review on Social Networks and Social Entrepreneurship. *Journal of Social Entrepreneurship* 5 (2): 214–237.

Fomina, Yulia A., and Eduard V. Fomin. 2014. The Capital Repair Issues of Apartment Building. *Innovative Economy and Society* 1: 54–60.

Germak, Andrew J., and Jeffrey A. Robinson. 2014. Exploring the Motivation of Nascent Social Entrepreneurs. *Journal of Social Entrepreneurship* 5 (1): 5–21.

Keohane, Georgia L. 2013. *Social Entrepreneurship for the 21st Century: Innovation Across the Nonprofit, Private, and Public Sector*. New York, NY: McGrow-Hill.

Krutikov, Valery K., and Maria V. Yakunina. 2013. *Non-commercial Sector of Economy and Innovative Development of the Region*. Kaluga: Polygraph-Inform.

Labour and Employment in Russia. 2017. *Statistical Collection*, ed. K.E. Laikam. Moscow: Federal State Statistics Service.

Leadbeater, Charles. 1997. *The Rise of the Social Entrepreneur*. London: Demos.

Lehner, Othmar M. 2014. The Formation and Interplay of Social Capital in Crowdfunded Social Ventures. *Entrepreneurship & Regional Development* 26 (5–6): 478–499.

Mair, Johanna, and Ernesto Noboa. 2006. Social Entrepreneurship: How Intentions to Create a Social Venture Get Formed. In *Social Entrepreneurship*, ed. Johanna Mair, Jeffrey Robinson, and Kai Hockerts, 121–136. New York: Palgrave Macmillan.

Makarevich, Anna N., and Tatyana Y. Sazonova. 2012. The Nature and Specificity of Social Entrepreneurship in Russia. *Journal of Russian Entrepreneurship* 24: 52–56.

McMullen, Jeffery S. 2011. Delineating the Domain of Development Entrepreneurship: A Market-Based Approach to Facilitating Inclusive Economic Growth. *Entrepreneurship Theory and Practice* 35 (1): 185–193.

Monzón, José L., and Rafael Chaves. 2012. *The Social Economy in the European Union* (Report). Brussel: European Economic and Social Committee. Accessed February 15, 2017. www.eesc.europa.eu.

Moskovskaya, Alexandra. 2011. *Social Entrepreneurship in Russia and the World: Practice and Research*. Moscow: Higher School of Economics.

Newth, Jamie, and Christine Woods. 2014. Resistance to Social Entrepreneurship: How Context Shapes Innovation. *Journal of Social Entrepreneurship* 5 (2): 192–213.

Robinson, Jeffrey. 2006. Navigating Social and Institutional Barriers to Markets: How Social Entrepreneurs Identify and Evaluate Opportunities. In *Social Entrepreneurship*, ed. Johanna Mair, Jeffrey Robinson, and Kai Hockerts, 95–120. New York: Palgrave Macmillan.

Roy, Abhijit, Alan Brumagim, and Irene Goll. 2014. Predictors of Social Entrepreneurship Success: A Cross-National Analysis of Antecedent Factors. *Journal of Social Entrepreneurship* 5 (1): 42–59.

Sharir, Moshe, and Miri Lerner. 2006. Gauging the Success of Social Ventures Initiated by Individual Social Entrepreneurs. *Journal of World Business* 41 (1): 6–20.

Stecker, Michelle J. 2014. Revolutionizing the Nonprofit Sector Through Social Entrepreneurship. *Journal of Economic Issues* 48 (2): 349–357.

Territorial Body of the Federal State Statistics Service in the Omsk Region. 2018. Gross Regional Product of the Omsk Region, May 7. Accessed June 8, 2018. http://omsk.gks.ru/wps/wcm/connect/rosstat_ts/omsk/ru/statistics/grp/.

The Government of the Omsk Region. 2010. Atmospheric Air and Public Health. Electronic atlas. Accessed June 6, 2018. http://msh.omskportal.ru/ru/RegionalPublicAuthorities/executivelist/MSH/the_state_control/ecology/realisation_nature_protection_actions/the_electronic_atlas.html.

The Government of the Omsk Region. 2018. Non-commercial Organizations of the Omsk Region. Accessed June 6, 2018. http://omskportal.ru/ru/government/society/society_topics/obshestv-obedenenija-omsk-obl.html.

U.S. Bureau of Labor Statistics. 2014. *The Economics Daily*, October 21. Accessed June 6, 2018. https://www.bls.gov/opub/ted/2014/ted_20141021.htm.

WCED (World Commission on Environment and Development). 1987. *Our Common Future*. Oxford: Oxford University Press.

Witt, Peter. 2004. Entrepreneurs' Networks and the Success of Start-Ups. *Entrepreneurship & Regional Development* 16 (5): 391–412.

Zhang, David Di, and Lee A. Swanson. 2014. Linking Social Entrepreneurship and Sustainability. *Journal of Social Entrepreneurship* 5 (2): 175–191.

Zhokhova, Valentina V. 2015. Social Entrepreneurship: Nature and Definition. *The Bulletin of the Far Eastern Federal University: Economics and Management* 73 (1): 85–98.

Part II

People, Practitioners and CSR Education

6

Yes, We Can! Encouraging Responsible Management Through Effective CSR Communication

Irene Garnelo-Gomez and Anastasiya Saraeva

6.1 Introduction

Business schools have gradually started incorporating corporate social responsibility-related modules into MBA programmes (Christensen et al. 2007; Larran and Andrades Peña 2014). A study published by Larran et al. (2017) found that 64% of top 100 MBA programmes ranked by the *Financial Times* offer stand-alone courses on corporate social responsibility (CSR) and ethics. Although this percentage appears to have increased in recent years, there is still a need to proactively integrate responsibility into business programmes (Waddock and Lozano 2013), and to encourage and develop education in responsible management (PRME 2007; Millar and Price 2018). This is particularly critical for business productivity. For example, effective CSR training (e.g. for managers) has a significant impact on business, specifically on brand image and the financial value of an organisation as, for instance,

I. Garnelo-Gomez (✉) · A. Saraeva
Henley Business School, University of Reading, Reading, UK
e-mail: i.garnelo-gomez@henley.ac.uk

© The Author(s) 2019
F. Farache et al. (eds.), *Responsible People*, Palgrave Studies in Governance,
Leadership and Responsibility, https://doi.org/10.1007/978-3-030-10740-6_6

"it is possible that properly trained managers can ensure sustainability while companies and their shareholders maximize their financial value" (López-Pérez et al. 2017, p. 442).

CSR practice suggests that it is essential that managers understand key aspects of CSR communication in order to create stakeholder awareness (Du et al. 2010). We thus argue that a similar approach should be followed in education, and, in particular, when delivering CSR modules to MBA students (referred to, in this chapter, as programme members). For instance, Henley Business School (University of Reading, UK), offers three modules related to CSR as part of its MBA curriculum. In one of them, namely Reputation and Responsibility, lecturers engage programme members in experiential learning (Kolb 1984). As such, programme members travel to Cape Town (South Africa) to conduct a consultancy project for local NGOs. In doing so, they not only develop their responsible management skills, but *experience* responsibility challenges in a novel and distinctive manner. Through immersing themselves in the daily lives of NGOs, MBA programme members help organisations to identify a responsibility challenge, analyse the problem, and offer a managerial solution. Most importantly, by engaging in conversations with diverse groups of individuals, from charity staff to beneficiaries, programme members have the fortunate opportunity of receiving first-hand insights on CSR practice; these insights then enrich their awareness of responsibility issues.

Henley Business School is also a participant in the Principles for Responsible Management Education (PRME) initiative. This platform, created in 2007 and coordinated by the UN Global Compact, aims to provide business students with the necessary awareness and understanding of sustainability and CSR to develop their ability to deliver change in the future (PRME 2007). As such, Henley Business School reports to the UN how the principles of PRME are being addressed, and how the research and teaching carried out at the institution facilitate the dialogue around CSR issues; in other words, how to create CSR knowledge and how to communicate it (Henley Business School 2017).

In spite of the growing tendency for CSR-related modules to be integrated into MBA curriculum, little is known about efficient ways to communicate CSR in management education (Setó-Pamies and

Papaoikonomou 2016). Most importantly, and to the best of the authors' knowledge, no study currently exists that explores the effects of the interplay between module content and lecturer in CSR communication—neither generally nor in the particular context of MBA education.

In this conceptual chapter, we reflect on practical CSR issues in MBA education and focus on the role of the individual in CSR practice. Specifically, we investigate how to encourage managers at the individual level to embrace CSR activities and become responsible agents who deliver change in the future. We then propose a theoretical framework, with the aim of shedding light on effective CSR communication in management education.

6.2 Communicating CSR in MBA Programmes

Various dimensions of CSR, such as citizenship, governance, and working conditions, are key drivers of corporate reputation (Reputation Institute 2018). These highlight the importance of communicating CSR in an effective way. According to Dawkins (2005), organisations should develop a clear strategy when designing CSR communications, and a CSR *message* should be tailored for each stakeholder group—that is, one based on information needs, interests, and preferred channels of communication.

Du et al. (2010) agree with Dawkins and include stakeholder characteristics in their Framework of CSR Communication. However, the authors focus their attention on the content of the message, which often emphasises what the company is doing, rather than focusing on the social issue itself. They suggest that when developing CSR communications, companies should indeed focus on the importance of the social issue but also on other factors. In particular, they mention the commitment the organisation has with the issue, the impact the company is making by getting involved, the motives driving the company to collaborate, and the congruence between the social issue and the business itself. Nevertheless, according to Morsing (2006), organisations should not merely inform stakeholders about CSR issues; rather, in order to build trust, companies might interact with stakeholders on a continuous basis. The scholar argues then that by establishing an "interaction strategy" (as a complement to the "information strategy"), stakeholders will positively identify with the company and the company will better understand stakeholders' expectations, contributing to the development of CSR strategies and the effective communication thereof.

We believe that a similar approach should be followed when communicating CSR in education. There should be a clear strategy behind the CSR communication, and the content of the message ought to focus on teaching business students how to embed social issues into the company's strategies. This argument is also aligned with existing approaches to CSR education. For instance, building on Lozano et al. (2006), we agree that the design of CSR-related modules should include not only relevant content, but also relevant learning processes that could encourage students to critically analyse CSR issues and the role of business in society.

Furthermore, we agree with Morsing's idea of establishing an "interaction strategy", which, in the context of this chapter, would involve communicating CSR messages not only in a classroom but also by interacting with the social issue itself and building relationships with key stakeholders. We also agree with Sims (2002), who suggests that ethics can be communicated effectively if an experiential approach is followed and if lecturers are able to create an environment in which students feel safe to share their experiences. In our view, the combination of a well-designed content that allows programme members to experience CSR, with the opportunity for interaction with others, both in the classroom and outside of it, leads to the creation of an effective message.

6.2.1 Effective CSR Message

Despite the significant existing research on CSR communications in the corporate world (Du et al. 2010; Tata and Prasad 2015) and in the education arena (Cornelius et al. 2007; Stubbs and Schapper 2011), little is known about how to effectively communicate CSR issues to MBA programme members. For the purpose of this conceptual chapter, we build on previous studies (Giacalone and Thompson 2006; Lozano et al. 2006) and argue that one of the key aspects when communicating CSR in higher education relates to the *content* of the CSR module.

In our view, and in accordance with the PRME principles (2007), the materials designed for communicating CSR in MBA programmes should not merely create awareness of past and current CSR issues. Rather they should aim to drive behavioural change as well. We believe in the idea that by the end of the programme, MBA programme members should have developed the necessary knowledge and belief around CSR issues that would translate at a personal level, and, as a consequence, at their place of work. As mentioned above, the first step to achieving this aim involves designing effective module content.

A few universities design the content of CSR modules not only to promote student acquisition of knowledge on social responsibility issues, but also to implement this knowledge through real case scenarios. Henley Business School's approach to MBA education could be an example of excellence in this area. As mentioned in the introduction, they offer three CSR-related modules as part of their MBA curriculum, one of them called Reputation and Responsibility. As part of this module, MBA programme members travel to Cape Town, where they work as consultants for a week with local charities, with the purpose of resolving existing organisational challenges. In doing so, they build an understanding of how to tackle social issues, which gives them strategies on how to apply CSR (Brew 2002; Stubbs and Schapper 2011). By working with these charities, MBA programme members interact with stakeholders affected by social issues, and it is through these experiences that they are able to build ideas and thoughts around social responsibility (Kolb 1984; Sims 2002).

The approach followed at Henley Business School allows MBA programme members to reflect on societal problems and to engage with them at a personal level. This learning approach contrasts with the standard design and content of CSR modules, which encourages students to examine CSR issues from a business perspective (Stubbs and Schapper 2011). We believe that by communicating CSR messages addressing both the personal and professional identities of MBA programme members, students will be more effectively engaged with module content which, ultimately, will lead to positive behavioural change.

While the content of the CSR message when communicating to MBA programme members is vital, we believe that the question of *who* is communicating the message is of particular importance (McDonald 2004). Indeed, the early studies on CSR communication have shown that effective messages may not necessarily lead to desired behaviours if they are not communicated by the "right" messenger. An example of this relates to Victoria State (Australia), where the local government attempted to proactively communicate the importance of wearing helmets while cycling. This resulted in a decrease of the number of young people cycling (and therefore exercising) and, as a consequence, a decrease in the overall national health rate (De Jong 2012). The question is, would have the outcome been different if the message was communicated by a different source?

In the next section of this chapter, we explore the notion of the messenger (i.e. lecturer), who has been hardly examined in the CSR arena (Groza et al. 2011), and who we argue is crucial to effectively communicate CSR in MBA programmes.

6.3   Identification with Lecturer as Key to Effective CSR Education

Despite the discussed importance of communicating CSR module content as an effective message, CSR education involves much more than "conveying information" (Benson 1994; Northcott 2001). In fact, various student surveys show that, despite advances in module materials, there are other attributes that make the module highly influential (Douglas et al. 2006; Butt and Rehman 2010). One of these attributes is *who* the lecturer is and whether and how students relate to them.

One may argue that the pedagogy literature has received a significant attention to the role of a teacher in higher education (Murray and Macdonald 1997; Hill et al. 2003). However, we believe that the role and significance of a lecturer as a *messenger* (i.e. an entity that communicates a message directly to the audience—see Saraeva 2017) in the context of education remains unclear and requires further investigation.

In general, communication literature suggests that a messenger appears as a critical "touchstone", which individuals use to evaluate or judge received messages (Groza et al. 2011). At the same time, various studies support that messengers can lead to changes in people's attitudes and behaviours (Lafferty and Goldsmith 1999; Ruth and York 2004). We argue that a communication approach that understands lecturers as messengers in CSR education may help MBA programme members to actively engage with the module content, which could contribute to greater commitment to CSR practice outside the classroom.

6.3.1 Unpacking the "Messenger"

One of the most discussed attributes of a messenger is *credibility* (Lafferty and Goldsmith 1999; Jones et al. 2003). For example, Fishbein and Ajzen (2011) find that individuals are more likely to engage in positive behaviours influenced by the information from a credible messenger (MacKenzie and Lutz 1989; Miller and Krosnick 2000). This is in line with the pedagogy literature, as subject knowledge, expertise, and organisation skills—that is, credibility—are found to be essential characteristics of a lecturer (Eggen and Kauchak 1993; Tootoonchi et al. 2002).

While, on the whole, lecturer credibility can positively impact how CSR messages are being perceived by MBA programme members, it is not yet clear why people still tend to react differently to the same lecturer. The communication literature suggests that perceptions of lecturers (as messengers) could be triggered by *unobservable determinants*, such as enthusiasm, energy and/or humour (Guolla 1999), impressions (Jones et al. 2003), or similarity between an individual and a messenger (Kwon et al. 2015), rather than credibility alone. For instance, Jones and Gerard (1967, p. 436) find that "when his [messenger's] values do not coincide with those of his audience, the force of his message is reduced". In other words, individuals would be more affected by what messengers communicate if there was a perceived overlap in values and/ or beliefs between a messenger and the audience (Basil 1996; Cheong and Morrison 2008).

Following the discussion on similarity, we suggest that a possible way of exploring underlying determinants of how individual MBA programme members perceive CSR lecturers may lie in studies related to *identification with the messenger* (Basil 1996; Saraeva 2017). In order to integrate the concept of identification with a messenger into the context of CSR education, it is important to review previous approaches to the phenomenon.

Burke's Drama Theory

Burke (1969) is one of the early theorists who indirectly focused on the role of a messenger. While studying drama, Burke finds that when the audience feels a certain connection—*rapport*—with a character on stage, this significantly induces the persuasiveness of their acting. Hence, we argue that when an MBA programme member feels a certain connection with a lecturer (similar to how the audience connects to a character on stage), then the communicated message about CSR (i.e. module content) may have a higher persuasive impact on the individual (Guolla 1999). Indeed, following the CSR education purpose, it seems crucial to ensure that the module content is well perceived. However, Burke does not elaborate on how the abovementioned rapport may impact individuals' behaviours. Furthermore, and building on the PRME principles (2007), MBA programmes (involving CSR communication) are expected to drive significant behavioural change among programme members. Thus, the drama theory lacks sufficient evidence on how a lecturer (as a messenger) could positively impact students' awareness of and behaviours towards CSR practice.

Bandura's Social Learning Theory

Further insight into understanding the rapport between a lecturer and MBA programme members is drawn from social learning theory (Bandura 1969). Bandura argues that people's behaviours are influenced or could be changed through learning from "role models", with whom an individual may feel a certain overlap of values. In other words, Bandura suggests that when a person *identifies* with the role model, they are more likely to engage in promoted behaviours. Drawing from this theory, a CSR lecturer may appear (deliberately or inadvertently) as a role model to MBA programme members (Tootoonchi et al. 2002). Thus, when a programme member feels identified with a lecturer, they would be more likely to engage in CSR behaviours and become agents who deliver change in the future.

Saraeva's Identification with Messenger

The identification with messenger framework by Saraeva (2017) is one of most recent developments in this area, which is successfully incorporated into corporate communication context. Saraeva believes that the framework may help to better understand how people perceive messages, and, in turn, to explain why they react differently to communication. She further argues that people's reactions and behaviours are driven by *interactions* between messages and various levels of identification with messengers.

Although the model of identification with messenger is developed and tested in the context of corporate communication about reputation, we believe that this framework is useful to the current context of CSR education. In particular, we argue that an *interplay* between module content (message) and identification with lecturer (messenger) may significantly influence MBA programme members' engagement with the CSR module, and, in turn, affect members' pro-CSR behaviours in the future (e.g. commitment to CSR practice).

Although establishing the role of MBA programme members' identification with a lecturer seems crucial, we believe that it is also important to explore consequences of the proposed interplay between module content and identification with a lecturer in communicating CSR to MBA programme members. In the next section of this chapter, we further address the proposed interplay and discuss possible outcomes of effective CSR communication in MBA education.

6.4   Message–Messenger Interplay and CSR Commitment

We have previously established that a CSR message may have a significant impact on MBA programme members when communicated in a way that addresses both the individuals' self-reflection and the business perspective. Building on the theory of reasoned action (Fishbein and Ajzen 2011) and the identification with messenger framework (Saraeva 2017), we believe that the interaction between identification with a lecturer and a CSR message may influence programme members' *commitment* to CSR practice.

Building on Garnelo-Gomez (2017), commitment in the context of responsibility is understood as high levels of engagement with the issues of consideration and long-term expressions of responsible behaviour. In this chapter, behaviours towards CSR practice involve engaging in CSR issues outside the classroom. This, in turn, may lead MBA programme members to becoming agents of change, which in our view includes actively responding to CSR issues in the workplace.

Bringing together messages and messengers in the context of CSR education, we propose a framework of a dynamic interplay between module content and identification with lecturer and their combined impact on commitment to CSR practice (see Fig. 6.1).

Previous studies on CSR and commitment have focused on understanding how competent CSR strategies and CSR communications could increase employee organisational commitment (Turker 2009; Du et al. 2010). We argue that this relationship between employees' commitment and CSR could be addressed from an earlier and alternative point of view. For instance, commitment could be understood as an antecedent instead of as a consequence of CSR strategies (i.e. employees' commitment to CSR could lead to a more effective CSR strategy and communication). By reaching what for the purpose of this chapter could be called a "perfect case scenario" (see Fig. 6.1 path (1)—effective message and high levels of identification with the messenger), MBA programme members would become the committed employees who would lead change and encourage the development of appropriate and efficient CSR strategies. In this case, employee commitment would lead to efficient CSR, which ultimately drives positive organisational performance

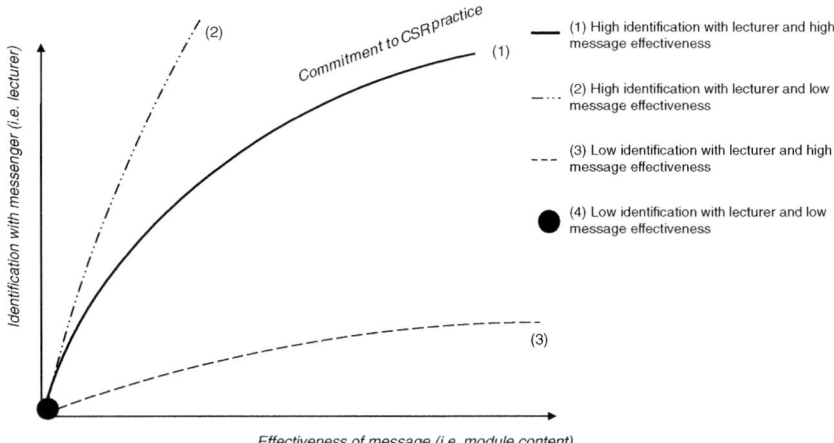

Fig. 6.1 Conceptual representation of an interplay between effectiveness of message (module content) and identification with messenger (lecturer)

(McWilliams et al. 2006). For example, a highly effective CSR message in the classroom would involve bringing real-life case studies to encourage students to critically analyse CSR issues and the role of business in society. Moreover, by explicitly communicating their values and beliefs as well as experience of CSR, lecturers would be able to establish a rapport with their students, which will arouse identification.

Another possible outcome of the proposed interplay would relate to the communication of a less effective or non-effective CSR message from the lecturer, whom MBA programme members feel highly identified with (see Fig. 6.1 path (2)). Given the high identification with a lecturer, one could expect MBA programme members to be strongly affected by the delivery of the module content. However, a less effective message would probably lead to a limited engagement with the CSR module and, in turn, scarce CSR experience outside the classroom. Interestingly, studies on identification with messenger suggest that identification may raise people's awareness and trigger *intentions* to change behaviours (see Basil 1996; Brown and Basil 2010). Thus, it can be suggested that in this scenario a possible (positive) consequence would be an increase of MBA programme members' intentions to further explore CSR topics as well as find ways to engage in responsible behaviours outside the classroom.

Looking at the third possible scenario (see Fig. 6.1 path (3)—effective CSR message and low or non-existent level of identification with the lecturer), we suggest that the possibility of the MBA programme members becoming committed to CSR practice would be limited. In particular, we expect students to understand, debate, and engage with the CSR message when in the classroom, but not necessarily to become agents of change in the long term. The communication literature, however, suggests that people tend to find messages more persuasive in situations when they are highly involved in a particular issue (Golob et al. 2008). Moreover, recent advances in CSR research suggest that individuals tend to engage in responsible behaviours if responsibility is somehow part of their personal identity (Garnelo-Gomez 2017). In other words, people who have CSR principles at the core of their identity (i.e. personal values and beliefs related to the defence of human rights, the environment, etc.) would be highly influenced by the communicated message, regardless of who the messenger is and how they feel towards them. Therefore, we argue that with the obtained knowledge (from module content) and personal values and beliefs, MBA programme members would be more likely to adopt and implement CSR strategies at their workplace, as well as become the agents of change (Hemingway and Maclagan 2004; Hemingway 2005).

Finally, in the least desirable scenario (see Fig. 6.1 path (4)—low levels of identification and less effective or non-effective CSR message), MBA programme members may develop a limited understanding and engagement with CSR issues. This may ultimately lead to lower levels of commitment to CSR practice—to include minor engagement with responsibility issues, short-term expressions of responsible behaviour, and limited application of knowledge outside the classroom—which would not comply with the PRME (2007) and the existing idea of effective CSR teaching (Sims 2002; Lozano et al. 2006). However, we believe that scenario (4) is highly unlikely to appear in CSR-related modules, especially in MBA education. More than 16,000 worldwide programmes (including MBA level) are committed to the PRME principles to "equip today's business students with the understanding and ability to deliver change tomorrow" (PRME 2007). Therefore, we believe that institutions participating in this initiative and beyond are increasingly interested in high-quality CSR teaching and learning.

To sum up, we believe that the proposed theoretical framework may help to anticipate MBA programme members' commitment to CSR practice. This also fits well with the PRME initiative (2007), which emphasises the long-term CSR education effect on proactive CSR change. While the proposed framework indicates that scenario (1), with high identification with the lecturer and highly effective CSR module content, would be most desirable for CSR-related modules within the MBA curriculum, it should be noted that scenarios (2) and (3) could also lead to positive outcomes. This would be the case if MBA programme members had the intention to further explore issues related to CSR (as in scenario (2)) or if CSR principles were already part of who they are as individuals (i.e. if their personal values and beliefs were aligned with those of responsibility) (as in scenario (3)).

6.5 Conclusion and Suggestions for Future Research

The growth of business schools' attention to CSR practice has led to an increasing integration of CSR-related modules into the MBA curriculum. However, effective ways of communicating CSR to MBA programme members have been greatly overlooked in the literature. In this chapter, we offer a novel theoretical framework, which unpacks nuances in effective communication of CSR-related messages in management education as well as outlines essential link to managers' commitment to CSR practice outside the classroom.

The journey towards effective communication starts with the message. In order to communicate CSR effectively, those in charge of designing the curriculum should carefully consider the content of the CSR-related module. We also argue that this type of module should have the aim of not only creating awareness, but also of driving change in behaviour (PRME 2007). In our view, the content of the module should be designed in such a way that programme members are able to critically analyse CSR from a business perspective, but which also allows them to reflect on social issues at a personal level. One of the ways in which this could be achieved (which is already established, for example, at the University of Leeds, University of Warwick, Cass Business School and EDHEC Business School) entails following an experiential approach (i.e. addressing CSR issues in a real case scenario). By facilitating the interaction between MBA programme members and stakeholders affected by social issues, the former are able to build their own argument around social responsibility (Sims 2002), which could contribute not only to higher levels of awareness but also to engagement and commitment.

We believe that "a messenger always accompanies a message" (O'Rourke 2013, p. 78). Thus, this chapter argues that the identification that audiences (such as MBA programme members) feel towards the lecturer communicating with them is key to understanding how and why students engage with CSR (Groza et al. 2011). In other words, when MBA programme members feel they identify with the lecturer, they may find the module content more influential, which, in turn, may contribute to higher levels of engagement and commitment to CSR practice.

Building on the premise of CSR communication, we offer a novel theoretical framework, which integrates the preceding discussed concepts. As such, the model reflects a dynamic interplay between module content and identification with the lecturer and their combined influence on commitment to CSR practice. Given this chapter is conceptual, we call for future empirical research to test the proposed framework and to cover additional issues that could influence the effectiveness of CSR communication in the context of MBA education. We believe that it will help to understand how to engage and develop modules in responsible management (Millar and Price 2018), contributing in this way to the PRME's principles.

6.5.1 Limitations

In light of the proposed framework, we acknowledge several limitations. Although incorporating the notion of a lecturer seems crucial, the framework is limited to identification with the lecturer and, as such, disregards other messenger characteristics. Future research should consider including additional factors (e.g. lecturer credibility, personal values, communication skills) and address how they might influence MBA programme members' engagement with the module as well as their future commitment to CSR practice. Furthermore, the characteristics of the individual who receives the message could also be taken into account by future researchers. For instance, the personal values and beliefs of the MBA programme members, as well as their motivations towards CSR practice, could influence the way the message is understood and processed.

The narrow scope of this study—applied as it is to CSR education at MBA level—also represents an important limitation. While it is crucial that MBA programme members become committed managers, leading change and encouraging the development of appropriate and efficient CSR strategies, it is essential to explore wider educational contexts. CSR-related modules are also implemented at the undergraduate and postgraduate levels. Thus, future research could explore how the proposed interplay between module content and identification with the lecturer influences bachelor and masters students' commitment to CSR practice.

The acknowledgment of these limitations and the presentation of these recommendations for future research are based on what we believe is an existing gap in the field of CSR communication in MBA education. We consider that the empirical testing of the theoretical framework proposed in this chapter could shed light on how to effectively communicate CSR messages to MBA programme members with the purpose of not only transferring knowledge, but encouraging behavioural change and an increase in the number of responsible people.

References

Bandura, Albert. 1969. Social-Learning Theory of Identificatory Processes. *Handbook of Socialization Theory and Research* 213: 262.

Basil, Michael D. 1996. Identification as a Mediator of Celebrity Effects. *Journal of Broadcasting & Electronic Media* 40 (4): 478–495.

Benson, M.J. 1994. Lecture Listening in an Ethnographic Perspective. In *Academic Listening: Research Perspectives*, ed. John Flowerdew, 181–188. New York: Cambridge University Press.

Brew, Angela. 2002. *The Nature of Research: Inquiry in Academic Contexts.* London and New York: Routledge.

Brown, William J., and Michael D. Basil. 2010. Parasocial Interaction and Identification: Social Change Processes for Effective Health Interventions. *Health Communication* 25 (6–7): 601–602.

Burke, Kenneth. 1969. *A Rhetoric of Motives*, vol. 178. Berkeley: University of California Press.

Butt, Babar Zaheer, and Kashif ur Rehman. 2010. A Study Examining the Students Satisfaction in Higher Education. *Procedia-Social and Behavioral Sciences* 2 (2): 5446–5450.

Cheong, Hyuk Jun, and Margaret A. Morrison. 2008. Consumers' Reliance on Product Information and Recommendations Found in UGC. *Journal of Interactive Advertising* 8 (2): 38–49.

Christensen, Lisa Jones, Ellen Peirce, Laura P. Hartman, W. Michael Hoffman, and Jamie Carrier. 2007. Ethics, CSR, and Sustainability Education in the Financial Times Top 50 Global Business Schools: Baseline Data and Future Research Directions. *Journal of Business Ethics* 73 (4): 347–368.

Cornelius, Nelarine, James Wallace, and Rana Tassabehji. 2007. An Analysis of Corporate Social Responsibility, Corporate Identity and Ethics Teaching in Business Schools. *Journal of Business Ethics* 76 (1): 117–135.

Dawkins, Jenny. 2005. Corporate Responsibility: The Communication Challenge. *Journal of Communication Management* 9 (2): 108–119.

De Jong, Piet. 2012. The Health Impact of Mandatory Bicycle Helmet Laws. *Risk Analysis: An International Journal* 32 (5): 782–790.

Douglas, Jacqueline, Alex Douglas, and Barry Barnes. 2006. Measuring Student Satisfaction at a UK University. *Quality Assurance in Education* 14 (3): 251–267.

Du, Shuili, Chitrabhan B. Bhattacharya, and Sankar Sen. 2010. Maximizing Business Returns to Corporate Social Responsibility (CSR): The Role of CSR Communication. *International Journal of Management Reviews* 12 (1): 8–19.

Eggen, Paul D., and Don Kauchak. 1993. *Educational Psychology: Classroom Connections.* London: Simon & Schuster Books for Young Readers.

Fishbein, Martin, and Icek Ajzen 2011. *Predicting and Changing Behavior: The Reasoned Action Approach.* New York: Psychology Press.

Garnelo-Gomez, Irene. 2017. 'I Live Sustainably': Exploring Sustainable Narratives Through the Lens of Identity Expression and Motivational Drives. PhD dissertation, University of Reading.

Giacalone, Robert A., and Kenneth R. Thompson. 2006. Business Ethics and Social Responsibility Education: Shifting the Worldview. *Academy of Management Learning & Education* 5 (3): 266–277.

Golob, Urša, Marko Lah, and Zlatko Jančič. 2008. Value Orientations and Consumer Expectations of Corporate Social Responsibility. *Journal of Marketing Communications* 14 (2): 83–96.

Groza, Mark D., Mya R. Pronschinske, and Matthew Walker. 2011. Perceived Organizational Motives and Consumer Responses to Proactive and Reactive CSR. *Journal of Business Ethics* 102 (4): 639–652.

Guolla, Michael. 1999. Assessing the Teaching Quality to Student Satisfaction Relationship: Applied Customer Satisfaction Research in the Classroom. *Journal of Marketing Theory and Practice* 7 (3): 87–97.

Hemingway, Christine A. 2005. Personal Values as a Catalyst for Corporate Social Entrepreneurship. *Journal of Business Ethics* 60 (3): 233–249.

Hemingway, Christine A., and Patrick W. Maclagan. 2004. Managers' Personal Values as Drivers of Corporate Social Responsibility. *Journal of Business Ethics* 50 (1): 33–44.

Henley Business School. 2017. Report to the United Nations Principles for Responsible Management Education 2015/16 & 2016/17. Accessed June 28, 2018. http://www.unprme.org/reports/HenleyBusinessSchool UNPRME2017.pdf.

Hill, Yvonne, Laurie Lomas, and Janet MacGregor. 2003. Students' Perceptions of Quality in Higher Education. *Quality Assurance in Education* 11 (1): 15–20.

Jones, Edward Ellsworth, and Harold Gerard. 1967. *Foundations of Social Psychology*. New York and London: Wiley.

Jones, Lee W., Robert C. Sinclair, and Kerry S. Courneya. 2003. The Effects of Source Credibility and Message Framing on Exercise Intentions, Behaviors, and Attitudes: An Integration of the Elaboration Likelihood Model and Prospect Theory 1. *Journal of Applied Social Psychology* 33 (1): 179–196.

Kolb, David. 1984. *Experiential Education: Experience as the Source of Learning and Development*. Englewood Cliffs, NJ: Prentice-Hall.

Kwon, Mina, Geetanjali Saluja, and Rashmi Adaval. 2015. Who Said What: The Effects of Cultural Mindsets on Perceptions of Endorser-Message Relatedness. *Journal of Consumer Psychology* 25 (3): 389–403.

Lafferty, Barbara A., and Ronald E. Goldsmith. 1999. Corporate Credibility's Role in Consumers' Attitudes and Purchase Intentions When a High Versus a Low Credibility Endorser Is Used in the Ad. *Journal of Business Research* 44 (2): 109–116.

Larran, Jorge Manuel, and Francisco Javier Andrades Peña. 2014. Determinants of Corporate Social Responsibility and Business Ethics Education in Spanish Universities. *Business Ethics: A European Review* 23 (2): 139–153.

Larran, Jorge Manuel, Francisco Javier Andrades Peña, and Muriel de los Reyes Maria Jose. 2017. Analysing the Inclusion of Stand-Alone Courses on Ethics and CSR: A Study of the MBA Curricula of the Financial Times Top-Ranked Business Schools. *Sustainability Accounting, Management and Policy Journal* 8 (2): 114–137.

López-Pérez, M. Eugenia, Iguácel Melero, and F. Javier Sesé. 2017. Does Specific CSR Training for Managers Impact Shareholder Value? Implications for Education in Sustainable Development. *Corporate Social Responsibility and Environmental Management* 24 (5): 435–448.

Lozano, Josep M., Daniel Arenas, and Alfons Sauquet. 2006. Educational Programmes in Corporate Social Responsibility. In *Corporate Social Responsibility, Volume 2: Performances and Stakeholders*, ed. J. Allouche, 241–259. London: Palgrave Macmillan.

MacKenzie, Scott B., and Richard J. Lutz. 1989. An Empirical Examination of the Structural Antecedents of Attitude Toward the Ad in an Advertising Pretesting Context. *The Journal of Marketing* 53 (2): 48–65.

McDonald, Gael M. 2004. A Case Example: Integrating Ethics into the Academic Business Curriculum. *Journal of Business Ethics* 54 (4): 371–384.

McWilliams, Abagail, Donald S. Siegel, and Patrick M. Wright. 2006. Corporate Social Responsibility: Strategic Implications. *Journal of Management Studies* 43 (1): 1–18.

Millar, Jill, and Margaret Price. 2018. Imagining Management Education: A Critique of the Contribution of the United Nations PRME to Critical Reflexivity and Rethinking Management Education. *Management Learning* 49 (3). https://doi.org/10.1177/1350507618759828.

Miller, Joanne M., and Jon A. Krosnick. 2000. News Media Impact on the Ingredients of Presidential Evaluations: Politically Knowledgeable Citizens Are Guided by a Trusted Source. *American Journal of Political Science* 44 (2): 301–315.

Morsing, Mette. 2006. Strategic CSR Communication: Telling Others How Good You Are. In *Management Models for Corporate Social Responsibility*, ed. Marco de Witte and Jan Jonker, 238–246. Berlin, Heidelberg: Springer.

Murray, Kate, and Ranald Macdonald. 1997. The Disjunction Between Lecturers' Conceptions of Teaching and Their Claimed Educational Practice. *Higher Education* 33 (3): 331–349.

Northcott, Jill. 2001. Towards an Ethnography of the MBA Classroom: A Consideration of the Role of Interactive Lecturing Styles Within the Context of one MBA Programme. *English for Specific Purposes* 20 (1): 15–37.

O'Rourke, James S. 2013. Corporate Reputation and the Discipline of Management Communication. In *The Handbook of Communication and Corporate Reputation*, ed. Craig E. Carroll, 72–80. Malden, MA: Wiley-Blackwell.

Principles for Responsible Management Education (PRME). 2007. About Us. Accessed May 28, 2018. http://www.unprme.org/about-prme/history/index.php.

Reputation Institute. 2018. 2018 Global RepTrak®—Most Reputable Companies in the World. Accessed June 28, 2018. https://www.reputation-institute.com/resources/pdf/2018-global-reptrak.

Ruth, Julie A., and Anne York. 2004. Framing Information to Enhance Corporate Reputation: The Impact of Message Source, Information Type, and Reference Point. *Journal of Business Research* 57 (1): 14–20.

Saraeva, Anastasiya. 2017. The Interactions Between Messages and Stakeholder (Dis)identification with Messengers: Exploring Their Moderating Impact on the Links Between Perceptions of Corporate Reputation, Organisational (Dis)identification, and Behavioural Outcomes. PhD dissertation, University of Reading.

Setó-Pamies, Dolors, and Eleni Papaoikonomou. 2016. A Multi-level Perspective for the Integration of Ethics, Corporate Social Responsibility and Sustainability (ECSRS) in Management Education. *Journal of Business Ethics* 136 (3): 523–538.

Sims, Ronald R. 2002. Business Ethics Teaching for Effective Learning. *Teaching Business Ethics* 6 (4): 393–410.

Stubbs, Wendy, and Jan Schapper. 2011. Two Approaches to Curriculum Development for Educating for Sustainability and CSR. *International Journal of Sustainability in Higher Education* 12 (3): 259–268.

Tata, Jasmine, and Sameer Prasad. 2015. CSR Communication: An Impression Management Perspective. *Journal of Business Ethics* 132 (4): 765–778.

Tootoonchi, Ahmad, Paul Lyons, and Abdalla Hagen. 2002. MBA Students' Perceptions of Effective Teaching Methodologies and Instructor

Characteristics. *International Journal of Commerce and Management* 12 (1): 79–93.

Turker, Duygu. 2009. How Corporate Social Responsibility Influences Organizational Commitment. *Journal of Business Ethics* 89 (2): 189.

Waddock, Sandra, and Josep M. Lozano. 2013. Developing More Holistic Management Education: Lessons Learned from Two Programs. *Academy of Management Learning & Education* 12 (2): 265–284.

7

Financial Education, Literary Fiction, and Corporate Social Responsibility

Maria Teresa Bosch Badia, Joan Montllor-Serrats
and Maria-Antonia Tarrazon-Rodon

7.1 Introduction: Decisions, Value, and Feelings

Corporate management has become increasingly sophisticated in a world aware of the challenges of sustainability where the claims of all stakeholders, their different interests, and their sensitivities influence any course of action. Corporate decisions are assumed to be taken with the traditional goal of financial value maximization in mind. Nevertheless, the strength of corporate value needs to make shareholders' wealth compatible with environmental and social requirements over the long term. The corporate social responsibility (CSR) challenge consists of making corporations environmentally, socially, and financially sustainable in order to achieve a satisfactory

M. T. Bosch Badia (✉)
Universitat de Girona, Girona, Spain
e-mail: mariateresa.bosch@udg.edu

J. Montllor-Serrats · M.-A. Tarrazon-Rodon
Universitat Autonoma de Barcelona, Bellaterra, Spain

© The Author(s) 2019
F. Farache et al. (eds.), *Responsible People*, Palgrave Studies in Governance,
Leadership and Responsibility, https://doi.org/10.1007/978-3-030-10740-6_7

triple bottom line of profits, people, and planet, as defined by Elkington (1994). Managers need to be prepared to face sustainability challenges with a strong sense of responsibility and sensitivity to deal with the human feelings of the different stakeholders involved in the complexity of this scenario. Additionally, shareholders, the managers of their portfolios, and stakeholders must share this sense of responsibility and sensitivity. Thus, CSR education has become a central need for business studies. However, it cannot be exclusively centered on acquiring knowledge. The modern educational goal of preparing students to "learn how to learn" must include to the development of the capacity to update knowledge, the even more important skill to be permanently sensitive to society and to the environment, i.e., to life in a single word.

This changing backdrop and set of expectations pose a challenge to managerial education. Often, business syllabuses are dominated by subjects where the goal is to prepare students for designing strategies, analyzing financial decisions, preparing marketing campaigns, managing human resources, and other topics with the focus on financial value creation. In short, the goal is to prepare them for a world of facts, which recalls the opening of Dickens' *Hard Times*, "Now, what I want is Facts…Plant nothing else and root out everything else" (Dickens 1995, p. 9). Although it is obvious that modern teaching is far from that of Mr. Gradgrind's school in *Hard Times*, there is also substantial evidence about the predominance of facts in business teaching.

However, the focus on business ethics and CSR, which is generally included in syllabuses today, may help to enlighten the nature of the world in which value creation takes place and help open students' minds beyond facts. Nevertheless, CSR is often addressed with respect to its contributions to corporate value because it is also a source of innovation, as pointed out by Porter and Kramer (2006), or because corporate stability requires a reasonable understanding between shareholders and stakeholders. As A. Rappaport (2012, p. 50) writes, "while there is no doubt that executives face difficult trade-offs, one point is clear: a company will not maximize shareholder value through the systematic exploitation of its stakeholders". The goal and the constraint are expressed very clearly in this statement. The problem is not only to teach ethics and CSR but also to teach them effectively in such a way that students make them part of their emotional intelligence, i.e., to their understanding and management of emotions. In this respect, business education should foster the development of students' empathy and emotional intelligence. Ioannidou and Konstantikaki (2008) stress the relevance of emotional training in general education. Its application to teaching CSR posits the following questions: How can one stimulate the development of emotional intelligence in a business classroom? Which case studies could be used? This chapter holds that a productive answer to these questions can be found in literary fiction and proposes to use literary works as case studies on CSR. The remainder of this chapter is structured as follows. Section 7.2 discusses the value of literature for management learning. Section 7.3 analyzes the connections among behavioral finance, CSR, and literary fiction. Section 7.4 analyzes *The Merchant of Venice* and Ibsen's *The Wild Duck* from the perspective of CSR. Section 7.5 discusses the capacity of literature to foster emotional intelligence in the classroom and its contributions to making students more empathetic and mature.

7.2 Literature and Management Learning

Art and literature convey human emotions and feelings, leading the reader to witness a myriad of different situations and to become aware of the behaviors of very different characters. Barter and Tregidga (2014) present a panorama on the capacity of fiction, art, and literary techniques to communicate business situations. They stress the capacity of storytelling and its analysis for advancing the knowledge of complex situations that cannot be accessed through conventional research. Younkins (2014, p. ix), in the preface of his book about capitalist fiction, holds that "reading novels and plays, and watching films are excellent ways to develop critical thinking, to learn about character, and to instill moral values". Kidd and Castano (2013), in an article published in *Science*, provide experimental evidence on the positive impacts of reading literary fiction on the capacity for understanding other people's beliefs and desires. Bal and Veltkamp (2013) develop an experimental study in which they find evidence for the positive effect of fiction reading on empathy under the condition that the reader becomes emotionally transported into the story. Their results are entirely in line with Younkins' arguments.

Harold Bloom (2001, p. 4), in an interview published in the *Harvard Business Review*, states that "by reading great imaginative literature, you can prepare yourself for surprise and even get a kind of strength that welcomes and exploits the unexpected". In this interview, Prof. Bloom insists on the fact that literature prepares readers for facing the unexpected. Guber (2007), in turn, praises the capacity of storytelling for corporate communication. According to this author, to be effective, storytelling must convey truth to the teller, to the audience, to the moment, and to the mission. In a nutshell, it must be credible. These requirements fit with scholarship on CSR (Wagner et al. 2009) that point out that marketing campaigns on CSR, if not credible, can be perceived by consumers as corporate hypocrisy and have adverse effects on sales. Badaracco (2006a) expresses the capacity of literary fiction to educate future leaders in ethics and applies literature to the analysis of leadership skills by emphasizing the challenges that leaders face (Badaracco 2006b).

Egan (2000) studies different Shakespearian characters, mainly the kings in historical plays, and analyzes their strong and weak points together with their achievements and mistakes from the perspective of modern management theories. Jennings (2013) analyzes how a background in reading the classics may help corporate leaders to become aware of the ethical dangers involved in their jobs. He stresses the relevance of the Bathsheba Syndrome, identified by Ludwig and Longenecher (1993). It consists of the ethical failures that originate from not being able to cope with success and, also, from the isolation that power brings. Jennings parallels Ishmael in *Moby Dick* ("I said nothing and tried to think nothing") with Enron's managers, who were both victims of the self-deception of Bathsheba Syndrome. He points out that the knowledge of literary stories can help to prevent these kinds of failures. Desai (2017) explores the connections between finance and literature, philosophy, and the arts in general. Among other topics, Desai relates literature to risk management, leverage, and competing obligations. Jane Austen's Lizzy Bennet (*Pride and Prejudice*) and

Anthony Trollope's Violet Effingham (*Phileas Finn*) are studied as risk managers. On the challenges that competing obligations pose to managers, Desai shows how the work by the philosopher Marta Nussbaum, *The Fragility of Goodness* (1986), enlightens these conflicts and takes Agamemnon sacrificing Iphigenia as an example.

Morson and Schapiro (2017) analyze the capacity of humanities to improve the understanding of economic phenomena. They counter the abstraction of economic mathematical models with the complexity of literature. Economics focuses on the analysis of evidence with the aim of generalizing it through theoretical models. Conversely, literature goes in-depth into complex, although specific, situations: "the novel... instead of showing the essential simplicity of things, it shows their complexity and teaches us to reason appropriately" (Morson and Schapiro 2017, p. 211). These authors stress the importance of taking culture into account to analyze economic scenarios. Ultimately, they advocate for a dialogue among disciplines to achieve a greater understanding of society. The implementation of CSR policies requires leadership to be able to analyze very complicated settings and the capacity to communicate to investors how essential sustainability is in the long run. Individual, corporate, and social ethics are central to this issue. In this respect, it is also relevant to the interaction among behavioral finance, CSR, and literary fiction. The next section centers on this interaction.

7.3   Marketing, Behavioral Finance, Literary Fiction, and CSR

The productive interaction between psychology and economics that has created the discipline of behavioral economics enlightens the analysis of CSR decisions and investors' decisions. The contribution of literary fiction to psychological analysis is well documented in several papers. Oatley (1999) argues that the separation between literature and psychology has impaired both. He underlines the creative facet of reading fiction by comparing literary works with simulations that lead their readers to explore emotions. In this line, Mar and Oatley (2008) consider narrative fiction as a simulation of life. They argue that literary stories arouse thoughts and emotions in their readers, and further-more, they abstract life in order to facilitate its comprehension. Beckert (2013) develops the concept of *fictional expectations*, which consists of structured narratives about the future states of the world through which individuals deal with uncertainty. Roy and Zeckhauser (2017) study the contributions of literature to the understanding of human behaviors and ignorance (scope, induction, cultural learning, anticipation, and insights into behavioral decision-making).

Marketing is a field in which studying literature can be highly pro-ductive. Understanding human emotions and persuasion is central to successful marketing. Bagozzi et al. (1999) explore the role of emotions in marketing. Virginia Woolf (1922, p. 126) masterly depicted the cen-trality of emotions in fiction signaling that "emotion is our material". Nünning (2017) studies the capacity of fiction for fostering the readers' empathy. Murphy (1999) identifies empathy among the core virtues for marketing. Stafford (1999) points out that "persuasion goes to the very heart of marketing as a technology and science". Works on fiction and rhetoric constitute an excellent basis for empowering persuasion, as Heinrichs (2017) argues drawing on Cicero and Shakespeare.

Behavioral finance contributes to explaining market bubbles and irrational behaviors, but it also contributes to a better understand-ing of ethical behaviors, beyond the supposed rational investors whose decisions are systematically made to maximize their profits. In the real world, many decisions are driven by the "spontaneous urge to action" that John M. Keynes labeled *animal spirits*. Akerlof and Shiller (2009, p. 3) enlarge this definition by signaling that the idea of animal spir-its "refers to a peculiar relationship with ambiguity and uncertainty. Sometimes we are paralyzed by it. Yet at other times it refreshes and energizes us, overcoming our fears and indecisions". In fact, the con-cept of *animal spirits* encapsulates the irrational and impulsive behav-iors observed during financial bubbles. Malkiel (2015, Chap. 10) explains the primary drivers of irrational behaviors as follows: overcon-fidence, biased judgments, herd mentality, and loss aversion. Nofsinger (2016) studies the psychology of investing by analyzing the impact of emotions on investment decisions and pointing out how psycholo-gists and economists have shown that feelings and emotions condition decision-making. Shiller (2017) points out the relevance of popular narratives for the analysis of economic fluctuations. Explicitly, he defines narratives as "human constructs that are mixtures of fact and emotion and human interest and other extraneous detail that form an impression on the human mind" (Shiller 2017, p. 973). We learn from this article the crucial importance for any decision-maker to become aware and analyze popular narratives that influence social behaviors at every moment. The knowledge of literature can be regarded as a useful background for the understanding of the generation and development of popular narratives and even how to generate counter messages. Shiller (2012, p. 106) also stresses the need for teaching ethics and facilitating a broad understanding of the complexity of the world among students. Literary fiction can contribute to this goal. In the next section, we explore how *The Merchant of Venice* and *The Wild Duck* can be respectively studied from the points of view of social and environmental sustainability.

7.4 CSR and Human Feelings Through *The Merchant of Venice* and *The Wild Duck*

Among the three pillars of sustainability, i.e., financial, environmental, and social, CSR aims to foster the environmental and social pillars. In fact, the ultimate goal of CSR is to improve human life and all forms of life on the planet as well. However, sustainable business strategies only can be fully implemented inside a society that is aware of the centrality of social and environmental sustainability for progressing toward an ethical world. The interaction among social rules, business decisions, and their impacts on human life can be explored through the analysis of literary fiction. This section analyzes *The Merchant of Venice* (Shakespeare 1955) and *The Wild Duck* (Ibsen 1980) from a CSR perspective. Business decisions that are linked with social and environmental sustainability play a central role in triggering their dramatic situations. Through both plays, the audience becomes aware of the fragility of human interactions and the tragic consequences that may follow from failing to act in a responsible manner.

7.4.1 *The Merchant of Venice* and Social Sustainability

The Merchant places the audience in front of a social setting that utterly lacks social sustainability. Shylock's attempt to enact revenge for the racial abuse he has suffered is at the center of the dramatic action. The leading causes of the social sustainability flaws in *The Merchant* stem from the political-economic system and social, racial, and religious discrimination at different levels. The system aims to promote the safety of mercantile contracts before human rights. In other words, we can say that it is centered on profit maximization. Venice is presented as a wealthy society that enjoys the prosperity of the commercial capitalism of its time, where human relations and money become inextricably intertwined. Dunne (2014) analyzes the connections between money and love in *The Merchant*. The legal system is designed to protect this prosperity, which is clearly put before human rights and prevents Antonio from being freed of his bond with Shylock, even by paying the debt several times over. Salanio stresses that the Duke only can save Antonio by asking Shylock to have mercy on him[1] ("none can drive him from the envious plea", Salanio, III.II.281). Antonio is perfectly aware of this fact ("the duke cannot deny the course of law", III.III.26). Shylock, in turn, reminds the Venetian establishment that their prosperity depends on the strict fulfillment of the law when claiming Antonio's flesh (the bond):

> If you deny it, let the danger light
> Upon your charter and your city's freedom. (IV.I.38–39)

Literary criticism has dealt with the legal and economic aspects of *The Merchant*. Harp (2010, p. 43) addresses the priority for businesses in Venetian society. Trepanier (2014, p. 209) concludes his study on the contracts, friendship, and love in *The Merchant* stating that this play "reveals the moral limitations of a commercial regime based on contract and the corrosive effects it has on noncontractual relationships like friendship, love, and marriage".

---

[1]All the quotations from *The Merchant of Venice* have been taken from the Arden Edition (Shakespeare 1955).

Discrimination, the other central feature of *Merchant's* society, not only adds more hindrances to noncontractual relationships but also has a perverse influence on business decisions. In this respect, we find three lines: race, homosexuality, and gender. Shylock is discriminated against for his race, Antonio is forced to hide his homosexuality, and Portia and Jessica, in different ways, are subjected to the limitations imposed on women. As stated, we consider the case of gender in Sect. 4.3. Discrimination leads Antonio and Shylock to make highly flawed decisions based on overconfidence (Antonio) and pride (Shylock), two of the drivers of irrational financial behaviors identified by behavioral finance.

Three traits define Antonio, namely, being a member of the Venetian upper class, his antagonism with Shylock, and his hidden homosexuality, although the latter is not universally accepted in Shakespearian criticism. As a ship owner and trader, Antonio manages a big business subjected to high risks, as stressed by Shylock (I.III.15–24). His decision to borrow money from Shylock to help Bassanio in courting Portia constitutes a case of overconfidence. By increasing the leverage, Antonio adds more risk to his risky business without changing its expected return. That is, he endangers its financial sustainability. Of course, this decision is based on the love that Antonio feels for Bassanio:

> My purse, my person, my extremest means
> Lie all unlock'd to your occasions. (I.I.138–139)

Bloom (1999, p. 185) stresses the two dominant traits of Shylock's character: hatred and intelligence. Both are widely displayed in his scheming against Antonio, who strongly scorns him in Act I ("to spet on thee again, to spurn thee too...", I.III.125–126). Shylock, in his famous moving soliloquy in Act III ("I am a Jew. Hath not a Jew eyes?" III.I.52–54), expresses the grief he feels for being an outcast due to his Jewish race while concurrently unveiling his wish for revenge ("If you prick us do we not bleed?...and if you wrong us shall we not revenge?" ... III.1.58 and 60). Shylock and Antonio have in common that they make business decisions based on feelings instead of rationality. Their feelings are, of course, opposite: Antonio is guided by his love for Bassanio, while hatred for Antonio guides Shylock. Both are victims of the imperfections of Venetian society but, at the same time, they are also unable to undertake any initiative to correct them. Antonio feels trapped in his sadness while Shylock remains a prisoner of his pride. Neither of them can think of changing society nor can they conceive that society may change. Instead of regarding Venice as a society, they view the city as a conglomerate of individuals.

Let us consider Antonio and Shylock from the viewpoint of CSR. When business decisions inside a society are not made with CSR in mind, it is practically impossible that a single firm or an individual becomes aware of the need for CSR. Antonio is a victim of Shylock but a victim that agrees on discriminating against Shylock because he is a Jew. Social sustainability neither exists in Antonio's mind nor is it present in his business decisions. Shylock does not claim the bond for discrimination but for revenge. Thus, he is unable to conceive that morally positive attitudes, as the ones required by CSR, could improve human relations. Antonio's donation to Bassanio raises the question of whether philanthropy is appropriate for business. This is a case of uncontrolled philanthropy that endangers financial sustainability. Feelings dominate the financial decisions made by Antonio and Shylock. Thus, they belong to System 1 thinking (intuition, thinking fast), as defined by Kahneman (2011). Analyzing decisions from the perspective of CSR leads to switching to System 2 thinking (considering issues in-depth and thinking slow). CSR focuses on the long-term impacts of business decisions by considering their effects on society and the environment. Thus, it makes strategic thinking absolutely necessary by analyzing the corporate future from the triple perspective of finance, environment, and society.

7.4.2 *The Wild Duck* and Environmental Sustainability

Environmental sustainability and the effects on human beings of business decisions that do not respect nature are at the center of *The Wild Duck*. The illegal felling of trees in the Hoydal Forest that triggers the tragedy shows two different negative attitudes to the environment. These attitudes are explored through the businessman Werle, whose central aim is making money, and Lieutenant Ekdal, whose central aim is dominating nature, even at the price of destroying it. Werle embodies the spirit of financialization. For him, the World is a market in which anything and anyone can be bought and sold. He bought the Hoydal Forest together with Ekdal but managed not to be involved in the illegal cut. In this respect, a question remains open: is Werle's help to Ekdal the outcome of his generosity or is it the way of purchasing his silence? When his relationship with Gina arrived at a point of no return due to her pregnancy, Werle managed to arrange her marriage with Hjalmar. His gift to Hedvig awakens the suspicion that he is her biological father. His announced marriage with Mrs. Sørby is also presented as a fair transaction: Werle sells welfare and buys love and care[2] ("I don't think that I'm taking more than I shall be able to give him", Mrs. Sørby to Gregers in Act IV, p. 189). Summarizing, for Werle anything is a trade. In his world, love does not exist, but hate does not exist either. Ekdal is the character who better encapsulates the lack of respect for nature. His loft at Hjalmar's home shows the miserable evolution of this wretched character: from a bear hunter in the forest to hunting domestic animals enclosed in the loft. Goldman (1994) highlights the self-deceiving function that the loft has for Ekdal, as it is also a metaphor for his decadence. Ekdal never shows any emotion; for him, any calamity remains explained by the revenge of the forest ("You see, the forest-the forest…the forest will have its revenge", Act II, p. 148). By cutting the forest, he has also cut his capacity for emotion.

The setting of *The Wild Duck* shows how the destruction of nature also destroys society. This connection constitutes an implicit message about the interrelated nature of life. Gregers substitutes his father's materialism for a fanatical idealism, "the claim of the ideal" (as doctor Relling defines it in Act III, p. 171), that combines the purity and the wilderness of nature. His pressure on Hjalmar to assume that Gina was Werle's lover and Hedvig was probably Werle's biological daughter introduces the wilderness of nature into the, until then, happy family of Hjalmar and Gina. After Gregers' revelations, Hjalmar opts for placing biology in front of love ("then I'd have known what a kind of woman you were", Act IV, p. 182). Indifferent to Gina's pleas and disregarding Gregers' advice of forgiving her ("nothing in the world can be compared

---

[2]All the quotations from *The Wild Duck* have been taken from the Methuen World Classics Editon (Ibsen 1980).

with the joy of forgiving", Act IV, p. 184), Hjalmar breaks off the family. At this point, Hjalmar becomes dominated by primitive feelings, even preferring revenge to reconciliation. Gregers shows his inner cruelty by proposing that Hedvig kills the wild duck. This is the start of family reconciliation through an act similar to an ancestral sacrifice ("suppose you sacrificed for him the most precious of your possessions - the thing that you love most dearly?" Act IV, p. 197) that would once more break the harmony of nature. Hedvig's suicide that follows can be regarded as the last link of the chain of negative human reactions that started after the cut of the forest. In Ekdal's words, it is the revenge of the forest. In summary, *The Wild Duck* represents a society unable to live in harmony with nature. Men's aggressiveness to nature is, inevitably, transmitted to human relations.

7.4.3 Gender in *The Merchant of Venice* and *The Wild Duck*

Gender inequality is central in both plays. We limit our analysis to Portia and Gina. The effects of gender discrimination on Antonio that have been considered in 7.4.1 rely on his central role in social discrimination. Portia and Gina have not been free to choose their husbands. Portia's father and Mr. Werle have imposed conditions (Portia's father) or manipulated the marriage (Werle). From Portia's point of view, *The Merchant* relates to the audience her struggle to achieve equality. The caskets scenes could be presented as a tragic situation in other circumstances. At this moment, Portia is a creature fettered to the will of her father. The excellent capacity she exhibits for managing complex situations proves the absurdity of her father's decision of limiting her freedom to select a husband. Korda (2009) studies Portia's language by showing that she often uses terms related to business and comparing her with the British women who, in early modern England, were money lenders at interest. This language suggests that Portia has remarkable expertise in managing her husbandry, which makes her capacity for defending Antonio against Shylock less surprising. In her exchange with Bassanio at Belmont, Portia shows the strictest determination of not enabling her future husband to manage her inheritance: *though yours, not yours*[3] (III.II.20). From the gender perspective, the trial scene constitutes a vindication of women's intelligence. Until Portia's arrival, the court (only integrated by men) has failed in its attempts to release Antonio from Shylock's bond. Portia, disguised as a man, enlightens the confused court by providing a deeper interpretation of the law. Antonio becomes free from the bond, and Portia demonstrates to the court how a woman can deal with legal affairs even better than men. Benston (1979, p. 379) stresses Portia's strategic skills that reach their peak when she defeats Shylock by turning the law against him and in the harmony that she creates for herself, Bassanio, and Antonio. In the ring scene that follows (Act V), Portia and Nerissa make Bassanio and Gratiano aware of the fact that they are their husbands but not their masters. The shared happiness that this scene conveys can be regarded as an implicit message on the value of equality over discrimination.

Conversely, in *The Wild Duck*, Gina remains continuously submissive to men, from Werle to Hjalmar. A central difference between Portia and Gina is that Gina is entirely alone. Her pathetic struggle to retain her husband ("what would have become of you if you hadn't had a wife like me?" Act IV, p. 183), the insensitive and proud Hjalmar, reveals a character full of inner sadness that only yearns for having some peace in her life. Her final words answer Hjalmar's despair after the suicide of Hedvig ("we must help each other. Now she belongs to both of us, you know", Act V, p. 215) again shows a sensitive woman who pleads not to be alone. In conclusion, the need to put environmental and social sustainability into practice becomes evident after the reading of both plays. Sustainability will not maximize the wealth of Shylock and Werle but will help to maximize harmony and contribute to a stable society. Table 7.1 summarizes the main issues on CSR that can be found in *The Merchant of Venice* and *The Wild Duck*.

---

[3]Interpreted in the Arden Edition as "yours de jure, not de facto" (p. 77, footnote 20).

Table 7.1 CSR in *The Merchant of Venice* and *The Wild Duck*

Issues on CSR	The Merchant of Venice	The Wild Duck
Environmental sustainability		(−) Tree felling in Hoydal Forest
Social sustainability	(−) Racism (anti-Semitic discrimination) (−) Gender discrimination (−) Homosexual's discrimination (implicit)	(−) Gender discrimination
Financial sustainability	(−) Financial decisions based on revenge feelings (Shylock) (−) Financial decisions based on overconfidence (Antonio)	(−) Business management only based on profit maximization (Werle)
Ethics	(−) Business-focused society (−) Shylock (−) Antonio (+) Portia (+) Gratiano	(−) Werle, Ekdal, Gregers, and Hjalmar (+) Gina (+) Society: reacting against the cut of Hoydal Forest
Philanthropy	(−) Antonio (excess of philanthropy: focused only in his own social class)	(−) Werle (hypocritical use of philanthropy)
Reputation	Shylock's revenge is part based on how Antonio has publicly traduced his honor and reputation in the market: Also noteworthy that Shylock protests he is not interested in Antonio's good character, but only his financial status, Act I Scene 3: 'Oh, no, no, no, no: my meaning in saying he is a good man is to have you understand me that he is sufficient'	(−) Werle: philanthropic strategies to control his reputation

7.5 Discussion

The value of literary fiction for business studies is currently widely accredited. Comparing the contributions of mathematics and literary fiction to the understanding of economics and business enlightens this issue. Mathematics has the power to summarize in equations the stable relationships among relevant variables. It contributes to modeling the logical connections that we may find in the complexity of the world of economics. Conversely, literary fiction does not simplify the complexity. Instead, it embeds economic decisions in a context that goes further than economics. The effects of feelings on decisions are depicted, and, by involving the reader in the story, she becomes aware of how unexpected outcomes may become real. In brief, it enlightens the relevant features of social scenarios that remain in the shadows when they are exclusively addressed using quantitative models. The discussions in the classroom focused on the links between CSR situations depicted in the literature are central to benefitting from this approach. Seeing the literary pieces under analysis performed on the stage or the screen stimulates the study and adds vividness to the discussions.

We have argued in this chapter that literary fiction can be applied explicitly to the analysis of CSR by approaching literary works as case studies. Social conflicts are one of the most common themes in literary fiction. Often, corporations, businesspeople, and bankers are involved in them. Politics and the social organization establish the context that frames the troubles experienced by the fictional characters. The relationship between men and nature is also a frequent topic in literary works. Reading fiction with CSR in mind helps to understand the roots of unsustainable scenarios, including how self-interest generates them and how indifference paves the way for environmental and social conflicts. Interweaving the central knowledge of business studies with the analysis of the complex situations presented in the literature creates an intellectual synergy that widens the skills for understanding the world and makes students more mature.

Focusing specifically on *The Merchant of Venice* and *The Wild Duck*, we corroborate the usefulness of literary fiction to the study of CSR.

In both plays, we realize how unethical behavior hinders individual and social harmony. Social discrimination pervades Venetian Society in *The Merchant*. Shylock is a victim of it. However, through his attempted revenge on Antonio, he argues against the need for empathy or compassion and, thus, seals his own fate. Antonio feels forced to hide his homosexuality while he simultaneously discriminates against Shylock. On the other hand, Portia successfully fights against gender discrimination and allows us to glimpse another possible world where women and men have equal power. *The Wild Duck* masterfully conveys to the audience how the lack of respect for nature cannot be dissociated from self-centered human tendencies and frivolous feelings that, not surprisingly, are a source of suffering and even of tragedy for the weakest characters of the play. The contribution of both plays to the understanding of the connection between human feelings and sustainability shows the power of literary fiction for enlightening the study of social and environmental issues. In conclusion, the analysis of literary pieces from the point of view of CSR constitutes an excellent pedagogical instrument for conveying to students that a fair and sustainable world can be constructed and maintained only by people who make responsible decisions in both personal and business matters.

Acknowledgements The authors thank three anonymous referees and the editors for their valuable comments. The usual disclaimer applies.

References

Akerlof, G., and R.J. Shiller. 2009. *Animal Spirits: How Human Psychology Drives the Economy, and Why It Matters for Global Capitalism.* Princeton: Princeton University Press.

Badaracco, J.L. 2006a. Leadership in Literature: A Conversation with Business Ethicist Joseph L. Badaracco, Jr. Interview by Diane L. Coutu. *Harvard Business Review* 84 (3): 47–55.

Badaracco, J.L. 2006b. *Questions of Character: Illuminating the Heart of Leadership Through Literature.* Boston: Harvard Business School Press.

Bagozzi, R.P., M. Gopinath, and P.U. Nyer. 1999. The Role of Emotions in Marketing. *Journal of the Academy of Marketing Science* 27 (2): 184–206. https://doi.org/10.1177/0092070399272005.

Bal, P.M., and M. Veltkamp. 2013. How Does Fiction Reading Influence Empathy? An Experimental Investigation on the Role of Emotional Transportation. *PLoS One* 8 (1): e55341. https://doi.org/10.1371/journal.pone.0055341.

Barter, N., and H. Tregidga. 2014. Guest Editorial Storytelling: Beyond the Academic Article: Using Fiction, Art and Literary Techniques to Communicate. *Journal of Corporate Citizenship* 54 (June): 5–10. https://doi.org/10.9774/gleaf.4700.2014.ju.00003.

Beckert, J. 2013. Imagined Futures: Fictional Expectations in the Economy. *Theory and Society* 42 (3): 219–240. https://doi.org/10.1007/s11186-013-9191-2.

Benston, A.N. 1979. Portia, the Law, and the Tripartite Structure of the Merchant of Venice. *Shakespeare Quarterly* 30 (3): 367–385. https://doi.org/10.2307/2869472.

Bloom, H. 1999. *Shakespeare: The Invention of the Human*. London: Fourth Estate.

Bloom, H. 2001. A Reading List for Bill Gates—and You. A Conversation with Literary Critic Harold Bloom. Interview by Diane L. Coutu. *Harvard Business Review* 79 (5): 63–68.

Desai, M. 2017. *The Wisdom of Finance*. London: Profile Books.

Dickens, Charles. 1995. *Hard Times*. London: Penguin Classics.

Dunne, D. 2014. 'O, My Ducats! O, My Daughter!' The Economics of Love in The Merchant of Venice. Accessed at 23 May 2018. http://2014.playing-shakespeare.org/o-my-ducatso-my-daughter-the-economics-of-love-in-the-merchant-of-venice.

Egan, M. 2000. Managers as Kings: Shakespeare on Modern Leadership. *Management Decision* 38 (5): 315–327. https://doi.org/10.1108/00251740010340490.

Elkington, J. 1994. Towards the Sustainable Corporation: Win-Win-Win Business Strategies for Sustainable Development. *California Management Review* 36 (2): 90–100. https://doi.org/10.2307/41165746.

Goldman, M. 1994. Eyolf's Eyes: Ibsen and the Cultural Meanings of Child Abuse. *American Imago* 51 (3): 279–305.

Guber, P. 2007. The Four Truths of the Storyteller. *Harvard Business Review* 85 (12): 52–59.

Harp, R. 2010. Love and Money in The Merchant of Venice. *Modern Age* 52 (1): 37–44.

Heinrichs, J. 2017. *Thank You for Arguing*. London: Penguin Books.

Ibsen, H. 1980. *The Wild Duck*. English translation by Michael Meyer. London: Methuen Drama.

Ioannidou, F., and V. Konstantikaki. 2008. Empathy and Emotional Intelligence. *International Journal of Caring Sciences* 1 (3): 118–123.

Jennings, M. 2013. Literature and Ethics in Finance. *Corporate Finance Review* 18 (3): 29–33.

Kahneman, D. 2011. *Thinking Fast and Slow*. New York: Farrar, Straus and Girou.

Kidd, D.C., and E. Castano. 2013. Reading Literary Fiction Improves Theory of Mind. *Science* 342 (18): 377–380. https://doi.org/10.1126/science.1239918.

Korda, N. 2009. Dame Usury: Gender, Credit, and (Ac)counting in the Sonnets and The Merchant of Venice. *Shakespeare Quarterly* 60 (2): 129–153. https://doi.org/10.1353/shq.0.0072.

Ludwig, D.C., and C.O. Longenecker. 1993. The Bathsheba Syndrome: The Ethical Failure of Successful Leaders. *Journal of Business Ethics* 12 (4): 265–273. https://doi.org/10.1007/bf01666530.

Malkiel, M. 2015. *A Random Walk Down Wall Street*. New York: Norton.

Mar, R.A., and K. Oatley. 2008. The Function of Fiction Is the Abstraction and Simulation of Social Experience. *Perspectives on Psychological Science* 3 (3): 173–192. https://doi.org/10.1111/j.1745-6924.2008.00073.x.

Morson, G.S., and M. Schapiro. 2017. *Cents and Sensibility: What Economics Can Learn from Humanities*. Princeton: Princeton University Press.

Murphy, P.E. 1999. Character and Virtue Ethics in International Marketing. *Journal of Business Ethics* 18 (1): 107–124. https://doi.org/10.1023/a:1006072413165.

Nofsinger, J.R. 2016. *The Psychology of Investing*. London: Routledge.

Nünning, V. 2017. The Affective Value of Fiction. *Writing Emotions*, 29–54. https://doi.org/10.2307/j.ctv1wxt3t.5.

Nussbaum, M. 1986. *The Fragility of Goodness: Luck and Ethics in Greek Tragedy and Philosophy*. Cambridge: Cambridge University Press.

Oatley, K. 1999. Why Fiction May Be Twice as True as Fact: Fiction as Cognitive and Emotional Simulation. *Review of General Psychology* 3 (2): 101–117. https://doi.org/10.1037/1089-2680.3.2.101.

Porter, M.E., and M.R. Kramer. 2006. Strategy and Society. *Harvard Business Review* 84 (12): 78.

Rappaport, A. 2012. *Saving Capitalism from Short-Termism*. New York: McGrawHill.

Roy, D., and R. Zeckhauser. 2017. Ignorance: Literary Light on Decision's Dark Corner. In *Routledge Handbook of Behavioral Economics*, ed. R. Frantz, S.H. Chen, K. Dopfer, F. Heulekom, and S. Mousavi, 230–249. London: Routledge.

Shakespeare, W. 1955. *The Merchant of Venice*, ed. John Russell Brown. Arden Edition. London: Methuen.

Shiller, R. 2012. *Finance and the Good Society*. Princeton: Princeton University Press.

Shiller, R. 2017. Narrative Economics. *American Economic Review* 107 (4): 967–1004. https://doi.org/10.1257/aer.107.4.967.

Stafford, T.F. 1999. Persuasion and Marketing. *Psychology & Marketing* 16 (2): 87–90.

Trepanier, L. 2014. Contract, Friendship, and Love in The Merchant of Venice. *Perspectives on Political Science* 43 (4): 204–212. https://doi.org/10.1080/10457097.2014.948735.

Wagner, T., R.J. Lutz, and B.A. Weitz. 2009. Corporate Hypocrisy: Overcoming the Threat of Inconsistent Corporate Social Responsibility Perceptions. *Journal of Marketing* 73 (6): 77–91. https://doi.org/10.1509/jmkg.73.6.77.

Woolf, V. 1922. On Re-reading Novels. In *Collected Essays* (1967), vol. 2, 122–130. New York: Harcourt, Brace & World.

Younkins, E.W. 2014. *Exploring Capitalist Fiction*. Lanham: Lexington Books.

8

A Practical Approach for Developing Social Consciousness and Responsibility in Marketing Students

Véronique Boulocher-Passet, Francisca Farache, Nadia Lonsdale and Wybe Popma

8.1 Introduction

There is a need for marketers who can drive change at organizations by coming up with new product or service ideas supported by business models that also help to address societal needs (Doyle 2008). Addressing grand societal challenges demands changing existing social paradigms, innovations that must create new social networks and capacities that evolve into new social structures and systems (Benneworth and Cunha 2015). This corresponds to a shift in society's expectations of business, forcing marketing educators to rethink curriculum content (Borin and Metcalf 2010). All the more since marketing has often been perceived as part of the problem, rather than the solution to societal problems such as pollution, overconsumption, the depletion of natural resources, unhealthy lifestyles, and human rights abuses

V. Boulocher-Passet (✉) · F. Farache · N. Lonsdale · W. Popma
Brighton Business School, University of Brighton, Brighton, UK
e-mail: V.Boulocher-Passet@brighton.ac.uk

© The Author(s) 2019
F. Farache et al. (eds.), *Responsible People*, Palgrave Studies in Governance,
Leadership and Responsibility, https://doi.org/10.1007/978-3-030-10740-6_8

(Markley Rowntree and Koernig 2015). After Schumacher (1973, p. 64) described education as the 'greatest resource' for achieving a just and ecological society, the Brundtland Report (WCED 1987) and *Agenda 21* both singled out education as an instrument for bringing about the social change necessary for sustainable development. If developing learners' capacities for social innovation has become part of universities' objectives and if particular courses have been designed in business schools to develop students as agents of change (Nicholls et al. 2013; Hesselbarth and Schaltegger 2014), the biggest part of core marketing modules taught in business schools throughout America and Europe still consist of strategic marketing, principles of marketing, marketing research, and marketing communications (Küster and Vila 2006). The field of nonprofit or social service marketing is less frequently included (Harrigan and Hulbert 2011). Socially conscious marketing practices are however no longer just a 'perk' or selling point for PR purposes. Both from a business and profitability standpoint, and from a moral standpoint, being socially conscious should be a requirement. Linked with the theme of this book on 'Responsible People: the Role of the Individual in CSR, Entrepreneurship, and Management Education', this chapter discusses what being socially conscious means for marketers and draws on the experience of enhancing social consciousness and responsibility within marketing students in one UK business school, with the aim of gaining deeper understanding of the role universities can play in developing future responsible marketing managers.

This chapter is organized as follows. First, the authors articulate their definition of social consciousness and draw upon literature on the aspects of social consciousness that are of importance to marketing learners. The authors then report on how qualitative data was collected via a case study approach, to capture how CSR and sustainability issues are incorporated into the marketing curriculum of Brighton Business School (BBS) in the UK. The third section of the chapter elaborates on the methods used by marketing lecturers of this institution to embed social consciousness within their teaching. The last section of the chapter explores how this case study can help inform the issue regarding the role of marketing educators in disseminating a CSR culture. The chapter concludes with identifying areas for future research.

8.2 What Does Social Consciousness Mean for Marketers?

Dating back to the mid-nineteenth century, with the earliest use found in *The North British Review*, the concept of social consciousness can be defined as 'awareness of and concern for the problems and injustices that affect society' (https://en.oxforddictionaries.com). Cooley (1907) defines it as the conscious awareness of being part of a larger whole, namely society. It includes the level at which one is aware of how one is influenced by others, as well as how your actions may affect others (Schlitz et al. 2010). Ammentorp (2007, p. 39) describes the development of social consciousness as a 'process involving increasing awareness of social-historical context, the ability to think abstractly about time and place, and beyond the immediate everyday conditions to understand individual experience as embedded in a broader system of social relations'. However, beyond the 'know-that' that social awareness refers to, Schneider et al. (2010) insist that management education also needs to address the more difficult 'know-how' and 'know-why' of socially responsible behavior in order to develop social consciousness. The authors used this key distinction between building social awareness and developing social consciousness in this research, and considered cognition, personal values and affect identified by Crilly et al. (2008) as the core elements of social consciousness and antecedents likely to encourage socially responsible behavior.

On a global scale, the need for a more sustainable world was unanimously acknowledged by United Nations members again in September 2015, when 17 Sustainable Development Goals were set, positioning education at the heart of the strategy to promote sustainable development (UN General Assembly 2015). Business leaders are being urged to apply their business acumen to come to grips with the social, moral, and environmental impact of their organizations (Mirvis 2008).

For most organizations, the three pillars of sustainability (social, economic, and environmental) are indeed now viewed as companywide necessities (Haugh and Talwar 2010). In particular, consequent to a range of factors such as consumer pressure, new legislation, and social evolution, environmental sustainability has increasingly become an issue of central importance to firms (Audebrand 2010). CSR strategies that encompass responsible or sustainable business practices, as recently adopted by many companies, demonstrate this (Deer and Zarestky 2017). Marketing managers are not exempt from this increasing focus on sustainability. Marketing has been rightfully implicated as a culprit in the over-consumption of resources and in the spread of western-style insatiability for goods among the world's developing and emerging nations. To the extent that it is part of the problem of unsustainable production and consumption, marketing can and must be a major part of the solution (Martin and Schouten 2014). Sustainable marketing means doing things differently to help bring about a society in which striving for environmental sustainability and social justice is the norm (Martin and Schouten 2012). According to Gordon et al. (2011, p. 146) it can be achieved in three principal ways:

- Green Marketing—Developing and marketing more sustainable products and services while introducing sustainability efforts at the core of the marketing and business process.
- Social Marketing—Using the power of upstream and downstream marketing interventions to encourage sustainable behavior.
- Critical Marketing—Analyzing marketing using a critical theory-based approach to guide regulation and control and stimulate innovation in markets with a focus on sustainability, but moreover challenging some of the dominant institutions of the capitalist and marketing systems, to construct a more sustainable marketing discipline.

It is important that Business Schools include ethics, CSR, and sustainability in their curricula to provide students with the necessary skills to contribute to a better society (Scullion 2017). The benchmark study by Nicholls et al. (2013) found ethics to be incorporated into more than 50% of the marketing courses at both the undergraduate and graduate levels in the United States. CSR was incorporated into about a third of undergraduate and half of graduate marketing courses. Sustainability was included in more than 40% of both undergraduate and graduate marketing courses. Thus, marketing students increasingly seem to be exposed to all three topics. How can social consciousness of those issues and a sense of responsibility be developed by marketing students within a business school environment? How can students be taught to be responsible people, and what role does management education play in the process? These questions were used as a starting point for our research.

8.3   Methodology

In order to analyze why and how ethics, CSR, and sustainability are incorporated in the curriculum at a business school level within an academic setting, a phenomenological case study approach (Yin 2018) was chosen. The selected 'case' in this study was the Marketing subject group within BBS in the UK. This group is made up of 16 academics, ranging in responsibility from part-time lecturers, through full-time senior lecturers to principal lecturers who will normally hold more senior administrative responsibility in addition to teaching and research roles. As a subject group, these academics are responsible for all marketing modules, both in the undergraduate and postgraduate programs. A total of around 2500 students study at BBS and a large majority of these will (usually at several points during their degree) take marketing modules taught by members of the Marketing subject group.

The choice for a holistic single-case design for this study was based on what Yin (2018) calls the 'critical case'. The Marketing subject group at BBS has a strong emphasis on social marketing and marketing ethics in both the background of its members (many of whom research and publish actively in areas like social marketing and CSR) and the content of the curriculum offered. As such there are only limited structural barriers to introducing learning content, which builds social consciousness in students. Researching in one UK business school made sense because the country is considered a leader in CSR and sustainability in management education (Matten and Moon 2004).

In order to increase construct validity (Yin 2018), we used several sources of evidence including interviews with relevant decision-makers and academic instructors, module descriptors that describe the content of each module and the University of Brighton strategic plan, which also includes BBS. Although the aim of this research is not directly to generalize results for other subject groups or business school environments within the UK, the external validity of the research is guaranteed, to some extent, considering that the course structures and module content within the business school is aligned to Higher Education Funding Council England (HEFCE) requirements, which apply to all recognized business degrees in England. In addition, the undergraduate degrees are accredited by two professional bodies, both the Chartered Institute of Marketing (CIM) and the Chartered Management Institute (CMI), which operate at a national level. To increase the reliability of our research results we developed, as suggested by Yin (2018), both a case study protocol and a case study database, which are available from the authors on request.

In order to get a good overview of all relevant issues within the subject group, we used a holistic case study design (Yin 2018) where we looked at marketing teaching in both the undergraduate and postgraduate business degrees. Primary data collection involved interviews with four key members of the Marketing subject group. The interviewees taught undergraduate and postgraduate modules.

- The in-depth interviews analysis was preceded by data analysis of all Marketing modules descriptors and related degree structures (BSc Business Management, BSc Business Management with Marketing, BSc Marketing, and MSc Marketing degrees) and followed by in-depth analysis of the university strategic plan, which applies to the business school. This design allowed for data triangulation, which is of paramount importance in a holistic single-case case study (Yin 2018).

8.4   Developing Social Consciousness and Responsibility of Marketing Students at Brighton Business School

The University of Brighton strategic plan for 2016–2021 speaks of four core values, which guide planning within the university: inclusivity, sustainability, creativity, and partnership. Sustainability underpins everything the university does: '*Our commitment to sustainability runs throughout all our practices, from the management of the university's campuses and facilities, through procurement, travel, food, ethical investment, community engagement, research, teaching and learning*' (University of Brighton 2016). The University of Brighton has a 158-year history as an educational institution operating in the unique environment that is Brighton (Shields 1990). From its earliest days as a tourist resort attracting visitors for the health cure of sea bathing in the nineteenth century, Brighton has been a location, which is open to new ideas, alternative lifestyles, and progressive social thinking. Interviewee 1 gives just two examples of many: '*in terms of "people and planet", Brighton is a hotbed for the "living wage" campaign with 321 businesses (and the local council as well) which signed up to pay a minimum wage around 15% higher than the national minimum living wage. In terms of the natural environment, Brighton was the first city to have a Green Party-led city council and since 2014 the Brighton and Lewes Downs Biosphere was recognised by UNESCO for its unique sustainable ecologic and socio-economic characteristics*'. All interviewees agreed that the environment of Brighton and the values of the University of Brighton play a key role in defining the relevant learning outcomes and objectives of the different courses and modules offered to students in the Business School. '*As marketing lecturers, we believe that a marketing manager who has as his/her sole aim to make profit is obsolete. We need professionals with strong knowledge of marketing techniques, capable of taking the best decisions, but also with a social conscience. Social consciousness is thus embedded everywhere in our courses*' (Interviewee 2). Experience at BBS is a testimony that this can start as early as the first year at undergraduate level, can be reinforced all throughout the curriculum, and even become a specialization at Master's level.

The efforts of the teaching teams to embed social consciousness in the Marketing curriculum at BBS are twofold.

8.4.1 Integration of Standalone Core and Elective Modules Within Courses

The first way BBS marketing lecturers try and develop social consciousness and responsibility among marketing students is within specific core and elective modules dedicated to sustainable marketing.

As core modules within their course, Business with Marketing, BSc students are required to study 'Marketing and Responsibility' in year two. As the name indicates, this module aims to sensitize students to the role of ethics within marketing decision-making. As Interviewee 1 explained '*We introduced this module as a way to infuse more ethics teaching into the core marketing curriculum. Students are very positive about this module and the in-class discussions are often very animated and instructive both to students and to the colleagues who teach the module*'. The module mixes both theoretical and practical approaches, with four main areas of sustainable marketing being covered—ethics, societal and not-for-profit marketing, environmental responsibility, sustainability, and responsible communication. Interviewee 4 stressed that this module offers students a broad perspective of various ethical marketing issues: '*We encourage students to examine every-day decisions of companies through the prism of CSR, sustainability and ethical decision making. In one of the assignment, students are tasked with producing financially viable recommendations for firms that tackle pressing moral and ethical issues, ranging from animal testing in cosmetics manufacturing, to on-line gambling, fair wages and female and male body image in advertising*'. Often the best-performing students in this second-year module will go on to do a research project in their final year related to topics they first encountered during 'Marketing and Responsibility' in year two.

As for the MSc Marketing degree at BBS, it offers a unique specialization in Social Marketing that combines marketing techniques to influence positive behavior for social good in a sustainable way (Kotler and Zaltman 1971). Through contacts with local government institutions and councils, BBS can offer students very interesting projects where they can apply their knowledge of social marketing to real cases, often to high praise of the commissioning organization. As Interviewee 2 clarified '*All students can enroll in this module and have contacts with charities that are developing a social marketing campaign. Therefore, all the students in the MSc Marketing course have the opportunity to research and learn about the not-for-profit experiences and social marketing issues*'.

At the BSc level, there is ample choice of elective modules linked to sustainability, ethics, and responsibility, with 'Social Marketing', 'Contemporary Issues in Marketing', 'Environmental Sustainability' or 'Working in the Voluntary and Not-for-profit Sector' to name the most popular. As Interviewee 1 explained: '*Looking at the popular business press and the academic literature, social consciousness has certainly gained attention over the last 10 years. Some of the (several hundred) topics covered by students in their assignments since we introduced those modules are; consumer decision making in relation to child labor, the effect of promotional campaigns around body image, peer pressure around alcohol consumption by students, and the societal impact of "fast fashion". Academics are often highly impressed by the work students deliver at the end of the year; once students are allowed to research a topic that really fits their interests (and BBS students perhaps more than others are interested in these social aspects of Marketing) they really run with it*'.

Besides integrating CSR in the curriculum and offering a Social Marketing pathway, the MSc marketing at BBS also offers one elective specifically devoted to ethics and CSR. Students in this module learn about business ethics and CSR theories. Interviewee 2 expanded on its content: '*The module explores up to date case studies from companies with good examples as well as bad ones. As part of their assessment, students have to discuss a current ethical or CSR issue, apply the theories they learned about and suggest ways to improve companies' behavior and actions*'.

8.4.2   Embedding Social Consciousness Everywhere in Subject-Specific Traditional Modules

More than designing specific modules to address main social concerns, individual faculty members at BBS use traditional marketing modules as places to raise awareness among future marketing managers about social issues. Interviewee 3 argued that, '*if specific modules are needed, that will rely on integrative frameworks that have some power for consolidating knowledge about CSR, ethics and sustainability, those concepts are important enough to be embedded in any marketing module offered*'. Interviewee 4 emphasized that sustainable marketing is at the heart of all subject-group teaching: '*Our aim in the Business School is for our students to develop a passion for practicing sustainable marketing. We do this through igniting the spark of interest in our undergraduate students the minute they come through the doors of the Business School. We continue to feed the fire of their interest during their time with us by embedding the principles of sustainability in all our modules*'.

Thus, in terms of social consciousness, nearly all of the subject-specific modules at the BSc level include one or more case studies related to CSR and sustainability issues as currently highly relevant matters in business thinking. As Interviewee 1 pointed out: '*In all of the core textbooks used in these first-year modules the student will find case studies around ethics, CSR and sustainability and often these will be subject of in-class discussions*'. Interviewee 4 insisted that not only integration of sustainability principles was important in any module, but also measuring of marketing success of such integration, as is done in 'Measuring Marketing Success' level 4 first year undergraduate module: '*Here we aim to introduce students to the idea that not only business now have to take responsibility seriously, they have to be able to measure the return on building long-term corporate value by integrating sustainability practices*'.

At the MSc level, students start their course with an Introduction to Marketing module. This module works as a refresher for students with a marketing background, but also as an introduction to the subject for students who have no previous marketing knowledge. In this short module, students are already introduced to the concept of CSR, and the idea of marketing for good. '*In introducing CSR together with the basics of marketing theory, we want to present the discussion around ethics awareness as an element of the marketing mix. Our idea is that students, from the start of the course, will perceive social responsibility as an important part of marketing*' Interviewee 2 explained. Similarly in the Communications and Branding module, one of the most popular within the course, students develop a communication project for a 'real life' client, which is a charity. As Interviewee 2 accentuated: '*Here students reflect on issues around marketing communication, ethics and CSR, such as high-pressure sales techniques directed to vulnerable groups, misleading advertising and green-washing techniques. As communication is one of the most recognisable marketing functions, it is important to prepare the future communicators and awaken their responsibilities as marketers*'.

Interviewee 3 gave concrete examples of how students' social consciousness can be enhanced in traditional marketing modules:

– Discussions can be used to bring up challenging topics for marketers. A discussion on the needs and wants of consumers by using mobile phones example can be very provocative. Mobile technology poses serious environmental challenges, because of the raw materials needed to produce the hardware, the energy used to power smartphone connectivity and the pollution associated with disposal. '*Do students, as consumers, worry about electronic waste they generate when updating to the latest, most innovative mobile each year? (…) What can marketing managers do about it? Are they responsible for this situation? As future marketing managers, how will students deal with this paradox of consumers wanting more and more innovations and this causing even more damage to society?*'
– The use of specifically chosen interesting case studies can also help develop students' social consciousness within core marketing modules. '*For example, I use Autolib (Paris's innovative electrical car sharing program) case study to illustrate the challenges and opportunities of public marketing, i.e. the application of marketing concepts and tools to public administration, also discussing the links between public administration and politics, and the difficulties of sustainable development projects*'.

As a result of the teaching team efforts to embed social consciousness in the Marketing curriculum, an increasing number of BBS students decide to write their final dissertation on issues related to ethics, CSR, sustainability, Social Marketing and/or the not-for-profit sector. '*BBS is thus offering degrees that still focus on the more traditional aspects of marketing, but the courses are shaping new graduates who are also capable of reflecting on the future impact of their marketing actions'*, Interviewee 2 clarified. This dissemination of a CSR culture within all marketing modules even reverberated on interdisciplinary projects within the Business School, such as the Business Project module, as explained by Interviewee 4: *'This module gives students an opportunity to come up with an app idea of their own, that has its potential for commercial success assessed not just by tutors but also by business executives. We encourage students to make CSR principles an integral part of their business proposal. This year's winners were the team who had placed the social need at the center of their business plan. They created a wearable tracking device and an accompanying app for relatives of those who suffer with Alzheimer's and dementia'.*

8.4.3 Discussion

The central issue of the relationship between education and 'the Good'—i.e. edification of citizens and future leaders for the health and welfare of the state—that Plato identified in *The Republic* millennia ago, seems nowadays even more vibrant since education can serve as the mechanism through which sustainability as public good can be advanced. If we want to educate responsible people, management education can play an important role in developing social consciousness in future managers. With its promotion of the *'Decade of Education for Sustainable Development'* between 2005 and 2014 (UNESCO 2005), there is no doubt that the United Nations has served as a catalyst to the development of sustainability thinking in education. Concrete application in the field of marketing education can be seen clearly in academic research that highlights the importance of incorporating sustainability in marketing curricula (Borin and Metcalf 2010), and in the publication of textbooks devoted to marketing and sustainability (Martin and Schouten 2012).

The aim of this chapter was to outline a practical example of how social consciousness and responsibility can be developed within the marketing curriculum of a business school. We presented an incursion into the why and how marketing lecturers at BBS do it. The case study demonstrates concrete ideas of how educators can help students more deeply understand the societal consequences of their decisions as future marketing managers. By creating an up-to-date and meaningful learning experience, the ultimate goal of the Marketing subject group at BBS is to make sustainability issues and values integral to future marketing decision-making, thus helping to push forward the sustainability agenda among current and future generations of marketing managers.

An ongoing debate exists regarding whether sustainability should be integrated into core marketing modules across the curriculum or developed as a standalone subject (Audebrand 2010). As proposed in the academic literature (Stubbs and Cocklin 2008), marketing lecturers at BBS are convinced that it is of central importance not only to increase student knowledge of sustainability, but also to challenge student views, and to encourage the analysis of student assumptions about marketing, the environment, and society. Experience at BBS shows that both routes complement each other when seeking to sow the seeds of a sustainability ethos. Sustainability needs to be integrated in the curriculum in a holistic way, rather than in a piecemeal one, thus facilitating critical, innovative, and creative learning spaces (Lambrechts et al. 2013).

Analysis unveiled that marketing lecturers at BBS act in accordance with Shrivastava's approach (2010, p. 446) where he suggests a 'holistic pedagogy of passion for sustainability', arguing against the fragmentation of management education and recommending the integration of analytical, physical, and emotional components. Some lecturers are even close to using a transformative learning approach as conceptualized by Mezirow (2000), one that begins with a disorienting dilemma that challenges the embedded meaning schemes and frames of reference that one uses to interpret experiences. With the aim to meet current sustainability challenges through educating students to be 'integrated catalysts' (who manage harmonization between thought, behavior, and action), who will have the capacity to lead business forward toward a socially oriented, ethical economy (Akrivou and Bradbury-Huang 2015).

If the provision of sustainability within the marketing curriculum reflects the commitment of BBS to the education and development of responsible marketing managers, expertise in CSR and sustainability issues also helps marketing lecturers achieve this ambitious objective. Surveys of business schools introducing sustainability and CSR into the curriculum continue to find that faculty with the right skills and knowledge are crucial to successfully integrating sustainability into the curriculum (Moon and Orlitzky 2011). The emphasis on sustainability in the overall strategy of the university clearly plays a role. Marketing lecturers at BBS insisted that this environment of the university, where sustainability is considered of strategic importance and embedded everywhere, also empowers graduates to leave the university with the skills and knowledge needed to be change-makers for a sustainable future. The university's award-winning sustainability campaign, c-change, engages not only staff, but also students in driving forward progress toward a fully sustainable university. The University of Brighton was ranked 7th in the People and Planet University League 2017, in recognition of its commitment to, and progress toward, sustainability. BBS also became a member of The Principles for Responsible Management Education (PRME), a United Nations-supported initiative founded as a platform to raise the profile of sustainability in schools around the world. This policy helps disseminating a sustainability culture among students. It also engenders changes in students' behavior, viewed as educating for sustainability (Thomas 2009). Thus addressing the already mentioned 'know-how' and 'know-why' of socially responsible behavior, evaluated by Schneider et al. (2010) as more difficult to achieve.

8.5   Conclusion

The main contribution of this chapter is to outline the implementation practice of sustainable marketing education in a UK business school. The findings offer valuable insights for other business schools into how to integrate sustainability into their marketing education and how to contribute to the United Nations Sustainable Development Goal number 4, namely quality education. This case study illustrates that business schools can and ought to be a place where responsible people can grow to become responsible managers. Responsible managerial decision-making will have a positive impact on society. Data analysis shows that, beyond creating explicit student opportunities around CSR and sustainability issues, universities can play an active role in embedding social consciousness and responsibility as part of their own strategic plan. There are further avenues to expand on this research. Firstly, a comparative study between experiences at other Business Schools in the UK could be conducted, to analyze how different universities approach this challenge in different ways. Other comparative studies could also be made with other cultures showing less concern for sustainability than in the UK, in order to evaluate better the important role universities do play when implementing a sustainability policy. Additionally, qualitative interviews and quantitative surveys with the BBS students on one hand, and alumni on the other hand, across different levels, would help understand and measure the real impact of the presented approach. From personal observation we know that quite a few graduates find jobs in social marketing, not-for-profit and charity organizations. It would be interesting to know what impact their education had on that career choice. Most importantly, every student who has completed a degree at BBS will have encountered aspects of sustainability and social consciousness every day in practically every module, through discussions with fellow students and professors in class, and outside the classroom, via sustainability initiatives throughout the university and within the city of Brighton itself. The combination of business school curriculum, university strategy, and city culture all allow individual students to develop their responsible self.

References

Akrivou, Kleio, and Hilary Bradbury-Huang. 2015. Educating Integrated Catalysts: Transforming Business Schools Toward Ethics and Sustainability. *Academy of Management Learning & Education* 14 (2): 222–240.

Ammentorp, Louise. 2007. Imagining Social Change: Developing Social Consciousness in an Arts-Based Pedagogy. *Outlines. Critical Practice Studies* 9 (1): 38–52.

Audebrand, Luc K. 2010. Sustainability in Strategic Management Education: The Quest for New Root Metaphors. *Academy of Management Learning & Education* 9 (3): 413–428.

Benneworth, Paul, and Jorge Cunha. 2015. Universities' Contributions to Social Innovation: Reflections in Theory & Practice. *European Journal of Innovation Management* 18 (4): 508–527.

Borin, Norm, and Lynn Metcalf. 2010. Integrating Sustainability into the Marketing Curriculum: Learning Activities that Facilitate Sustainable Marketing Practices. *Journal of Marketing Education* 32 (2): 140–154.

Cooley, Charles H. 1907. Social Consciousness. *American Journal of Sociology* 12 (5): 675–694.

Crilly, Donal, Susan C. Schneider, and Maurizio Zollo. 2008. Psychological Antecedents to Socially Responsible Behavior. *European Management Review* 5 (3): 175–190.

Deer, Shannon, and Jill Zarestky. 2017. Balancing Profit and People: Corporate Social Responsibility in Business Education. *Journal of Management Education* 41 (5): 727–749.

Doyle, K. 2008. Job Market Sees Growing Demand for Sustainability Managers. *Grist Magazine*.

Gordon, Ross, Marylyn Carrigan, and Gerard Hastings. 2011. A Framework for Sustainable Marketing. *Marketing Theory* 11 (2): 143–163.

Harrigan, Paul, and Bev Hulbert. 2011. How Can Marketing Academics Serve Marketing Practice? The New Marketing DNA as a Model for Marketing Education. *Journal of Marketing Education* 33 (3): 253–272.

Haugh, Helen M., and Alka Talwar. 2010. How Do Corporations Embed Sustainability Across the Organization? *Academy of Management Learning & Education* 9 (3): 384–396.

Hesselbarth, Charlotte, and Stefan Schaltegger. 2014. Educating Change Agents for Sustainability—Learnings from the First Sustainability Management Master of Business Administration. *Journal of Cleaner Production* 62: 24–36.

Kotler, Philip, and Gerald Zaltman. 1971. Social Marketing: An Approach to Planned Social Change. *The Journal of Marketing* 35 (3): 3–12.

Küster, Inés, and Natalia Vila. 2006. A Comparison of Marketing Teaching Methods in North American and European Universities. *Marketing Intelligence & Planning* 24 (4): 319–331.

Lambrechts, Wim, Ingrid Mulà, Kim Ceulemans, Ingrid Molderez, and Veerle Gaeremynck. 2013. The Integration of Competences for Sustainable Development in Higher Education: An Analysis of Bachelor Programs in Management. *Journal of Cleaner Production* 48: 65–73.

Markley Rountree, Melissa, and Stephen K. Koernig. 2015. Values-Based Education for Sustainability Marketers: Two Approaches for Enhancing Student Social Consciousness. *Journal of Marketing Education* 37 (1): 5–24.

Martin, Diane M., and John W. Schouten. 2012. *Sustainable Marketing*. Upper Saddle River, NJ: Pearson Prentice Hall.

Martin, Diane M., and John W. Schouten. 2014. The Answer Is Sustainable Marketing, When the Question Is: What Can We Do? *Recherche et Applications en Marketing* (English Edition) 29 (3): 107–109.

Matten, Dirk, and Jeremy Moon. 2004. Corporate Social Responsibility. *Journal of Business Ethics* 54 (4): 323–337.

Mezirow, Jack. 2000. *Learning as Transformation: Critical Perspectives on a Theory in Progress*. The Jossey-Bass Higher and Adult Education Series. San Francisco, CA: Jossey-Bass.

Mirvis, Philip. 2008. Executive Development Through Consciousness-Raising Experiences. *Academy of Management Learning & Education* 7 (2): 173–188.

Moon, Jeremy, and Marc Orlitzky. 2011. Corporate Social Responsibility and Sustainability Education: A Trans-Atlantic Comparison. *Journal of Management & Organization* 17 (5): 583–603.

Nicholls, Jeananne, Joseph F. Hair, Jr., Charles B. Ragland, and Kurt E. Schimmel. 2013. Ethics, Corporate Social Responsibility, and Sustainability Education in AACSB Undergraduate and Graduate Marketing Curricula: A Benchmark Study. *Journal of Marketing Education* 35 (2): 129–140.

Schlitz, Marilyn Mandala, Cassandra Vieten, and Elizabeth M. Miller. 2010. Worldview Transformation and the Development of Social Consciousness. *Journal of Consciousness Studies* 17 (7–8): 18–36.

Schneider, Susan C., Maurizio Zollo, and Ramesh Manocha. 2010. Developing Socially Responsible Behaviour in Managers. *Journal of Corporate Citizenship* 39: 21–40.

Schumacher, Ernst Friedrich. 1973. *Small Is Beautiful: A Study of Economics as if People Really Mattered*. London: Blond & Briggs.

Scullion, Richard. 2017. Embedding Social Responsibility in HE Corporate Communications Degrees. The Place of CSR in Teaching Corporate Communications Programs (Advertising, Branding and Public Relations). In *Corporate Social Responsibility in the Post-Financial Crisis Era*, 3–23. Cham: Palgrave Macmillan.

Shields, Rob. 1990. The 'System of Pleasure': Liminality and the Carnivalesque at Brighton. *Theory, Culture & Society* 7 (1): 39–72.

Shrivastava, Paul. 2010. Pedagogy of Passion for Sustainability. *Academy of Management Learning & Education* 9 (3): 443–455.

Stubbs, Wendy, and Chris Cocklin. 2008. Teaching Sustainability to Business Students: Shifting Mindsets. *International Journal of Sustainability in Higher Education* 9 (3): 206–221.

Thomas, Ian. 2009. Critical Thinking, Transformative learning, Sustainable Education, and Problem-Based Learning in Universities. *Journal of Transformative Education* 7 (3): 245–264.

UNESCO. 2005. *United Nations Decade of Education for Sustainable Development (2005–2014): International Implementation Scheme.* Paris: United Nations Educational, Scientific and Cultural Organisation.

UN General Assembly. 2015. *Transforming Our World: The 2030 Agenda for Sustainable Development.* New York: United Nations.

University of Brighton. 2016. *Practical Wisdom: University Strategy 2016–2021.* Available at https://www.brighton.ac.uk/practical-wisdom/index.aspx.

WCED (World Commission on Environment and Development), Bruntland Commission. 1987. *Our Common Future.* Report of the World Commission on Environment and Development.

Yin, Robert K. 2018. *Case Study Research and Applications: Design and Methods.* Los Angles: Sage.

Part III

Citizens, Consumers, Stakeholders— Shaping the Future of CSR

9

Frack Off: Climate Change, CSR, Citizen Activism and the Shaping of National Energy Policy

David McQueen

Efforts to introduce hydraulic fracturing (or 'fracking') for oil and gas to Europe in recent years have met fierce public resistance, as well as worries from various commercial interests—such as brewers—about impacts on local water quality on which they depend. A combination of persistent protest, political lobbying and developing scientific concerns around the impacts of fracking have contributed to government-imposed moratoria and bans in a growing number of countries. In contrast to the shale boom in the US, particularly, but also in some Canadian and Australian states, shale oil and gas extraction in Europe has failed to gain the required political and public support to ensure widespread development. Concerns over noise, air and water pollution, tanker traffic and the industrialisation of the countryside in a densely populated continent, alongside urgent calls to switch from fossil fuels to preserve humanity's future, have led many to reject fracking as socially irresponsible and environmentally unacceptable.

D. McQueen (✉)
Faculty of Media and Communication,
Bournemouth University, Poole, UK
e-mail: dmcqueen@bournemouth.ac.uk

© The Author(s) 2019   **175**
F. Farache et al. (eds.), *Responsible People*, Palgrave Studies in Governance,
Leadership and Responsibility, https://doi.org/10.1007/978-3-030-10740-6_9

October 2018 saw the first British fracking operation at the Preston New Road site in Lancashire operated by Cuadrilla Resources since a 2011 national moratorium following earth tremors around a drilling site close to Blackpool (*The Telegraph* 2017). Preston New Road has been a focal point for protest since 2016 when the government overturned a decision by Lancashire county council and gave Cuadrilla consent to extract shale gas at two wells on the site. The resumption of fracking in the UK has been met by public protests, controversial imprisonments, close scrutiny of seismic activity and media commentary on the British government's failure to implement effective policies in the fight against climate change. It also comes at a critical juncture in Europe for the development of shale gas and oil exploration and this chapter reflects, at this key moment, on the forces at play as well as the work of key individuals in the fight over fracking. The chapter concludes by considering if the technology can ever win the social licence required to be widely deployed in England, or further afield in Europe and ponders who holds responsibility for the future of this controversial process.

The fossil fuel sector has a long and well-documented history of pollution and destructive impacts on the environment and communities around the world with the paradoxical terms 'resource curse' or 'oil curse' often used to describe the negative effect of discovery and exploitation (Khanna 2017). Oil companies are consistently ranked among the least trusted corporations and most in need of more regulation (Corso, cited Spangler and Pompper 2011). Furthermore, much of the industry's CSR activity is dismissed as 'greenwashing' (Spence 2017, p. 397) designed to provide a buffer against criticism, regulation and efforts to scale back fossil fuel use. Indeed, the urgent requirement to drastically reduce reliance on fossil fuels has been underscored in the latest in a long line of UN Intergovernmental Panel on Climate Change Reports (IPCC 2018). The IPCC report noted that global net emissions of carbon dioxide would need to fall by 45% from 2010 levels by 2030 to keep global warming below 1.5 degrees Celsius. Without 'rapid, far-reaching and unprecedented changes in all aspects of society' (IPCC, cited CNN 2018) the world will face more heat waves for tens of millions of people, enormous species loss, extreme weather events, increased water scarcity, food shortages, a ten-fold increase in Arctic ice-free summers and a total wipe-out of the world's coral reefs by 2040 (IPCC 2018; *New York Times* 2018a). Despite repeated warnings of this kind since the 1980s, meaningful action on climate change remains 'painfully slow' with the oil and associated industries alongside other corporations with heavy environmental footprints attempting to 'frustrate meaningful progress' (Miller and Dinan 2015, p. 86).

While the use of all fossil fuels, and especially coal, has come under increased scrutiny with this rising sense of urgency around climate change, the process of natural gas exploration by hydraulic fracturing of shale formations, or 'fracking', has taken on a number of specific concerns. There is alarm among environmentalists that the availability of cheaper gas undermines the economic viability of sustainable energies. In addition, the energy-intensive, unconventional techniques deployed in fracking for natural gas mean not only increased carbon dioxide but, more worryingly, methane emissions which are more than a hundred times greater at absorbing heat than CO_2 (Howarth 2015). However, it is the experience of the *local* impacts of shale gas extraction and transportation that has helped galvanise powerful and sustained opposition to fracking. These impacts include the industrialisation of the countryside, the toxic contamination of drinking water, noise, light and air pollution, chronic illness, seismicity, the poisoning of agricultural land, chemical spills, accidents and explosions (Hannigan 2014; McQueen 2017). Evidence of these impacts has been widely shared using a variety of media through a dense network of local, regional and national protest movements, connected around the world through the internet and social media.

Public resistance to fracking in the United Kingdom has, therefore, been informed particularly by the US and Australian experiences where fracking has a longer history of development and where both the industry and associated protests have been growing rapidly apace (Short and Szoluchab 2017). As recently as 2009, the words 'shale gas' did not even appear in the annual US government energy outlook, yet by 2010 23% of US natural gas production had come from shale (Gross 2013) surging to nearly 70% of gas production in 2015 (EIA, cited U.S. EPA 2016, p. 4) Hydraulic fracturing also accounted for more than 50% of domestic oil production (ibid.) and the technology has enabled an important shift away from dependency on imported oil and gas and supports an estimated 725,000 jobs (Reuters 2015). It is estimated by the International Energy Agency (IEA) that US oil output could surpass Saudi Arabia's by 2020, making the country almost self-reliant (Bloomberg 2012). However, as Spence (2017, p. 390) observes, while this dramatic increase has undoubtedly benefitted the US economy, local communities around the rigs sustaining America's shale boom now experience some of the same the socioeconomic disruptions and environmental risks typically associated with the oil curse overseas.

Alongside the noise, lights, flares and odours from fracking rigs, each time a well is fracked millions of litres of fresh water and chemicals must be delivered and toxic, often radioactive, fracked water needs to be stored in giant waste water pools, or removed from the site entirely. An average of more than 1000 tanker truck trips are required per frack thereby taking a toll on local, often rural infrastructure not build for heavy traffic of this kind (Spence 2017), as well as increasing the number of road traffic accidents. In the development of The Energy Policy Act signed into law by George W. Bush in 2005 the fracking industry successfully lobbied to be exempt from certain sections of the Clean Air Act (1970), Clean Water Act (1972) and Safe Drinking Water Act (1974) through the so-called 'Halliburton Loophole'. Controversially, companies do not have to disclose the chemical composition of their fracking fluids. This is justified on the basis of commercial sensitivity, yet many of the chemicals used in the fracking process are known to be 'caustic, poisonous or explosive' (Wilber, cited Hannigan 2014, p. 189). An EPA report in 2016 found 'scientific evidence that hydraulic fracturing activities can impact drinking water resources under some circumstances' which has added pressure on fracking companies to publish a list of the more than 1000 chemicals used in the fracking process (U.S. EPA 2016, p. 16).

A large part of the struggle against the fracking industry involves control over knowledge—the ability to define what is and what isn't a threat to health and the environment. The shale gas and oil drilling discourse is filled with struggles over 'facts', such as the toxicity of chemicals used in fracking fluids. As Gullion (2015) argues, while the foundations of policymaking appear to rest on science; the science in question is mutable, particularly when cloaked by commercial confidentiality or underpinned by industry research grants. Even among scientists the facts are in dispute (see McQueen 2017) and 'epistemic privilege' is often granted to the more powerful (and well-funded) groups, while 'the groups in power try to eliminate all expressions of emotional pain from the discussion' (Gullion 2015, p. 173).

Gullion uses the term 'reluctant activists' to describe the group of people she interviewed in Texas who are disproportionally burdened by the negative effects of natural gas development. The people in her research are neither poor nor (for the most part) members of racial or ethnic minority groups, but 'are living in a sacrifice zone' albeit one that is relatively prosperous:

> Environmental problems can be a shock to these people, because they are typically sheltered from industrial activities. Used to buying their way to safety […], they are often not aware of the difficulties of living in proximity to polluting industries. (Gullion 2015, p. 173)

Gullion pinpoints the struggle over disputed scientific knowledge and the industry's efforts to close down discussion of lived experience of local fracking. Fear of health threats, confusion and a sense of powerlessness experienced by residents and farmers living close to fracking sites is a common theme in much of the critical scholarship and media coverage of the shale industry. Where local wells and ground water is contaminated by fracking the industry has sometimes provided bottled water on condition such supplies are not taken as an admission of liability. Payments for damage caused by seismicity, leaks and accidents are also often agreed with non-disclosure clauses that prevent those most affected from sharing their experiences with others (Insurance Journal 2013; DutchNews.nl 2016). Resistance to local fracking is expensive, stressful and traumatic (Short and Szoluchab 2017) and networks of fellow protestors often provide the only sympathetic venue to express frustration. Yet resistance in the US and Australia continues to grow and the efforts of individuals captured in documentaries, blogs and creative protest has inspired those in neighbouring states and other countries facing the same issues.

A series of powerful and disturbing films documenting local experience of shale gas exploration in the US and beyond have helped galvanise domestic and international opposition to fracking. These include *Split Estate* (2009), *Gasland* (2010), *Gasland Part 2* (2013), *Fractured Land* (2015), and *Frackman* (2015), as well as hundreds of low-budget, locally produced reports and documentaries made in areas affected by, or threatened with the possibility of fracking. The most influential of these is undoubtedly Academy-Award-nominated *Gasland* written and directed by Josh Fox who travels across twenty-four US states impacted by unconventional hydrocarbon extraction talking to people whose lives have been blighted by polluted air and drinking water, destruction of property value, ill health and even an exploding well (Hannigan 2014). Mazur (2014) argues that before April 2010 major US news organisations paid little attention to the issue of fracking, but that following the offshore Deepwater Horizon disaster of that month *The New York Times* and other media outlets began to report more frequently on potential risks of the onshore exploration of shale gas that *Gasland* had exposed.

The continuing effect of Josh Fox's individual contribution to the fracking debate is hard to measure, but what is clear is the filmmaker's tenacity and skill in collating and publicising the hidden fallout of shale gas development across the country. *Gasland* and Fox's follow-up documentary *Gasland 2* explore the negative impacts of fracking that the mainstream media had often failed to report on, alongside the emotional toll that challenging the industry has taken on families and communities. His films and other documentaries that came in their wake have been used by environmental activists to help mobilise local communities against the threat of fracking around the world.

The shale industry quickly woke to the 'Gasland effect' and has fought back against the films and the movement they spurred in a number of ways. They sponsored films such as *Shale Gas and America's Future* (2010) released by the American Clean Skies Foundation, a pro-natural gas industry group (Natural Gas Intel 2012) and *Truthland* (2013), which benefitted from a $1 million grant from America's Natural Gas Alliance (*The Nation* 2013). *Fracknation* (2013) another film made in direct response to the *Gasland* films, alongside *Not Evil Just Wrong: the True Cost of Global Warming Hysteria* (2009) by the same director

Phelim McAleer, were also promoted and received logistical support by industry lobbyists.

A loose coalition of free-market foundations and fossil fuel lobbyists have also funded so-called AstroTurf groups, educational material for schools, think tanks, academic and industry research, online and media campaigns in favour of fracking. Americans for Prosperity Foundation and The Heartland Institute, both funded by the Koch brothers, The Heritage Foundation, The Cato Institute, The Competitive Enterprise Institute, Koch Industries and the American Petroleum Institute (API) are among the US organisations championing unconventional oil and gas drilling as well as promoting climate change denial and scepticism. These and other conservative foundations press for accelerated investment in domestic oil and gas exploration, extolling the security virtues of reducing dependency on imported fossil fuels, while casting doubt on climate change science and frustrating policy efforts on climate action (Miller and Dinan 2015). The success of these groups can partly be measured by the decision in 2017 by President Donald Trump, who describes climate change as a 'hoax', to withdraw from the Paris Agreement on climate change mitigation and prioritise fossil fuel infrastructure projects which had been held up by the Obama administration (Piper and McQueen 2018). The close cooperation of the US Environmental Protection Agency (EPA) with The Heartland Institute and other climate sceptic groups (AP News 2018) under Scott Pruitt and the slashing of environmental regulations under Andrew Wheeler, the new acting chief of the agency, a former coal lobbyist (*New York Times* 2018b), is further indication of the Trump administration's close cooperation with fossil fuel lobby groups.

A study by Robert Brulle in the journal *Climatic Change* (2014) shows 91 organisations in the US that make up what he describes as 'the climate change counter-movement' (CCCM) received an annual income of just over $900 million between 2003 and 2010, much of which came through trusts or other mechanisms that assure anonymity to donors. Researching such funding is problematic, but one estimate indicated the Koch Brothers alone have donated $61million to the CCCM (Cave and Rowell 2014, p. 224) suggesting the power individuals can have in shaping public discourse around climate change.

Many US conservative foundations and fossil-fuel lobby groups have developed ties with members of the British political establishment directly, or via the Global Warming Policy Foundation (GWPF) founded by Lord Nigel Lawson, The Institute of Economic Affairs (IEA), Economists for Free Trade (EFT) and other think tanks. Their pro-fossil fuel, anti-climate action agenda can be seen in the Conservative Party's shift away from the 'Vote Blue, Go Green' strategy led by David Cameron and encoded in a statement of Conservative principles, *Built to Last*, published in August 2006 (Carter and Clements 2015, p. 207). Cameron who in 2010 promised, as the head of the Conservative-Liberal Democrat Alliance to lead the 'greenest government ever' was by 2013 failing to challenge the growth of climate science denial in his own party and reportedly demanding that aides 'get rid of all the green crap' (green levies and regulations) that he regarded as responsible for pushing up energy prices (Carter and Clements 2015, p. 215). A Downing Street source allegedly remarked: 'We used to say: "Vote blue, go green", now it's: "Vote blue, get real"' (cited *The Guardian* 2013).

As Hannigan (2014) notes, the ruling Conservative/Liberal Democrat coalition was divided between a pro-growth wing and an environmental wing. The former enthusiastically embraced fracking, seeing it as the key to energy security and economic prosperity. The latter faction worried that fracking would industrialise the countryside and make it difficult to justify subsidies for renewable energy projects. In addition, Tory Members of Parliament from rural constituencies who tended to be hostile to renewable energy projects such as wind farms, were unlikely to welcome fracking rigs in their backyards—'especially in the "stockbroker belt", the rolling countryside in Surrey and Sussex south of London where an estimated 700 million barrels of recoverable shale oil have been forecast' (Hannigan 2014, p. 179).

Influenced by the pressures from within the party, the right-wing press, and a more sceptical Conservative-supporting base, the Conservative Governments under David Cameron from 2015 and Teresa May from 2016 appeared to lose interest in meaningful efforts at tackling climate change. The government ended much of its support for renewable energy—dramatically cutting subsidies to the solar industry leading to 12,000 job losses in the sector in a single year (*The Guardian* 2016) and effectively prohibiting onshore wind turbines whilst 'going all out for shale' (McQueen 2017, p. 222). For Carter and Clements this direction of travel was an unsurprising development:

> The right is climate sceptic or 'climate go-slow' because it is anti-regulation, pro-market, anti-state, anti-EU, anti-taxes, so it is very hard to construct a 'conversation' or 'narrative' where positive action to mitigate climate change fits comfortably. (Carter and Clements 2015, p. 217)

Potential future leaders of the Conservative Party and arch-Brexiteers Boris Johnson, Michael Gove and Jacob Rees-Mogg are widely regarded as climate change sceptics, or at least sceptical of legislation designed to reduce greenhouse gas emissions. Yet their 'go-slow' on climate action can trace its roots back at least to 2011 with a speech by George Osborne at the Conservative Party Conference in Manchester that year, which put him on a collision course with the government's then coalition partners the Liberal Democrats (*The Independent* 2011). The downgrading of green energy schemes and the 'dash for gas' announced in 2012 by David Cameron quadrupled the amount of power expected to be generated from gas by 2030 and made it more likely that the UK would be unable to meet its carbon emission targets (*The Observer* 2012). Blocking the development of onshore and even some offshore wind farms, such as Navitus Bay (*The Telegraph* 2015), whilst offering tax incentives to frack for gas struck many environmentalists as perverse, but it indicates that the gap between the policies of the Trump administration in the US and that of the UK's British Conservative Government may be more a matter of presentation than of substance.

Protests against fracking and associated pipeline construction have, arguably, contributed in some cases to state or county-wide bans or moratoria in the US (see McQueen 2018), but they have failed to prevent both Democrat and Republican administrations from encouraging the shale boom across the nation. Opposition to shale gas drilling is, however, much more intense in Western Europe than it is in southern Ohio or upstate New York (Levi 2013). Environmental concerns and protests, particularly related to the danger to water supplies and impacts to the countryside in a densely populated continent, have slowed adoption of the practice in Europe. The European Union currently lacks a unified stance on fracking and while banned in Germany and France, Poland, for one has resisted calls for restrictive European legislation on shale gas to protect its energy independence from Russia (*New York Times* 2012).

Have public protests played a part in slowing the progress of hydraulic fracturing across the continent? France, for instance, has the twelfth biggest reserves of shale gas in the world and yet protests and 'a highly charged and emotional debate' (Chaineau and Lennock 2016, p. 1) resulted in an effective ban on hydraulic fracturing by the centre-right government of former President Nicolas Sarkozy in 2011, which was upheld by the constitutional court in 2013. While the nation's reliance on nuclear energy meant that France was perhaps not as anxious to develop locally fracked gas resources as other nations, the likelihood of further protest action from farmers, wine producers and citizens with a history of militant protest is likely to have been a strong consideration.

Bulgaria became the second country in Europe to ban fracking in January 2012 following large-scale and persistent street protests against Chevron (BBC 2012). Chevron was also forced to suspend its plans to drill an exploratory well in neighbouring Romania in the village of Pungesti, in an economically depressed area near the Moldovan border following sustained opposition by local residents and farmers. The local community protested and blocked the company from entering the area for two months. In a detailed report on EJ Atlas (2018) noted how:

> An activist in Bucharest, who acts as a liaison with people in Pungesti, said people in remote areas are now knowledgeable about the well-publicized problems like water pollution that opponents say fracking has caused in the United States and they are well-connected with a European network and international network.

After weeks of intense policing and allegations of brutality against protestors Chevron finally pulled out of Romania 'due to poor exploration results and prolonged protests by environmentalists'. This withdrawal from the fracking project marked the end of the company's shale gas exploration in Europe (EJ Atlas 2018). Other protests in Poland and Ukraine are far less likely to halt unconventional hydrocarbon extraction in countries which are anxious to end their dependency on Russian imported gas, but they may have also slowed progress in developing the countries' shale gas resources.

In Germany long-running and large-scale protests against nuclear energy undoubtedly contributed to Angela Merkel's CDU government decision in 2011 to phase out nuclear power stations by 2022, but it was not the only factor. The Fukushima disaster of 2011 was proclaimed as the immediate catalyst for the Merkel administration to accelerate an earlier commitment by the government of Gerhard Schroeder (SPD) to phase out nuclear power. Merkel won early support for the suspension with an ARD poll showing 80% support for the decision, with 53% backing closure of all German reactors as soon as possible (Reuters 2011). However, this represented a handbrake turn on energy policy for the CDU and opposition parties accused Merkel of 'transparent trickery' in response to the prospect of the CDU faced losing control of Baden-Württemberg in imminent regional elections. Nuclear power plants were unpopular nationally and the move was seen as an effective method of neutralising the anti-nuclear opposition. The decision, described as 'overly hasty' by former Chancellor Helmut Kohl (*Spiegel* 2011), did not prevent electoral defeat for the CDU in the Baden-Württemberg state election of 27 March 2011 which saw a doubling of the Green vote. The sudden reversal in policy position taken by the Christian Democrats in the field of nuclear energy policy 'simply lacked credibility', while the media and public mostly agreed that the catastrophe in Fukushima mobilised people to vote, and especially to vote for The Green Party which has rejected the use of nuclear energy since its foundation (Keil and Gabriel 2012, p. 240).

Similarly, it is likely that citizens' protests alone did not cause the German government to ban fracking in 2016 and that other electoral and commercial concerns, as in France, have played a role. In May, 2013, the Association of German Breweries voiced its grave concern to the federal cabinet that fracking could violate the 500-year-old Bavarian purity law, which only allows water, barley, hops and yeast, and endanger the water supply that more than half Germany's breweries currently take from private wells (Nicola, cited Hannigan 2014, p. 177). Unpicking the various factors that lead to legislative change is undoubtedly, a complex process. In October 2018, neither 50,000 anti-coal demonstrators in the Hambach Forest, nor the presence of tree-house protestors for several years on the threatened site have (at the time of writing) halted German energy giant RWE's plans to begin clearing half of the forest's remaining 200 hectares of woodlands (Deutsche Welle 2018), nor its support from the German government. Other political and economic factors and opposition forces may have to come into play.

In the Netherlands a complex of factors are thought to have helped sway the Dutch government to impose a moratorium in 2015 and confirm the permanent end to shale gas drilling in 2018. As in Germany, objections by brewing groups like Heineken, alongside opposition by a number of local councils, water boards and citizen groups played their part. The experience of residents affected by strong earth tremors and subsidence in the Groningen area where 100,000 homes are estimated to have suffered damage as a result of decades of gas exploration has also helped focus the minds of legislators on the probable long-term seismic impact of fracking (DutchNews.nl 2016, 2018; Deutsche Welle 2017).

In Spain, grassroots opposition to fracking has led to bans on fracking in four regions—Cantabria, La Rioja and Navarra (since 2013) and Catalonia (since 2014). According to a report in EJOLT (2013) the use of community workshops to explain the threat of fracking were highly effective in a decentralised campaign in Cantabria and nationwide public opposition to fracking is rapidly spreading with more than 400 towns declaring themselves fracking-free towns. In the Basque Country and in Asturias and Burgos several fracking companies have, the report states, 'given up due to opposition and public pressure'. Similarly, a 2012 moratorium on fracking in Denmark was due to come to an end in 2015, but the French oil and gas giant Total decided to abandon its shale gas exploration plans in 2016 'following poor results from initial drilling in north Jutland and overwhelming public resistance' (*Copenhagen Post* 2016).

Despite these setbacks for the fracking industry on the continent, fracking recommenced in Britain on the 15 October 2018 after a seven-year pause. This followed a moratorium imposed by the British government after minor earthquakes were detected in the Blackpool area close to Cuadrilla's Preece Hall site in the spring of 2011 which was lifted at the end of 2012. Protests against Cuadrilla in 2013 at Balcombe in West Sussex, against Third Energy's exploratory drilling at Kirby Misperton in Yorkshire, against the drilling of a shale well at Barton Moss in Salford by iGas and in Lancashire at Cuadrilla's Preston New Road and Roseacre Wood sites have failed, so far, to halt the British government's determination to support the shale industry. This determination was bolstered by lobbying and interventions by industry personnel and experts at the heart of Whitehall ministries and the Cabinet Office (McQueen 2017). Westminster's policy rhetoric emphasises economic development, regulatory oversight and distribution of benefits to local communities, while minimising discussion of the implications of shale gas for anthropogenic climate change (Cotton et al. 2014), among other impacts discussed above.

Nevertheless, the scale and determination of day-to-day protests has slowed work at the drilling sites in Lancashire and Yorkshire and may have halted operations at Balcombe where Cuadrilla denied ever wanting to frack due to the nature of the rock. While day-to-day protests rarely made news headlines, the arrest of individuals sometimes did. Great-grandmother Jackie Brookes, 79, who set up a table for serving tea and cakes to both protesters and police at the Kirby Misperton site in North Yorkshire in September and October 2017 was arrested on 9th October after she and other protesters refused orders by police to 'step away from the picnic table' set up near the site (*The Metro* 2017). Even pro-conservative and pro-fracking newspapers *The Sun* and *Daily Mail* considered the arrest an over-reaction—with 'TWELVE' (emphasis in original) policemen noted in the *Daily Mail* headline which also quoted protestors as shouting 'This is England, not 1930s Germany'. *The Sun* strapline described the arrest shown in a large photograph which dominated coverage in several papers as follows: 'This is the shocking moment an elderly tea lady was forcibly moved from her month-long post set up at a controversial fracking site by police'. Here the power of images played a part as photographs of young uniformed police arresting an innocuous-looking, white-haired lady at her tea stall clearly disturbed a faction of Middle England normally unsympathetic to anti-fracking protestors.

The following day, across the Pennines in Lancashire outside Cuadrilla's Preston New Road site, an 81-year-old disabled protester Anne Power was sitting in a folding chair by the side of the road. Campaigners were listening to speeches at what has become a regular 'Green Monday' event when a tanker reportedly drove through the crowd, waved in by Cuadrilla security staff. This prompted people to sit down in protest, which led to the arrest of Anne Power who was photographed being dragged across the road by three uniformed police officers. The arrest also gained some mainstream media coverage, but social media widely recirculated the image side-by-side to that of a Suffragette being dragged by policemen in a strikingly similar pose with the text: 1910—Suffragette; 2017 anti-fracker under each photo. The meme strapline was 'Over 100 years and the police are still on the wrong side of history'.

The most media coverage however went to three protestors imprisoned for their part in a four-day direct action protest that blocked a convoy of trucks carrying drilling equipment from entering the Preston New Road fracking site in Little Plumpton, near Blackpool. Simon Blevins, 26, and Richard Roberts, 36, were sentenced to 16 months in prison and Richard Loizou, 31, received a 15-month sentence after being convicted of causing a public nuisance climbing onto lorries outside Cuadrilla's fracking site by a jury at Preston crown court. Another defendant, Julian Brock, 47, was given a 12-month suspended sentence after pleading guilty to the same offence in a trial where the defendants could not talk about why they were concerned about fracking, 'or explain that many people in the community welcomed being mildly inconvenienced if it delayed and deterred the much greater threat of fracking and climate change' (Lucas 2018). According to a lawyer representing them, the three men were the first environmental campaigners to be jailed for a protest in the UK since the mass trespass on Kinder Scout in the Peak District in 1932. Judge Robert Altham was widely criticised for the draconian sentence against non-violent protestors and for allegedly having a conflict of interest due to his family's links to the gas and oil industry. The sentence was deemed 'manifestly excessive' (*The Times* 2018) on appeal and the three were released a week later to a hero's welcome from anti-fracking protestors. Widespread media coverage for their arrest and release gave them a rare opportunity to explain their reasons for protesting to the mainstream media. The fact that one, Simon Blevins, was a soil scientist alarmed at the impact fracking would have on the soil lent further credence to those who doubted the government's claim science supported the case for fracking. Have these protests and attendant publicity had any impact on the government's plans to go 'all out for shale'?

In 2018 the Conservative Government under Teresa May enjoys a slim majority in Parliament with the support of the Democratic Unionist Party (DUP), which Ian Johnston of *The Independent* described as 'a far-right party with a track record of Donald Trump-style climate change denial'. Indeed, the DUP's former environment minister once described global warming as a 'con' and the Paris Agreement on climate action as 'a delusion' in language reminiscent of President Trump (*The Independent* 2017). Yet the government has faced protracted legal battles and protests against the return of fracking across the UK and the other major Parliamentary parties have now vowed to oppose fracking. In 2016 the Labour Party announced it would ban the process and the Liberal Democrats added a ban to their 2017 manifesto. The same year the Scottish SNP government banned fracking after a consultation found overwhelming public opposition and little economic justification for the industry (*The Guardian* 2017). This followed a two-year moratorium on fracking in Scotland from 2015. In 2015 the Welsh government also imposed a moratorium and are likely to permanently ban the process, or indeed any coal bed methane extraction, arguing that the 'benefits of petroleum extraction are not great enough to outweigh its commitment to sustainably manage natural resources' (National Assembly for Wales Research Service 2018). Northern Ireland ruled out fracking in 2014 following sustained protests in County Fermanagh (*Belfast Telegraph* 2014) and in the Republic of Ireland legislation banning fracking was passed in 2017 in the first Private Members' Bill to be passed by both Houses during the lifetime of the minority Government (*Irish Times* 2017). These bans followed protest and pressure from civil society that has been harder to resist or ignore in national parliaments than in Westminster. England remains the sole country in the British Isles where fracking is permitted and the scale of opposition in the regions—Lancashire, Yorkshire and Sussex where exploratory drilling has taken place—suggests drilling on a large scale across the English countryside is an unrealistic ambition. Craig Bennett writing in *The Independent* in reaction to Ireland's vote to ban shale gas exploration argued:

> Leaders of the Labour, Liberal Democrat and Green parties have all said they would oppose fracking in their manifestos. In addition, Scotland, Wales, and Northern Ireland have all put in place their own suspensions of fracking, which means whatever the election result large sections of the UK are already off the table as a source of shale gas. (Bennett 2017)

It certainly appears that, while just under 50% of the population continues to hold no strong views either for or against fracking, public opinion has been turning against it and it is now regarded as the least favoured potential source of energy for the UK with more than double the amount of people opposed (33%) to fracking than support it (16%) in 2017—a complete turnaround from 2013 when more were in favour of fracking than opposed it. A sign of the government's discomfort at these poll findings is the decision in 2018 to no longer ask this question in surveys.

The success or failure of the government's current energy strategy may ultimately be down to the level and intensity of local protests where sustained direct action requires huge time and energy commitment by groups of dedicated individuals. At Preston New Road Henry Owen, who locked himself to the top of a scaffold to impede Cuadrilla's work at the site in October 2018, told *The Guardian* it was important to continue demonstrating:

> "It's absolutely vital because this industry has no social licence in the UK," he said. "It's being pushed through by government who don't care about their commitments to take action on climate change. They're not interested in what local communities have to say. After all democratic avenues have been exhausted over a seven-year campaign, there is a place for direct action to stop this industry." (*The Guardian* 2018a)

This sums up some of the core arguments of protestors who have been on the front line of protests against fracking in the UK. This chapter has indicated that their arguments have gained traction across the

British Isles with bans or moratoria now operating in Ireland, Scotland and Wales. Media coverage of fracking in the UK has often echoed industry reassurances on the safety of the technology (McQueen 2017). In Britain as in the US and Poland journalists have, for the most part, offered framing of the debate set by the government and representatives from the fracking industry, which focus on the benefits of the process for the economy and for national energy security and which downplay potential hazards. Matthews and Hansen (2018) note this generic framing occupies a privileged position in the overall reporting of hydraulic fracturing and resonates with the publics' concerns over 'affordable energy' whilst countering the communication of the associated risks.

However, they also note problems in sustaining a pro-fracking discourse in media reporting over time or challenging environmental concerns with trusted spokespersons independent of the fracking industry. Anti-fracking views now find a place among the general influences shaping media coverage and fracking is now reported as a mainstream, and controversial, news story rather than a business story. The authors indicate that research points to the influence of anti-fracking media, whether by documentary via YouTube or social media:

> Observing the mobilized protest activities that have emerged alongside online media and conversation and their interests in "local issues, local concerns and local needs" of affected citizens (Bomberg, 2017: p. 86), helps to reveal the interconnected influences that are informing the media reporting of environmental risks and the potential threats associated with the hydraulic fracturing process'. (Matthews and Hansen 2018)

At the end of this short survey of the present state of the debate around fracking in Europe and the UK at a crucial turning point in its development it is worth reflecting on the power of individuals. Politicians, such as President Donald Trump and powerful, wealthy lobbyists, such as the Koch brothers, have enormous power to shape public perceptions and political decision-making in the US and beyond. However, individual protestors, such as 79-year-old Jackie Brookes, 81-year-old Anne Power, or Simon Roscoe Blevins, Richard Roberts and Richard Loizou whose arrests achieved national media coverage can also help shape the debate around fracking in the UK. These citizens' commitment to a collective protest, even at the expense of their liberty, may be helping to change the terms of the national conversation on the country's energy strategy, a policy area usually left to the expertise of government and energy specialists. Public support for fracking is falling and protests continue to make headlines and to slow progress at drilling sites, such as Preston New Road, dogged by daily earth tremors in October 2018. This combination of factors may see the political will to push fracking through tested to the limits. Conservative MP Zac Goldsmith has already indicated the possibility that fracking may damage his party in forthcoming elections if local planning rules are changed to allow fracking. In an interview with *The Guardian* in October 2018, Goldsmith said:

> Fracking is an issue that has the potential to turn whole regions against the government. The drilling rigs and pollution, the industrial equipment and sheer volume of trucks all make it an alarming prospect for communities up and down the country.

Goldsmith noted that some Conservative MPs had been angered by the proposed planning changes, which would allow shale gas wells to be drilled without the need for planning permission and class fracking sites as nationally significant infrastructure, adding:

> If the government's answer is simply to change the planning rules so that even elected local representatives have no say on the issue, then it will have to be prepared for a huge backlash. (*The Guardian* 2018b)

This chapter has noted a fast-moving and fluid situation in Europe around unconventional hydrocarbon extraction with many countries banning hydraulic fracturing between 2011 and 2018. The snapshot of the current situation provided here offers a chance to reflect on the forces at play in the contentious debate around fracking. Critical studies of the energy sector pay attention to the alarming warnings coming from the IPCC and other scientific bodies on the need to dramatically slash our dependence on fossil fuels. These studies describe energy intensive technologies such as fracking as unsustainable and irresponsible. The 'responsible people', in this debate, this chapter suggests, are those who oppose these technologies, often at great cost to themselves and with little personal reward. The protestors in Lancashire, Yorkshire and across Europe who challenge environmentally unsustainable energy development, such as fracking, are protecting scarce natural resources and challenging corporate irresponsibility. As individual researchers and citizens we too need to take responsibility for our collective future and challenge corporate interests where they are clearly at odds with the public interest and the future of this planet as they are in the fracking industry.

References

AP News. 2018. Emails Show Cooperation Among EPA, Climate-Change Deniers. *AP News*, May 25. Accessed October 10, 2018. https://apnews.com/64cd37b0503440c0b92e6ca075f87dd4.

BBC. 2012. Bulgaria Bans Shale Gas Drilling with 'Fracking' Method. *BBC*, January 19. Accessed October 12, 2018. https://www.bbc.com/news/world-europe-16626580.

Belfast Telegraph. 2014. Fracking: Drilling Will Not Be Allowed in Northern Ireland Unless It's Proven Safe, Warns Environment Minister Mark H. Durkan. *Belfast Telegraph*. Accessed October 12, 2018. https://www.belfasttelegraph.co.uk/business/news/fracking-drilling-will-not-be-allowed-in-northern-ireland-unless-its-proven-safe-warns-environment-minister-mark-h-durkan-30469238.html.

Bennett, Craig. 2017. Ireland Is the Latest European Country to Ban Fracking—The Tories Need to Follow Suit. *The Independent*. Accessed October 14, 2018. https://www.independent.co.uk/voices/fracking-environment-ireland-theresa-may-a7771956.html.

Bloomberg. 2012. U.S. Oil Output to Overtake Saudi Arabia's by 2020. *Bloomberg*, November 12. https://www.bloomberg.com/news/articles/2012-11-12/u-s-to-overtake-saudi-arabia-s-oil-production-by-2020-iea-says.

Brulle, Robert. 2014. Institutionalizing Delay: Foundation Funding and the Creation of U.S. Climate Change Counter-Movement Organizations. *Climatic Change* 122 (4): 681–694.

Carter, Neil, and Ben Clements. 2015. From 'Greenest Government Ever' to 'Get Rid of All the Green Crap': David Cameron, the Conservatives and the Environment. *British Politics* 10 (2): 204.

Cave, Tamasin, and Andy Rowell. 2014. *A Quiet Word: Lobbying, Crony Capitalism and Broken Politics in Britain.* London: Random House.

Chaineau, Claude-Henri, and Jean Lennock. 2016. Stakeholder Engagement on Shale Gas in Europe: Has It Already Failed? *SPE International Conference on Health, Safety & Environment in Oil and Gas Exploration and Production,* 1620.

CNN. 2018. *Planet Has Only Until 2030 to Stem Catastrophic Climate Change, Experts Warn.* Accessed October 21, 2018. https://edition.cnn.com/2018/10/07/world/climate-change-new-ipcc-report-wxc/index.html.

Copenhagen Post. 2016. Total Gives Up Fracking Plans in Denmark. *Copenhagen Post,* June 1. Accessed October 21, 2018. http://cphpost.dk/news/total-gives-up-fracking-plans-in-denmark.html.

Cotton, Matthew, Imogen Rattle, and James Van Alstine, J. 2014. Shale Gas Policy in the United Kingdom: An Argumentative Discourse Analysis. *Energy Policy* 73: 427–438.

Deutsche Welle. 2017. Earthquake Damage in the Netherlands. *DW,* September 21. Accessed October 13, 2018. https://www.dw.com/en/earthquake-damage-in-the-netherlands/av-40597733.

Deutsche Welle. 2018. Germany: Thousands Hold Anti-Coal Protest in Hambach Forest. *DW,* October 6. Accessed October 13, 2018. https://www.dw.com/en/germany-thousands-hold-anti-coal-protest-in-hambach-forest/a-45779366.

DutchNews.nl. 2016. Shored-Up Homes are a Common Sight in Earthquake-Hit Groningen. *DutchNews.nl,* June 2. Accessed October 10, 2018. https://www.dutchnews.nl/features/2016/06/91027/.

DutchNews.nl. 2018. Dutch Minister Confirms Ban on Drilling, Shale Gas 'Not an Option'. *DutchNews.nl,* October 26. Accessed October 10, 2018. https://www.dutchnews.nl/news/2018/02/dutch-minister-confirms-ban-on-drilling-shale-gas-not-an-option/.

EJOLT. 2013. Fracking Ban Expanded in Spanish Regions. *Environmental Justice Organisations, Liabilities and Trade,* February 10. Accessed October 10, 2018. http://www.ejolt.org/2014/02/fracking-ban-expanding-in-spanish-regions/.

EJ Atlas. 2018. Pungesti's Resistance to Chevron Gas Fracking, Romania. *Environmental Justice Atlas.* Accessed October 10, 2018. https://ejatlas.org/conflict/resistance-to-shale-gas-fracking.

Gross, Michael. 2013. Dash for Gas Leaves Earth to Fry. *Current Biology* 23 (20): 901–904.

Gullion, Jessica Smartt. 2015. *Fracking the Neighborhood: Reluctant Activists and Natural Gas Drilling*. Cambridge: MIT Press.

Hannigan, John. 2014. *Environmental Sociology*. London: Routledge.

Howarth, Robert W. 2015. Methane Emissions and Climatic Warming Risk from Hydraulic Fracturing and Shale Gas Development: Implications for Policy. *Energy and Emission Control Technologies* 3: 45–54. Dove Press.

The Guardian. 2013. David Cameron at Centre of 'Get Rid of All the Green Crap' Storm. *The Guardian,* November 21. Accessed October 7, 2018. https://www.theguardian.com/environment/2013/nov/21/david-cameron-green-crap-comments-storm.

The Guardian. 2016. Solar Subsidy Cuts Lead to Loss of 12,000 Jobs. *The Guardian*, July 25. Accessed October 7, 2018. https://www.theguardian.com/environment/2016/jul/25/solar-subsidy-cuts-lead-to-loss-of-12000-jobs.

The Guardian. 2017. Scottish Government Bans Fracking After Public Opposition. *The Guardian*, October 3. Accessed October 12, 2018. https://www.theguardian.com/uk-news/2017/oct/03/scottish-government-bans-fracking-scotland-paul-wheelhouse.

The Guardian. 2018a. Anger and Blockades as Fracking Starts in UK for First Time Since 2011. *The Guardian,* October 15. Accessed October 20, 2018. https://www.theguardian.com/environment/2018/oct/15/fracking-protesters-blockade-cuadrilla-site-where-uk-work-due-to-restart.

The Guardian. 2018b. Fracking Risks Turning Country Against Tories, Says Zac Goldsmith. *The Guardian*, October 28. Accessed October 28, 2018. https://www.theguardian.com/environment/2018/oct/28/fracking-turning-country-tories-zac-goldsmith-conservative-drilling.

The Independent. 2011. Osborne's Anti-Green Agenda Splits Coalition. *The Independent*, October 26. Accessed October 20, 2018. https://www.independent.co.uk/environment/green-living/osbornes-anti-green-agenda-splits-coalition-2375993.html.

The Independent. 2017. DUP Condemned for Climate Change Denial of Trump-Style Proportions. *The Independent*, June 9. Accessed October 14, 2018. https://www.independent.co.uk/news/uk/politics/dup-climate-change-denial-hung-parliament-election-results-trump-a7781681.html.

Insurance Journal. 2013. Fracking Companies Silence Water Complaints with Sealed Settlements. *Insurance Journal,* June 10. Accessed October 17, 2018. https://www.insurancejournal.com/news/national/2013/06/10/294608.htm.

IPCC. 2018. *IPCC Special Report.* Accessed October 18, 2018. http://www.ipcc.ch/report/sr15/.

The Irish Times. 2017. Ireland Joins France, Germany and Bulgaria in Banning Fracking. *The Irish Times,* June 28. Accessed October 15, 2018. https://www.irishtimes.com/news/politics/oireachtas/ireland-joins-france-germany-and-bulgaria-in-banning-fracking-1.3137095.

Keil, Silke, and Oscar Gabriel. 2012. The Baden-Württemberg State Election of 2011: A Political Landslide. *German Politics* 21 (2): 239–246.

Khanna, Arpita Asha. 2017. Revisiting the Oil Curse: Does Ownership Matter? *World Development* 99 (November): 214–229.

Levi, Michael A. 2013. *The Power Surge: Energy, Opportunity, and the Battle for America's Future.* New York: Oxford University Press.

Lucas, Caroline. 2018. The Jailing of Fracking Protesters Tells Us We Are Winning This Fight. *The Guardian,* September 26. Accessed October 18, 2018. https://www.theguardian.com/commentisfree/2018/sep/26/jailing-fracking-protesters-fight-caroline-lucas.

Mazur, Allan. 2014. How Did the Fracking Controversy Emerge in the Period 2010–2012? *Public Understanding of Science* 25 (2): 207–222.

Matthews, Julian, and Anders Hansen. 2018. Fracturing Debate? A Review of Research on Media Coverage of "Fracking". *Frontiers in Communication* 3 (41): 1–11.

The Metro. 2017. Tea Lady 79 Is Grabbed by 12 Police While Supplying Tea to Anti-Fracking Protestors. *The Metro,* October 10. Accessed October 15, 2018. http://metro.co.uk/2017/10/10/tea-lady-79-is-grabbed-by-12-police-while-supplying-tea-to-anti-fracking-protesters-6990204/.

McQueen, David. 2017. Fear, Loathing and Shale Gas. The Introduction of Fracking to the UK: A Case Study. In *Corporate Social Responsibility in the Post Financial Crisis—CSR Conceptualisations and International Practices in Times of Uncertainty,* ed. A. Theofilou, G. Grigore, and A. Stancu. London: Palgrave Macmillan.

McQueen, David. 2018. Turning a Deaf Ear to the Citizen's Voice. Digital Activism and Corporate (Ir)responsibility in the North Dakota Access Pipeline Protest. In *Corporate Responsibility and Digital Communities—An International Perspective Towards Sustainability,* ed. Georgiana Grigore, Alin Stancu, and David McQueen. London: Palgrave Macmillan.

Miller, David, and William Dinan. 2015. Resisting Meaningful Action on Climate Change. In *The Routledge Handbook of Environment and Communication,* ed. Anders Hansen and Robert Cox. London: Routledge.

The Nation. 2013. The Fracking Industry's Dishonest Response to 'Gasland'. November 18. Accessed October 10, 2018. https://www.thenation.com/article/fracking-industrys-dishonest-response-gasland/.

National Assembly for Wales Research Service. 2018. *Drilling Down: The Welsh Government Proposes Policy to Ban Petroleum Extraction.* Accessed October 12, 2018. https://seneddresearch.blog/2018/09/06/drilling-down-the-welsh-government-proposes-policy-to-ban-petroleum-extraction/.

Natural Gas Intel. 2012. *Industry-Funded Truthland Film Opens in Ohio Sunday.* Accessed October 9, 2018. https://www.naturalgasintel.com/articles/3246-industry-funded-truthland-film-opens-in-ohio-sunday.

The New York Times. 2012. Shale Gas Search Divides Romania. *New York Times*, April 22. Available at: https://www.nytimes.com/2012/04/23/business/global/shale-gas-search-divides-romania.html.

New York Times. 2018a. Major Climate Report Describes a Strong Risk of Crisis as Early as 2040. *New York Times*, October 7. Available at: https://www.nytimes.com/2018/10/07/climate/ipcc-climate-report-2040.html.

New York Times. 2018b. 76 Environmental Rules on the Way Out Under Trump. *New York Times,* July 6. Accessed October 9, 2018. https://www.nytimes.com/interactive/2017/10/05/climate/trump-environment-rules-reversed.html.

The Observer. 2012. Huge Scale of UK's 'Dash for Gas' Revealed. *The Observer,* November 3. Accessed October 12, 2018. https://www.theguardian.com/environment/2012/nov/03/uk-dash-gas.

Piper, Ben, and David McQueen. 2018. How Successful Have Lobbyists Been at Influencing State and National Policy to Further the Completion of the Dakota Access Pipeline, Since the 2008 US Election? *Journal of Promotional Communications* 6 (1): 46–71.

Reuters. 2011. Germany to Shut Down Pre-1980 Nuclear Plants. *Reuters*, March 15. Accessed October 12, 2018. https://www.reuters.com/article/germany-nuclear/update-3-germany-to-shut-down-pre-1980-nuclear-plants-idUSLDE72E17620110315.

Reuters. 2015. U.S. Fracking Boom Added 725,000 Jobs—Study. *Reuters*, November 6. Accessed October 10, 2018. https://www.reuters.com/article/usa-fracking-employment-study-idUSL8N13159X20151106.

Short, Damien, and Anna Szoluchab. 2017. Fracking Lancashire: The Planning Process, Social Harm and Collective Trauma. *Geoforum*. Available at: https://www.sciencedirect.com/science/article/pii/S0016718517300519.

Spangler, Ingrid S., and Donnalyn Pompper. 2011. Corporate Social Responsibility and the Oil Industry: Theory and Perspective Fuel a Longitudinal View. *Public Relations Review* 37: 217–225.

Spence, David B. 2017. Corporate Social Responsibility in the Shale Patch? *Lewis & Clark Law Review* 21 (2): 387–425.

Spiegel. 2011. Helmut Kohl Weighs in on Reactor Debate. *Spiegel Online*, March 25. Available at: http://www.spiegel.de/international/germany/nuclear-moratorium-overly-hasty-helmut-kohl-weighs-in-on-reactor-debate-a-753125.html.

The Telegraph. 2015. Jurassic Coast 'Saved from Industrialisation' as Navitus Bay Wind Farm Rejected. *The Telegraph*, September 11. Accessed October 15, 2018. https://www.telegraph.co.uk/news/earth/energy/windpower/11859736/Jurassic-Coast-saved-from-industrialisation-as-Navitus-Bay-wind-farm-rejected.html.

The Telegraph. 2017. Cuadrilla Lancashire Fracking Plans Cleared by High Court. *The Telegraph*, April 12. Accessed October 12, 2018. https://www.telegraph.co.uk/business/2017/04/12/cuadrillas-lancashire-fracking-plans-cleared-high-court/.

The Times. 2018. Fracking Protesters Freed After Judge Criticises 'Excessive' Jail Sentence. *The Times*, October 18. Accessed October 22, 2018. https://www.thetimes.co.uk/article/fracking-protesters-freed-after-judge-criticises-excessive-jail-sentence-v8tl9nl3n.

U.S. EPA (U.S. Environmental Protection Agency). 2016. *Hydraulic Fracturing for Oil and Gas: Impacts from the Hydraulic Fracturing Water Cycle on Drinking Water Resources in the United States. Executive Summary.* Washington, DC: Office of Research and Development. EPA/600/R-16/236ES. Accessed October 2, 2018. https://cfpub.epa.gov/ncea/hfstudy/recordisplay.cfm?deid=332990.

10

Leveraging CSR to Gain MNE Legitimacy in Post-Arab Spring Morocco

Rick Molz, Gwyneth Edwards and Salma Msefer

10.1 Introduction

Every market has a set of institutions that govern societal interactions, including business transactions, which may undergo changes over time (Oliver 1992). This research employs an actor-centered approach, using theory of institutional work, to better understand the interplay between multinational enterprise (MNE) actors and their

R. Molz (✉)
John Molson School of Business, Concordia University,
Montreal, QC, Canada
e-mail: Rick.molz@concordia.ca

G. Edwards
HEC Montreal, Montreal, QC, Canada
e-mail: gwyneth.edwards@hec.ca

S. Msefer
Business Development Bank of Canada, Montreal, QC, Canada

© The Author(s) 2019
F. Farache et al. (eds.), *Responsible People*, Palgrave Studies in Governance,
Leadership and Responsibility, https://doi.org/10.1007/978-3-030-10740-6_10

local institutional environments during times of institutional change. Institutional work refers to the purposeful actions and practices of individual and collective actors, which are aimed at creating, maintaining, and disrupting institutions (Lawrence et al. 2011). By using the setting of post-Arab Spring Morocco, we investigate MNE strategic responses to local institutional pressures. The research is based on the argument that MNEs have to manage various elements in their institutional environment, including political and legal elements, in addition to the more traditional product and market-focused variables (Baron 1995); however, MNE actors are not only constrained by regulations and norms within their institutional environment, but also may strive to shape these very institutions through institutional work (Lawrence and Suddaby 2006).

MNE strategic behavior in response to institutional pressures may vary from conforming to active resistance, depending on the type of pressure exerted on the organization (Oliver 1992). In this study, we are particularly interested in how MNEs engage in corporate social responsibility (CSR) to respond to and shape the local institutional environment, during institutional change. Our retrospective qualitative study investigates how ten Moroccan subsidiaries of developed-nation MNEs engage in institutional work, through CSR activities. The study examines the strategies employed by the MNE subsidiaries during the institutional changes that took place following the protests and institutional upheaval known as the Arab Spring, which took place in the Middle East and Africa.

This chapter is structured as follows. We first discuss the literature on institutional change, institutional work, and the role of CSR within this context. We then present the arguments for a multiple case study methodology, provide a description of the 10 MNEs and the sources of data, and explain how the data was analyzed. We then present the findings of the study by first discussing the responses of the MNE to institutional pressures (pre-Arab Spring) and institutional change (post-Arab Spring), following by the specific role of CSR within their institutional work. We conclude with a summary of contributions and ideas for further research.

10.2   Literature Review

MNEs play a key role in the global economy, with over one-third of all international trade represented by transfers between MNE subsidiaries (Xu and Shenkar 2002). MNE subsidiaries are embedded not only within the corporate organization, but also within their local environment, which MNE actors rely on for resources and administrative practices (Rosenzweig and Singh 1991). Within this environment, MNE subsidiaries operate within a local institutional framework, defined as a "set of fundamental political, social, and legal ground rules that establish the basis for economic activities" (Davis and North 1971, p. 6). MNEs seek to gain legitimacy from different sources in their local environment by adopting local institutional practices.

MNEs originating from developed countries and operating in developing countries (i.e. emerging economies) face specific challenges because the business and cultural environments in developing countries can be very different and the influence of socio-political institutions relatively (Sheth 2011). For example, governments, business groups, religion, and local communities have an important influence on market competition (Hoskisson et al. 2000). MNE subsidiary actors newly entering a developing country face uncertainty, as the local government can change laws and regulations quickly and without warning (Yu Xie and Boggs 2006; Tarnovskaya 2012). Moreover, although many developing countries have experienced extensive growth due to liberalization, and represent attractive investment opportunities for MNEs, these countries can also be accompanied by social and political disturbances. However, social ties and political connections may also emerge as strategic options that can enable MNEs to manage environmental uncertainties (Sheth 2011); when formal institutions fail to deliver necessary MNE resources (e.g. legitimacy), informal governance, such as cooperation between MNEs and social organizations, can be used in its place.

The complex institutional environments that exist at the local MNE subsidiary level can be understood using Scott's (2005) framework of institutions, articulated through three institutional pillars: regulative (written rules and regulations), normative (social understood norms and behaviors), and cultural-cognitive (taken-for-granted beliefs). Organizations must manage institutional pressures that are exerted from these three pillars to gain or maintain legitimacy within institutional environments. Institutional pressures can come from government agencies, interest groups, public opinion, and social, business, and professional networks (Oliver 1997); arguably, organizations must conform to these pressures to be perceived as legitimate.

Management scholars, however, have shown an interest in moving beyond the emphasis on institutional stability and conformity, to focus on the processes of institutional change and the specific role of actors in enabling or preventing change (Oliver 1992; Seo and Creed 2002). Research suggests that organizational actors do not simply respond to institutional demands with passive compliance but employ a range of strategic responses such as acquiescence, compromise, avoidance, defiance, and manipulation (Oliver 1992), which we argue can now be understood as institutional work.

Rapid institutional reforms and institutional changes are one of the main sources of uncertainty for companies in emerging and developing economies (Chung and Beamish 2005), but at the same time present opportunities for institutional work. MNEs are more likely to pursue idiosyncratic ways of organizing within host and home environments when faced with institutionally weak environments. For example, in order to mitigate some of the risks associated with uncertain and volatile markets, MNEs may build relationships with local actors. For firms entering and operating in emerging economies, it is important to develop relationships not only with local business partners but also with national and local governments; the institutional work is thus complex.

The notion of institutional work (Lawrence and Suddaby 2006) complements the research on organizations and institutional change and has become an important area of research in the new institutional theory, as it provides insights pertaining to the structure–agency debate (Gawer and Phillips 2013). Institutional work is intentional—some of it is highly visible, but most types are mundane such as in the day-to-day adjustments, adaptations, and compromises of actors that are trying to maintain institutions (Lawrence et al. 2011). Institutional work includes lobbying for resources, promoting agendas, and challenging existing or proposing new legislation (Lawrence and Suddaby 2009). Individuals and collective actors try to adjust to, change, or re-create the institutional structures within which they exist, and which give them their roles, relationships, resources, and routines (Lawrence et al. 2011). Institutional work considers that there is a recursive relationship between institutions and agency but its focus is on how action affects institutions; it allows for a deeper investigation of the relationship between actors and their environment and the ways that strategic action and institutions affect each other. Research on institutional work, however, is relatively new, and the role of CSR within this domain has yet to be investigated within the context of institutional change.

In this research, we are specifically interested in how MNE actors leverage CSR in their institutional work, as a mechanism to seek legitimacy and influence the direction of institutional change; arguably CSR practices can be a mechanism to attain organizational goals. Current CSR research supports this argument; CSR research has been moving away from a focus on legal compliance and maximizing profits (Greenfield 2004) to looking at organizations as agents of change, concerned about stakeholders and related issues that are embedded within their institutional environments (Bies et al. 2007; Pettit 2005). As such, in this research, we seek to understand how CSR strategies are employed by MNE actors to both respond to and shape institutions during periods of institutional change.

For the purposes of this chapter, CSR will refer to the firm's propensity to consider stakeholder concerns in its business activities and decisions, and its inclusion of not only the primary stakeholders such as employees, customers, and suppliers, but also the larger community of stakeholders, such as formal and informal institutions in the local environment. Further, CSR initiatives or stakeholder relations (relationships with government, political groups, NGOs) are treated as institutional work when they are undertaken to influence the firm's external environment, allowing the firm to (1) gain legitimacy, (2) repair a damaged reputation, (3) accompany changing societal expectations, or (4) influence existing (albeit changing) institutions.

10.3 Research Design and Methods

10.3.1 Context—Morocco and the Arab Spring

Morocco is a country in North Africa that straddles both the Atlantic Ocean and Mediterranean Sea. It is a constitutional monarchy with an elected parliament and a hereditary King (that is, not elected) who holds executive and legislative powers over the military, foreign policy, and religious affairs (Economist Intelligence Unit 2012). The term "Arab Spring" refers to the wave of spontaneous uprisings, strikes, and revolutions that broke out in the different countries of the Middle East and North Africa, as a result of numerous and varied institutional failings. Morocco was home to popular protests that were inspired by the events in Tunisia and Egypt. The first major demonstrations occurred on February 20, 2011, when thousands of Moroccans called on Mohamed VI, the King of Morocco, to give up some of his powers, followed by weekly protests in multiple cities across the country to demand greater democracy and a crackdown on government corruption. After significant protests, the King agreed to a referendum on a new constitution, which was adopted in 2012 and impacted institutions, as shown in Table 10.1.

The constitution had an impact on several formal institutions. It granted the government executive powers, but retained the King as head of the army, religious authorities, and the judiciary (Economist Intelligence Unit 2011). In addition, it incorporated the claims of key social groups such as Amazigh individuals (Berbers) and recognized Amazigh as an official language. It also acknowledged some fundamental human rights for both men and women and institutionalized gender equality by encouraging the creation of women's rights organizations and giving women more legal rights (e.g. the right to sue for divorce and to maintain custody of their children even if they remarry). CSR as an institution gained normative strength. Firms began to gradually embrace responsibility for the impact of their activities on the environment, communities, employees, and consumers. Our research project sought to understand the impact of these institutions on the MNE subsidiaries and their institutional work, within the context of CSR and engaging the firm's stakeholders.

Table 10.1 Institutional evolution in Morocco following the Arab Spring

	Institutions	
	Formal	Informal
2011 Arab Spring protests	Constitutional reforms: Prime Minister and the Parliament are granted more power (Economist Intelligence Unit 2011) The recognition of cultural and linguistic plurality; Amazigh (Berber language) recognized as an official language (Lewis 2011) Entrenchment of equality of civil, economic, and cultural rights of both men and women (Economist Intelligence Unit 2011)	Norms: Use of social media to denounce government repression and to organize protests (Browning 2013) Anti-American sentiment (KPMG Country, Report 2013)
2012	New Institutions: Rise of religious political powers (new government elected in legislative elections was the Party of Justice and Development, an Islamist conservative party) (Economist Intelligence Unit 2011) New constitution makes commitments to gender parity in government (Economist Intelligence Unit 2011)	Norms: Greater awareness about the importance of CSR programs (Avina 2013) Rise of religious groups/Islamist ideology (Economist Intelligence Unit 2011)

Source Table compiled by the authors using sources identified in table

10.3.2 Research Design

A comparative multiple case study approach was used to investigate the MNE institutional work, within the context of Morocco's institutional environment, both just before and then post the Arab-Spring period. Collecting rich data through qualitative research allows for the consideration of context-specific factors and the identification of complex patterns (Yin 2003). A multiple case study was performed as a means to seek patterns of MNE behavior and broaden the transferability of the results. MNEs were selected based on three conditions: (1) the MNE originated in a developed nation, (2) the MNE's Moroccan subsidiary was in operation since at least 2011, when the Arab Spring events took place, and (3) the MNE informant was willing to provide internal corporate documents that would inform the research question.

For each case, we studied (1) the MNE interactions relating to local regulative, normative, and cognitive institutional demands, (2) the impact of the Arab Spring on these institutions, and (3) the ways that MNE subsidiary employees responded to the institutional changes (i.e. engaged in CSR activities) through institutional work. Data was gathered through visits and face-to-face interviews at the Moroccan subsidiaries and through secondary data sources (documents).

10.3.3 Data Collection and Methods

The sample of ten firms was developed from two sources. First, we contacted the American Chamber of Commerce in Morocco for suggestions, and second, the third author poled professional associates for personal contacts in firms meeting our research criteria. Interviewees were recruited through email. Fourteen in-depth, semi-structured interviews were performed between November 2013 and June 2014. Interviewees were selected based on their depth of knowledge, expressed through their position title, and included executives from human resources, communications, subsidiary (country) managers, general managers, and finance directors. Interviews were supplemented by publicly available annual reports and other secondary sources that included company histories, internal MNE documents, industry reports, and press releases (see Table 10.2 for details).

Table 10.2 MNE Corporate and Moroccan subsidiary descriptions, interviewees

MNE	Corporate information	Moroccan subsidiary and data sources
1	Industry: Hospitality and Tourism Company size: 170,000 employees International presence: Present in 92 countries 2014 revenue: $6.141 billion US Headquarter location: France Founded in: 1967	Company size: 3500 employees Organizational age: 1993 Ownership: Joint Venture Interviewee: Business Development Director Secondary sources: 11 plus 2 annual reports
2	Industry: Electrical Industrial Services Company size: 22,000 employees International presence: presence in 30 countries 2014 Revenue: $43.58 billion US Headquarter location: Saint-Denis, France Founded in: 1913	Company size: 2500 employees Organizational age: 1946 Ownership: Wholly owned subsidiary Interviewees: General Manager; Finance Director Secondary sources: 7 plus 2 annual reports
3	Industry: Express Logistics Company size: 480,000 employees International presence: Operates in 220 countries 2014 revenue: $63.6 million US Headquarter location: Bonn, Germany Founded in: 1969	Company size: 300 employees Organizational age: 1987 Ownership: Wholly owned subsidiary Interviewee: Country Manager Secondary sources: 6 plus 2 annual reports
4	Industry: Telecommunications Company size: 118,706 employees International presence: Offices in 180 countries 2014 revenue: $27.74 billion Headquarter location: Stockholm, Sweden Founded in: 1876	Company size: 200 employees Organizational age: 1984 Ownership: Wholly owned subsidiary Interviewee: Human Resources Director Secondary sources: 9 plus 2 annual reports

(continued)

Table 10.2 (continued)

MNE	Corporate information	Moroccan subsidiary and data sources
5	Industry: Computer software and hardware Company size: 128,000 employees International presence: Offices in 100 countries 2013 revenue: $86.83 billion Headquarter location: Albuquerque, New Mexico Founded in: 1975	Company size: 60 employees Organizational age: 1984 Ownership: Wholly owned subsidiary Interviewee: Country Manager Secondary sources: 4 plus 2 annual reports
6	Industry: Consumer goods Company size: 118,000 employees International presence: Offices in 70 countries 2013 revenue: $83.06 billion Headquarter location: Cincinnati, Ohio Founded in: 1837	Company size: 210 employees Organizational age: 1958 Ownership: Wholly owned subsidiary Interviewee: Human Resources Director Secondary sources: 4 plus 2 annual reports
7	Industry: Automotive Company size: 121,807 employees International presence: Present in 128 countries 2013 revenue: $46.1 billion US Headquarter location: Hauts-de-Seine, France Founded in: 1899	Company size: 8500 employees Organizational age: 1966 Ownership: JV with institutional owners Interviewee: Communications Director CSR Manager Secondary sources: 10 plus 2 annual reports
8	Industry: Pharmaceuticals Company size: employees International presence: Presence in 100 + countries 2014 revenue: $38 billion US Headquarter location: Paris, France Founded in: 1973	Company size: 900 employees Organizational age: 1965 Ownership: Wholly owned subsidiary Interviewee: Communications Director Secondary sources: 5 plus 2 annual reports

(continued)

Table 10.2 (continued)

MNE	Corporate information	Moroccan subsidiary and data sources
9	Industry: Energy Company size: 2000 permanent, 1185 retail International presence: presence in 16 countries 2013 revenue: $192 million US Headquarter location: London Founded in: 2011	Company size: 710 employees Organizational age: 2011 Ownership: Joint Venture Interviewee: Communications Director Communications Coordinator Secondary sources: 5 plus 2 annual reports
10	Industry: Environmental Services Company size: 330,000 employees International presence: Offices in 48 countries 2013 revenue: $26.2 billion US Headquarter location: Paris, France Founded in: 1853	Company size: 4000 employees Organizational age: 2002 Ownership: Wholly owned subsidiaries Interviewee: Communications Director, Director of Branding and Reputation Secondary sources: 12 plus 2 annual reports

The interview protocol was modeled after a study by Alimadadi et al. (2012). The interview guide had three foci: (1) the institutional pressures and associated MNE responses, (2) the impact of the Arab Spring on MNE operations, and (3) MNE strategic responses to the institutional changes that occurred following the Arab Spring events. The interviews were semi-structured, with open-ended questions, to allow the interviewer to probe for specific issues of interest. Each interview lasted about 45 minutes (see Appendix 1 for interview guide).

Case narratives describing the findings of the above three foci were created from the interview data and secondary sources, including annual reports (two consecutive years per company), financial reports, press releases, and news reports. The combination of interviews (primary data) and documents (secondary data) allowed for triangulation across, as well as within, data sources (Welch 2004).

10.3.4 Data Coding and Analysis

Eight of the fourteen interviews were conducted in French, while six were conducted in English. After translating the French interviews into English, the data was transcribed and uploaded into Hyper Research software, for coding purposes. The data was analyzed in three stages, using a thematic approach. In the first stage, we identified the types of institutional demands faced by each MNE subunit by identifying and categorizing these demands into institutional pillars (regulative, normative, and cognitive). Second, we identified the MNEs' strategic responses to manage each of the institutional demands that they faced. Third, we identified the ways that the Arab Spring led to institutional change or had an impact on institutional conditions. In the final stage of the analysis, we identified how the institutional change provoked by the Arab Spring extended opportunities for MNEs to engage in institutional work through CSR. Cross-case synthesis was used to contrast firms across multiple categories (Yin 1994).

10.4   Research Findings and Discussion

10.4.1 Overview of Findings

The study set out to investigate the institutional pressures experienced by MNEs, as well as strategies that these firms employed to overcome them. The research also investigated how the institutional changes provoked by the Arab Spring influenced MNE strategic behavior and, more specifically, their institutional work. Findings indicated that the MNEs faced institutional pressures that stemmed from regulative, normative, and cognitive demands within the Moroccan institutional context. Consistent with one of the main premises of institutional theory, many of these institutions were found to constrain the actions of MNEs. For instance, in terms of regulative pressures, many firms indicated that the bureaucracy had a direct impact on their business operations. However, the study also found that the MNE subsidiaries were not simply products of their institutional environment; rather, these firms employed specific strategies, such as advocacy and relationship building, to overcome institutional constraints.

The analysis also indicated that institutional instability caused by the Arab Spring aggravated some of the institutional pressures experienced by MNEs; for example, many MNEs suffered payment delays for products and services provided to public sector clients, along with delays in decision-making for pending contract bids. However, in many instances, the institutional changes also provided the MNEs with an opportunity to engage in institutional work to advance their own interests. In the following sections we discuss the MNE responses to the institutional pressures both pre- and post-Arab Spring, and then discuss the specific CSR strategies that they employed.

10.4.2 MNE Responses to Institutional Pressures

Through the data analysis, several themes emerged with regards to the type of institutional work that MNEs employed to overcome institutional demands within their institutional environments. The research found that the MNEs employed specific strategies to influence institutions favorably to their business needs. In support of the notion of institutional work, we found that MNE actors sought to manipulate their institutional environments in order to overcome existing pressures and create new opportunities. However, results indicated that the MNE actors focused their institutional work on managing regulatory demands, while conforming to normative and cognitive-cultural demands such as adapting to religious norms. We describe this institutional work as follows and highlight examples in Table 10.3.

Advocacy. All MNEs indicated that Morocco had made some progress in strengthening its formal institutions and improving the business environment, however, issues related to excessive bureaucracy, red tape, and corruption remained. MNEs were confronted with these institutional challenges and continued to manage them in their everyday operations, by starting and maintaining a dialogue with government, political actors, and stakeholders and engaging in advocacy to promote corporate interests.

Leveraging local organizations. According to Lawrence and Suddaby (2006), interest associations or organizations that are formally created to represent constituencies also engage in institutional work. This work involves lobbying for resources, pushing for agendas, and proposing new legislation to represent the interests of specific actors. All of the MNEs in our study were members of local business groups, which provided guidance on how to navigate the local environment, lobby for material resources or seek the social and political capital required to create new institutional structures or practices.

Use of Internal Dedicated Departments. Several MNEs indicated that they had internal dedicated departments that worked with external stakeholders to simplify and facilitate processes for the company. These dedicated organizations were unique to the Moroccan subsidiaries and allowed the local actors to respond to institutional constraints as they arose. These specialized departments allowed the MNEs not only to

Table 10.3   Examples of institutional pressures and institutional work

Institutional conditions	Representative quote	Subsidiary response	Institutional work
MNE 2 *regulative*: existing laws to penalize companies for delays in payments for services or products is ineffective	"We were involved in many meetings with government officials to discuss application of the law. However, in practice, this law could not be applied"	Lobbied the government to put in place measures that would lead to the application of the law (as member of an employer association)	Advocacy
MNE 3 *regulative*: existing regulation stipulates that companies in the express logistics sector must pay royalties to the National Post Office	"At the moment we have no choice but to pay but we've been in discussions with the government and the head of the National Post Office who agrees with us… But the law needs to go through a certain process…"	Lobbied the government to change the law	Advocacy
MNE 3 *regulative*: minimum value of declaration for packages is excessively low	". If the value of an item is less than 50 Euros, you don't need any documents with it. We are trying to increase that to 100 Euros or more"	Lobbied the government to update regulation	Advocacy
MNE 10 *regulative*: existing law stipulates that percentage of profits must be reinvested for the first ten years of operation	"..The way they were doing it was by having two [local] companies…. These two companies are tied to the contract. MNE 10 is not a public service, so if it makes profit, it is entitled to take money out of the country"	Ignored law	

(continued)

Table 10.3 (continued)

Institutional conditions	Representative quote	Subsidiary response	Institutional work
MNE 2 cognitive: prevalence of Wasta (systems of preferment, nepotism/cronyism) practices	"In Morocco, there are relationships that are man to man, if you don't have the right contacts, it is difficult to get things moving… the emotional relations that develop are what gets things to move smoothly for the MNC"	Conform: adapted to local institution	Conform
MNE 5 *regulative*: Government proposal to limit access to the Internet	"…we do lobbying, talk to people, explain to them the dangers of stopping innovation in our country, our lobbying is related to this"	Lobbying government and political actors to explain the importance of innovation	Advocacy
MNE 1 *regulative*: length of time to obtain permits	"To overcome this, we continue to do what we have to do…. We know a lot of people…. The Ministry of Tourism also implicates itself personally…. So we have to engage in lobbying and to develop relationships with people at high levels"	Lobbying to obtain permits more rapidly	Advocacy
MNE 1 *regulative and cognitive*: lack of transparency in government contracts procurement procedures	"If there is a tender for a piece of land that becomes available, it is important to do some lobbying with the Ministry, so that they push for us to win the business…it is an explaining kind of lobbying, we don't show up with a briefcase"	Lobbying to obtain contracts	Advocacy

(continued)

Table 10.3 (continued)

Institutional conditions	Representative quote	Subsidiary response	Institutional work
MNE 4 *normative*: Islamic practice	"We have a program of adaptation of new employees…I explain that you should avoid scheduling meetings on Friday afternoons because people go to prayer…We ask expatriates to respect the month of Ramadan and avoid drinking coffee in front of others"	Conform: adapted to local institutions	Conform
MNE 4 *cognitive*: lack of understanding about technological services	"We try to push everything that is technology. And for these types of services we need to explain our expertise…They don't always see the benefits of some of the services. That's why we need to explain"	Lobbying the government and telecommunications operators	Advocacy
MNE 6 *regulative*: lack of regulation of informal economy	"We fight against that [counterfeit goods] by hiring outside agencies. and training customs officers so they can identify fake products… authorities are very keen on this, we provide them with the tools to do that…"	Training customs officials	Educating
MNE 8 *regulative*: delays in getting authorizations	"The public affairs department manages relationships with public authorities… so we do a little lobbying and try to influence things but in a transparent and ethical way"	Lobbying authorities	Advocacy

simplify processes, but also to manage and anticipate problems that may arise with the authorities.

Educating. According to Lawrence and Suddaby (2006), "educating" is a form of institutional work aimed at creating institutions that involve teaching actors the skills and knowledge necessary to support new institutions. One key strategy to engage in educating is to create templates or frameworks that will provide actors with an outline to guide action. The study identified several instances of MNEs engaging in this type of institutional work. For example, MNE 6, in an effort to tackle counterfeit goods, partnered with the government to teach customs officers how to recognize fake products.

CSR. CSR strategies enable MNEs to build relationships with different stakeholders, which further serve to legitimize their presence in the local institutional context. Results indicated that, in many instances, the MNE subsidiary actors worked in partnership with the government and with local non-governmental organizations (NGOs) to implement their CSR initiatives. These initiatives were significant. Some examples:

- MNE 1 supported the integration of youth into the workforce and became a sponsor of Action for Aids in Morocco and of agricultural cooperatives of women in the South of the country;
- MNE 2 donated school supplies and computers to schools, and subsidized summer camps for the children of staff;
- MNE 3 supported educational programs in Moroccan cities and villages and partnered with an international NGO that supported Morocco's vulnerable young population;
- MNE 4 brought e-learning technology to remote villages and teachers;
- MNE 5 provided associations with the tools and the training so they could use technology in their organizations;
- MNE 6 painted schools, sponsoring an association that aids single mothers;
- MNE 8 subsidized after school classes to support the children of employees; and,

- MNE 9 initiated road safety and environment programs, promoted entrepreneurship among youth, provided children with backpacks and bicycles, supported education initiatives, and the installation of a water purification units in rural areas.

It is important to note that the above list is not exhaustive; most MNE subsidiaries in the study had well-developed CSR programs that were adapted to the local institutional setting. According to most respondents, the subsidiaries received general CSR guidelines from headquarters, with program decisions made by local subsidiary managers. Notably, the CSR programs were philanthropic in nature and adapted to the institutional context. MNE 3's Country Manager stated: "… there should be an active social responsibility program to give back to the poor and needy or to the environment of this country."

The study also found that MNEs collaborated with government for some of their CSR projects. For example, MNE 6, a consumer goods firm, collaborated with the Ministry of Youth and Sports to organize a football tournament for marginalized youth. "We involved the authorities because it was a constructive project for Moroccan society. They went into small villages to choose youth and build teams that would participate in the football tournament" (Human Resources Director, MNE 6). MNE 7, an automotive manufacturer, collaborated with the Ministry of Equipment to promote road security though the launch of road safety campaigns that targeted youth and professional drivers.

In terms of CSR geared toward employees, the research found that MNEs promoted employee satisfaction. For example, in 2011, MNE 3 was recognized by an employer's association as one of the best employers in Morocco for its communications program, working conditions, and proximity to management. We also found that many of the MNEs were increasingly looking to hire local individuals, even for high-level management positions. According to the Business Development Director of MNE 1, "It is a willingness of [MNE] to say, we are a responsible corporate citizen, we come to Morocco and we have the responsibility to develop local talents." Like MNE 1, MNE 3 also expressed an effort to hire local individuals and to replace expatriates: "We believe that locals serve their markets better and therefore localization is becoming high in the agenda" (Country Manager, MNE 3). Several MNEs indicated that they were able to hire locally due to a growing population of highly educated individuals.

CSR and key stakeholders. Many of the MNEs indicated that they had a strategy for stakeholder management, to include stakeholder matrices. MNE 9, for example, had identified its most important stakeholders and monitored relationships throughout the year. The Country Director managed the relationships with the Ministry of Energy, while the Human Resources Director managed relationships with unions. The most pressing issues were tracked every trimester to anticipate possible issues and action plans were put in place to prevent potential crises.

10.4.3 CSR Strategies as Institutional Work

This research demonstrates that although the ten MNEs constantly engaged in institutional work to adapt to or create a more favorable institutional environment, institutional change brought about by the Arab Spring events provided these MNEs with opportunities to extend their institutional work. We provide examples of these opportunities in Table 10.4 and discuss as follows.

The Arab Spring had an impact on societal-level institutions as it raised awareness of existing social inequalities in Morocco and, particularly, on the youth unemployment issue. At the time, young people between the ages of 15 and 29 made up 30% of the Moroccan population, yet 49% were neither in school nor in the workforce (World Bank 2012). Many youth participated in the Arab Spring events to voice their discontent concerning lack of opportunity in Morocco. The Arab Spring in Morocco signaled a greater democratic opening, as people were able to protest and voice their opinions, with relatively little resistance from the regime. Furthermore, during the Arab Spring, questions were raised in regards to acceptable corporate behavior and the role of corporations in society, and there was a demand for greater transparency and less corruption. According to the General Manager and Finance Director at MNE 2, companies were impacted by changes in normative

Table 10.4 Examples of institutional pressures and institutional work Post-Arab Spring

Institutional conditions	Representative quote	Subsidiary response	Institutional work
MNE 1 *regulative*: government instability and change in government/political actors	"So when you have a person that comes out of nowhere after the Arab Spring and that you didn't know, you have to invest a great deal in the relationship so that it becomes closer"	Lobbying and relationship building	Advocacy
MNE 10 *normative*: negative attitudes toward the company (for charging high prices, etc.)	"we decided on a grassroots communications campaign, which is mainly socially oriented. We launched a CSR campaign… We decided to target the elements that we felt were the most intelligent for our strategy"	Launched CSR campaign, exerted effort for rapprochement with authorities	CSR Advocacy
MNE 5 *cognitive*: youth employability issues should be addressed by the private and public sectors	"We had to focus on youth employment… we introduced certifications in Morocco at a very subsidized price.. we are also investing in youth.. So there was a refocusing…"	Launched CSR activities	CSR
MNE 5 *cognitive*: recognition of different cultures and greater pluralism	"We lobbied [parent company] so that inside Morocco you don't see the separation of the Sahara on the map… We introduced Amazighe [Berber] language on [operating system]"	Launched CSR activities	CSR
MNE 3 *normative*: Arab world perceived as no longer safe to invest in	"Along with the new Minister of Transport and other businessmen, we tackled a few conference exhibitions in France…and promoted Morocco as a stable place to invest in"	Engaged in promotion/lobbying at conferences	Marketing Advocacy

institutions: "There is a greater awareness about social issues and about redistributing wealth. Companies do not want to have problems due to the great social inequalities and realize that wealth should be redistributed within society."

Although all MNEs surveyed had been working on CSR programs in Morocco for a couple of years, several respondents indicated that, following the Arab Spring events, they both increased and re-oriented their CSR programs to better address the current societal problems. Several MNEs specifically put in place CSR programs to address the socio-economic issues brought to the fore following the Arab Spring. For example, MNE 4 indicated that the adherence to human rights was a major preoccupation, leading to human rights meetings with various stakeholders and the adoption of the UN Guiding Principles on Business and Human Rights. MNE 5 explained that although they had engaged in CSR for over a decade, since the Arab Spring, their CSR was geared more toward society and individuals (rather than government). MNE 7 enhanced its CSR activities within the realm of education and road safety, in partnership with government institutions, for the local communities (employees, youth, and professional drivers).

10.4.4 Discussion

Historically, studies of international management have focused on the importance of institutions and the ways in which institutions influence MNE activities. However, less is understood on how foreign MNE subsidiaries influence local (host country) institutions, particularly in developing countries and specifically through the use of CSR activities. This study explored the dynamic interaction that takes place between MNE actors and local institutions, as a process of institutional work, during a period of marked institutional change. The research demonstrated that MNEs are constantly engaging in institutional work by interacting with the various constituents in their local environments, including government and social actors. During and following the period of the Arab Spring, the research showed that these 10 MNEs had to redirect their institutional work to either maintain or rebuild their legitimacy.

Some MNEs capitalized on the institutional change to engage in advocacy and bring about more favorable regulatory changes. MNE 3, for example, succeeded in obtaining their own customs office at Casablanca airport, staffed with government officials who were solely dedicated to MNE 3's business. The study illustrates that although institutions may constrain firm behavior MNE actors can also actively engage in institutional work to bring about change.

Most of the MNEs in the sample engaged in advocacy within their institutional environment, which involved mobilizing political and regulatory support through strategies of social persuasion. The MNEs maintained a collaborative relationship with the authorities to overcome regulatory constraints, such as administrative slowness, and to be able to engage successfully in advocacy when they needed to advance their projects. The MNEs also leveraged professional organizations, or interest organizations composed of companies in the same sector, that could be effective in lobbying the government for changes. Following the Arab Spring, when many government actors were replaced, some MNEs indicated that they made a deliberate effort to develop ties with the new authorities as to be able to collaborate with them and engage in lobbying in the future. In addition, some MNEs capitalized on the uncertainty to lobby the government to improve some business regulations.

In the study, CSR strategies were treated as institutional work because actors specifically employed CSR strategies to gain legitimacy by seeking to be more responsible economic actors. CSR also includes the strategies that MNEs employ to manage their different stakeholders. The study found that MNEs have well-developed CSR programs in Morocco that they have been working on for several years. Many of the CSR initiatives launched by the MNEs involved supporting local NGOs and subsidizing social projects; this is consistent with previous research that argues that CSR in developing countries tends to be less formalized and more philanthropic in nature (Jamali and Neville 2011) and is often related to deeply ingrained cultural and religious values and primarily targets local communities. These findings are important because MNEs can use CSR strategies to become more local and to capitalize on the religious and cultural nuances in their institutional context to gain greater legitimacy.

10.5 Conclusion

This research study investigated the institutional pressures experienced by MNEs in Morocco, a developing country, as well as the strategic responses, through institutional work, employed by MNEs to manage these pressures. The research found that the Moroccan MNE subsidiaries actively engaged with local actors to influence practices and, more broadly, institutions, through CSR. During and following the Arab Spring events that affected many countries in the Arab world, many MNEs were faced with a changing institutional environment that modified the local norms, regulations and cognitive behaviors of individuals and institutions. These changes provided MNEs with extended opportunities to influence the direction of institutional change, which (in this study) they undertook by extending their institutional work through CSR activities.

The study highlighted how the context of the MNE subsidiaries, that is, the post-Arab Spring environment, influenced the type of institutional work that they performed. The Arab Spring came about due to failed institutions and civil unrest. The MNE subsidiaries responded to the institutional changes, within this context, by approaching their institutional work as CSR activity. By taking a stakeholder approach to their institutional work, and broadening their definition of stakeholders beyond the traditional (e.g. customers, suppliers, employees, and government) to society as a whole, these MNEs were able to take advantage of the uncertainty created by institutional change and influence the direction of that change, not only for their own benefit but for the benefit of society as a whole. Although the results of a multiple case study such as this, set within a relatively unique context (post-Arab Spring), are not easily generalizable across all contexts, the study highlights the role of CSR within institutional work, specifically during periods of social upheaval, and the benefit of such work to society in general.

Given the impact of institutional work by the ten MNEs under study, it would be worthwhile extending this type of research across all countries affected by the Arab Spring and associated institutional changes. Although to do so as a qualitative could be somewhat prohibitive, given the investment required (e.g. for this project, travel and time were significant constraints, which influenced the number of cases), alternative methods could include: (1) an in-depth single case study of an MNE with subsidiaries in many Middle East and African countries (to assess differences across countries), (2) an industry-specific study to understand how different types of MNEs respond to institutional change caused by civil unrest, or (3) a combined researcher-MNE-institution conference where MNEs and institutions could present their stories of institutional work and debate their respective roles in regards to CSR and institutional change.

Appendix 1: Interview Guide

I. Information about the respondent

- What is your position in the company?
- How long have you been working at the company?
- How much experience do you have working in Morocco or in another emerging market?

II. General company information

- Is the multinational enterprise a wholly owned subsidiary? To what extent are decision-making procedures influenced by the parent company?
- How long has the company been operating in Morocco?
- What are the main projects of the subsidiary in Morocco?
- How many employees does the company have in Morocco?
- What is the proportion of local stuff versus expatriate staff?

III. International experience of the multinational enterprise

- What are main obstacles, barriers, or challenges to doing business in Morocco? (Example: regulative, normative, cognitive demands)
- How does the company manage the challenges that it encounters?

IV. Relationships

- What are the subsidiary's most important relationships (ex. customers, suppliers, politicians, NGOs, other subunits, parent company)?
- How does the company manage these relationships?
- How does the company manage relationships with political/government units? Do they present opportunities/challenges?
- Does the company belong to an industry, trade, or business association?
- Do these relationships allow the company to overcome some of the obstacles to doing business mentioned above?

V. Critical events

- In 2011, the Arab region experienced political and economic instability due to the 'Arab Spring' events.
- Did the Arab Spring have an impact on the company's business operations in Morocco? (Examples: canceled contracts, delays, regulatory changes)
- Did these events have an impact on how the company managed its relationships with key actors? If so, how?

VI. Corporate Social Responsibility (CSR) as a legitimacy tool

- I saw on your website that you have established *(x)* program to assist in the development of the country. What other kinds of social activities does the company have in Morocco? Please provide examples of these programs.
- Did the company undertake more social activities after the Arab Spring events?

VII. Looking forward

- How does the company view its future operations in Morocco? Are there any major concerns in terms of the social/governmental environment for doing business in Morocco?

References

Alimadadi, Siavash, Christer Forsling, Cecilia Pahlberg, and Firouze Pourmand Hilmersson. 2012. Business and Political Interactions in Emerging Markets: Experiences from China South Africa and Turkey. In *Business, Society and Politics: International Business and Management*, vol. 28, ed. Amjad Hadjikhani, Ulf Elg, and Pervez Ghauri, 209–230. Bingley: Emerald Group Publishing Limited.

Avina, Jeffrey. 2013. The Evolution of Corporate Social Responsibility (CSR) in the Arab Spring. *Middle East Journal* 67 (1): 77–92.

Baron, David P. 1955. *Business and Its Environment*. Upper Saddle River, NJ: Prentice-Hall.

Bies, Robert J., Jean M. Bartunek, Timothy L. Fort, and Mayer N. Zald. 2007. Corporations as Social Change Agents: Individual, Interpersonal, Institutional and Environmental Dynamics. *Academy of Management Review* 32 (3): 788–793.

Browning, John G. 2013. Democracy Unplugged: Social Media, Regime Change, and Governmental Response in the Arab Spring. *Michigan State International Law Review* 21 (1): 63–86.

Chung, Chris C., and Paul W. Beamish. 2005. The Impact of Institutional Reforms on Characteristics and Survival of Foreign Subsidiaries in Emerging Economies. *Journal of Management Studies* 42 (1): 35–62.

Davis, Lance E., and Douglass C. North. 1971. *Institutional Change and American Economic Growth*. Cambridge: The University Press.

Economist Intelligence Unit. Country Profile 2011—Morocco. London: The Economist Intelligence Unit.

Economist Intelligence Unit. Country Profile 2012—Morocco. London: The Economist Intelligence Unit.

Gawer, Annabelle, and Nelson Phillips. 2013. Institutional Work as Logics Shift: The Case of Intel's Transformation to Platform Leader. *Organization Studies* 34 (8): 1035–1071.

Greenfield, W.M. 2004. In the Name of Corporate Social Responsibility. *Business Horizons* 47 (1): 19–28.

Hoskisson, Robert E., Lorraine Eden, Chung M. Lau, and Mike Wright. 2000. Strategy in Emerging Economies. *Academy of Management Journal* 43 (3): 249–267.

Jamali, Dima, and Ben Neville. 2011. Convergence Versus Divergence of CSR in Developing Countries: An Embedded Multi-layered Institutional Lens. *Journal of Business Ethics* 102 (4): 599–621.

KPMG Africa. Country Profile 2012–2013—Morocco (KPMG).

Lawrence, Thomas B., and Roy Suddaby. 2006. Institutions and Institutional Work. In *Handbook of Organization Studies*, 2nd ed., ed. Stewart R. Clegg, Cynthia Hardy, Thomas B. Lawrence, and Walter R. Nord, 215–254. London: Sage.

Lawrence, Thomas B., Roy Suddaby, and Bernard Leca. 2009. *Institutional Work: Actors and Agency in Institutional Studies of Organizations*. Cambridge: Cambridge University Press.

Lawrence, Thomas B., Roy Suddaby, and Bernard Leca. 2011. Institutional Work: Refocusing Institutional Studies of Organization. *Journal of Management Inquiry* 20 (1): 52–58.

Lewis, Aidan. 2011. Why Has Morocco's King Survived the Arab Spring? *BBC News Middle East*. November 24. Accessed June 12, 2018, http://www.bbc.com/news/world-middle-east-15856989.

Oliver, Christine. 1992. The Antecedents of Deinstitutionalization. *Organization Studies* 13 (4): 563–588.

Oliver, Christine. 1997. Sustainable Competitive Advantage: Combining Institutional and Resource-Based Views. *Strategic Management Journal* 18 (9): 697–713.

Pettit, Philip. 2005. Responsibility Incorporated. Paper presented at the Kadish Center for Morality.

Rosenzweig, Philip M., and Jitendra V. Singh. 1991. Organizational Environments and the Multinational Enterprise. *Academy of Management Review* 16 (2): 340–361.

Scott, W. Richard. 2005. Institutional Theory: Contributing to a Theoretical Research Program. In *Great Minds in Management: The Process of Theory Development*, ed. Ken G. Smith and Michael A. Hitt, 460–484. Oxford: Oxford University Press.

Seo, Myeong-Gu, and W.E. Douglas Creed. 2002. Institutional Contradictions, Praxis, and Institutional Change: A Dialectical Perspective. *Academy of Management Review* 27 (2): 222–247.

Sheth, Jagdish N. 2011. Impact of Emerging Markets on Marketing: Rethinking Existing Perspectives and Practices. *Journal of Marketing* 75 (4): 166–182.

Tarnovskaya, Veronika V. 2012. Activating Stakeholders: An Approach by MNCs in Emerging Markets. In *Business, Society and Politics*, vol. 28, ed. Amjad Hadjikhani, Ulf Elg, and Pervez Ghauri, 45–68. International Business and Management. Bingley: Emerald Group Publishing Limited.

Welch, Catherine, and Ian Wilkinson. 2004. The Political Embeddedness of International Business Networks. *International Marketing Review* 21 (2): 216–231.

World Bank. 2012. The Challenge of Youth Inclusion in Morocco Article. May 14. Accessed June 12, 2018. https://www.worldbank.org/en/news/feature/2012/05/14/challenge-of-youth-inclusion-in-morocco.

Yu Xie, Henry, and David J. Boggs. 2006. Corporate Branding Versus Product Branding in Emerging Markets: A Conceptual Framework. *Marketing Intelligence & Planning* 24 (4): 347–364.

Xu, Dean, and Oded Shenkar. 2002. Institutional Distance and the Multinational Enterprise. *Academy of Management Review* 27 (4): 608–618.

Yin, Robert K. 1994. *Case Study Research*, 2nd ed. London: Sage.

Yin, Robert K. 2003. *Case Study Research: Design and Methods*, 3rd ed. Thousand Oaks, CA: Sage.

11

Identifying the Root Causes of Human Rights Violation for Workers in International Supply Chains: A Systematic Literature Review

Nizar Shbikat

11.1 Introduction

The impacts of globalization and neoliberalism on global businesses have gained considerable attention in academia in the last two decades. More recently, there has been a burgeoning literature focusing on labor rights and working conditions in international supply chains. As companies tend to expand their operations globally, the ethical integrity of their supply chains becomes questionable (Bremer and Udovich 2001). Many multinational corporations (MNCs) in developed countries prefer to keep the extensive-knowledge operations (e.g. product design and development) in-house while outsourcing or offshoring the more routine activities (e.g. production) to less developed countries (Frenkel 2001) in order to achieve competitive advantages. Consequently, this shift in production strategies intensifies the "race to the bottom" between global buyers.

N. Shbikat (✉)
University of Kassel, Kassel, Germany

© The Author(s) 2019
F. Farache et al. (eds.), *Responsible People*, Palgrave Studies in Governance,
Leadership and Responsibility, https://doi.org/10.1007/978-3-030-10740-6_11

Although a lengthy debate is evident in existing literature regarding the issue of labor rights and workplace conditions in global value chains, this chapter is the first, to the best of my knowledge, to adopt a systematic literature review to identify the root causes of this issue. I argue that improving working conditions in global businesses is a "wicked problem" due to the complexity of labor governance structure and the conflict of interests of different stakeholders.

As a response to labor rights issues in their supply chains, MNCs adopted corporate social responsibility (CSR) initiatives such as code of conduct (COC), certification, and multi-stakeholder initiatives (Lillywhite 2007) to improve labor conditions (Posthuma and Bignami 2014). However, most CSR initiatives have failed to meet their objectives. The chapter contributes to the theme of this book by investigating the factors that hinder individuals in supply chains (e.g. workers, social auditors, management, unionists) from being socially responsible. The results indicate that the failure of CSR initiatives stems not only from institutions but also from individuals, including workers. The chapter is structured as follows: the following section highlights some academic perspectives regarding workers' standing in global supply chains. Section 11.3 explores the complex structure of labor governance and outlines some initiatives which have been developed as a means of empowering workers. Section 11.4 describes the systematic literature review as a methodological framework. The results are presented in Sect. 11.5 and discussed in Sect. 11.6. The chapter ends by summarizing the key points and suggesting possibilities for further research.

11.2 Labor Status in International Supply Chains

The existing literature has highlighted and discussed many accidents that have occurred in regions where labor regulations are weak. For example, several Chinese workers at Foxconn, one of the leading electronics manufacturers, committed suicide in 2010 due to the inferior labor conditions (Smyth et al. 2013; Donaghey et al. 2014). Another disaster occurred in 2012, when 300 workers died as a result of an accidental fire at the Ali garment factory in Pakistan; this incident was caused by the lack of safety procedures (Lund-Thomsen and Lindgreen 2014). A year later, the Rana Plaza garment manufacturing facility in Bangladesh collapsed, and the death toll exceeded 1000 (Perry et al. 2015). Such unfortunate events demonstrate the current reality of the limited human rights of workers in global value chains especially in dark zones where media coverage and anti-sweatshop movements are scarce.

Suppliers in emerging economies usually encounter internal pressures from local rivals and the government, and external pressures from global buyers to reduce costs and to tighten lead times which eventually leads to a ruthless, competitive race to the bottom (Khara and Lund-Thomsen 2012) by transferring these pressures to laborers in the form of wage reductions, excessive overtime, and outsourcing workforce from labor contractors. Prieto-Carrón (2008) argues that the workers most vulnerable to abuse of human and labor rights are those with the least amount of relational power in the supply chain. In line with this argument, Wicaksono and Priyadi (2016) state that young, female migrants with low skills are most likely to be subjected to substandard working conditions. Female workers are usually employed in repetitive low-skill jobs (Lillywhite 2007) because they are more obedient and skillful in performing manual operations (Prieto-Carrón 2008). Such mainstream practices of allocating a workforce to certain jobs based on gender classification diminish equal employment opportunities and intensifies discrimination.

The literature reviewed reflects a consensus among scholars that weak working conditions, anti-union activities and violations of human rights are evident and common in labor intensive sectors, such as the garment and textile industries (Knorringa and Pegler 2006; Merk 2009; Robinson 2010; Barrientos et al. 2011; Drebes 2014; Lebaron 2014) (see Sect. 11.5.3).

11.3 Labor Governance: A "Wicked Problem"

The concept of "wicked problem" was first introduced by Rittel and Webber (1973). It refers to the kind of problem that has no clear definitive formulation to solve it. Additionally, there is no final solution for such a problem because there is no "stopping rule" (Rittel and Webber 1973, p. 162). Another characteristic of a wicked problem is that its solution is not true or false but rather good or bad. Furthermore, if there is a solution, it cannot be tested easily. Global labor governance is a type of wicked problem due to the complexity of governance structures and conflicts of interests of different stakeholders. It could be argued that improvement in labor rights cannot be achieved without the involvement of numerous stakeholders at national and international levels. The global community has paid more attention to labor standards since 1919 (Weil and Mallo 2007). However, the exponential increase in the awareness of global community on human rights issues in global production networks only started in the early 1990s when anti-sweatshop movements and "name and shame" campaigns by civil society organizations criticized and publicized the harsh working conditions in the supply chains of athletic footwear brand companies (Schrempf-Stirling and Palazzo 2016). Subsequently, global brands have engaged in different activities to guard their image through unilateral initiatives (e.g. COC), bilateral initiative (e.g. International Framework Agreement), and multilateral initiatives (e.g. OECD Guidelines for Multinational Enterprises [Lillywhite 2007]). Doubtlessly, such initiatives can lead to some improvements in core labor rights such as abolition of child labor, yet they don't override or substitute local laws and regulations. One critique of private regulatory mechanisms (such as COC) is that they are designed to limit the legal liability of global brands rather than protecting workers' rights (Locke et al. 2013).

According to Barrientos and Smith (2007), a code of conduct (COC) can lead to improvements in outcome standards such as wages, but has little impact on process rights such as freedom of association. Similarly, Locke et al. (2009) suggest that the effectiveness of COC is driven by three factors; the power of the MNC, the effectiveness of an audit in making changes, and the incentives needed for change. Brand companies take advantage of their superior bargaining power in order to require suppliers to promote labor rights as a necessity to preserve the business relationship. Thus, suppliers are forced, because of the asymmetrical power relations in the supply chain, to embrace COC and undergo several audits (also known as private social audits [Lund-Thomsen and Lindgreen 2014]) to ensure their compliance. Section 11.5.4 addresses the causes of the failure of COC in global supply chains.

11.4 Methodology

This chapter adopts the systematic literature review guidelines proposed by Denyer and Tranfield (2009). Figure 11.1 depicts the review stages.

11.4.1 Question Formulation

A review question specifies the area of the research. In light of Denyer et al.'s (2008) work, CIMO-logic (see below) is used to formulate the following review question:

RQ: in the context of international supply chains, what are the possible causes that create, persist or escalate the violations of labor rights?

CIMO stands for Context-Intervention-Mechanism-Output. The context in this chapter refers to international or global supply chains. Output represents violated labor rights that are based on International Labor Organization (ILO) core conventions. Interventions and mechanisms are replaced by causes to serve the purpose of the research.

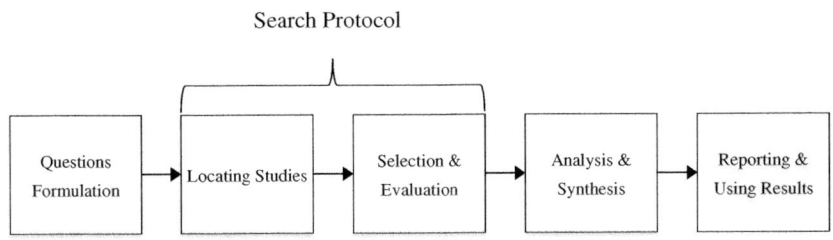

Fig. 11.1 Steps of conducting a systematic literature review. *Source* Adopted from Denyer and Tranfield (2009)

11.4.2 Search Protocol

The identification of relevant studies from the existing literature is a vital element to answer the review question. Thus, the author randomly selected 13 articles of systematic literature review in the field of supply chain management in order to identify the relevant academic databases. Accordingly, the following databases were identified: Emerald, EBSCO, ScienceDirect, Sage, Web of Science, and Wiley. The next step was determining the keywords or search strings to be used in the search engines of the databases. Table 11.1 outlines the keywords that were derived from the review question.

The keywords and synonyms pertaining to violations were excluded to increase search sensitivity and allow more studies to be included. However, further inclusion criteria are necessary to limit the number of resulting studies. Therefore, articles should be peer-reviewed, the language is English and search scope is set to title-abstract-keywords (Jafari 2015; Ntabe et al. 2015; Cerchione and Esposito 2016; Schmeisser 2013; Delbufalo 2012).

According to Cragg et al. (2012), the significant attention that academia and scholars gave to human rights in business commenced in the early 1990s. Consequently, the date of publication was restricted to the period 1990–2016. After implementing the search protocol, the meta-search results are summarized in Table 11.2. Eventually, 90 articles were found to be relevant and fully reviewed. Furthermore, two articles were included as a result of backward search due to their importance to the field of this research.

Table 11.1 Identification of search strings

Human rights		International		Supply Chain
Human right* OR labor* OR labour*, OR employee*, OR work* OR social responsibility* OR CSR OR sweatshop* OR slavery	AND	International OR multinational OR global OR transnational	AND	Supply chain* OR supply network* OR supply channel* OR value chain* OR logistics OR SCM OR supplier* OR procurement OR pur-chas* OR sourcing

Source Bouchet et al. (2015), Gold et al. (2015), Hemphill and Kelley (2016), Hu (1992), Kembro et al. (2014), and Phau et al. (2015)

Table 11.2 Meta-search results

Database	Result
Emerald	526
EBSCO	454
ScienceDirect	293
Sage	406
Web of Science	101
Wiley	110
Total	1890

11.4.3 Analysis and Synthesis

Following the previous work of scholars (Pilbeam et al. 2012; Abidi et al. 2014; Zimmermann et al. 2016), data were synthesized and presented into descriptive analysis to capture common attributes that all articles share such as date of publication (see Sects. 11.5.1, 11.5.2, 11.5.3, 11.5.4). Additionally, thematic analysis was undertaken to collect and synthesize data based on specific content or theme (see Sect. 11.5.4). Data analysis refers to fully reviewing articles for locating and extracting the data of interest. On the other hand, data synthesis groups the extracted data into categories. With the help of MS Excel, articles were coded and the extracted data were tabulated. For thematic analysis, data were assigned to different stakeholders and further synthesis levels were added for the ease of graphical representation. Moreover, when one data extract was obtained from several articles, the article with the earliest publication date was selected. The graphical representations of the results are presented in the next section.

11.5 Results

11.5.1 Contribution by Countries

According to Zimmermann et al. (2016), analyzing articles based on geographical dispersion provides an indication regarding the level of global interest in the research topic.

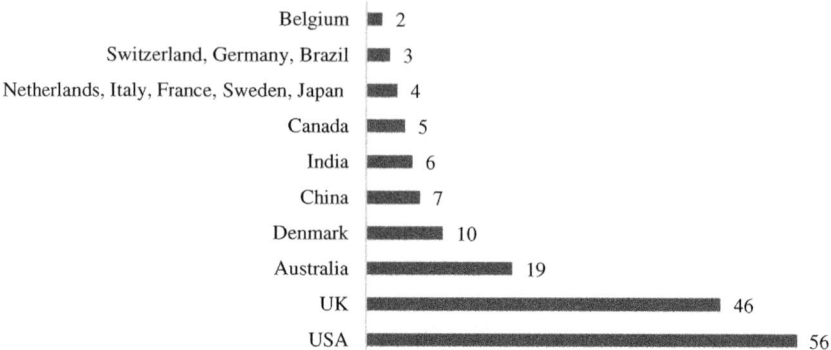

Fig. 11.2 Contribution by countries

Figure 11.2 shows the contribution of countries by affiliation to the academic debate on human rights in the international supply chains. Contribution refers to the number of authors contributing by affiliation. Thus, one author can have more than one contribution. For example, if an article has three authors from American institution(s), then the total contributions of the USA will be incremented by three. In addition to the countries in Fig. 11.2, Korea, Finland, Spain, Chile, Indonesia, Ethiopia, South Korea, Ecuador, and Poland have one contribution each. It should be remembered that only articles written in English were included in the data synthesis; therefore, it is unsurprising that the three nations making the largest contribution are English speaking countries.

11.5.2 Publication Year

With reference to the search scope and the exclusion criteria of the search protocol, the distribution of publication years for the articles reviewed is illustrated in Fig. 11.3, which indicates a continuous growth in literature publications in relation to the issue of interest in this chapter.

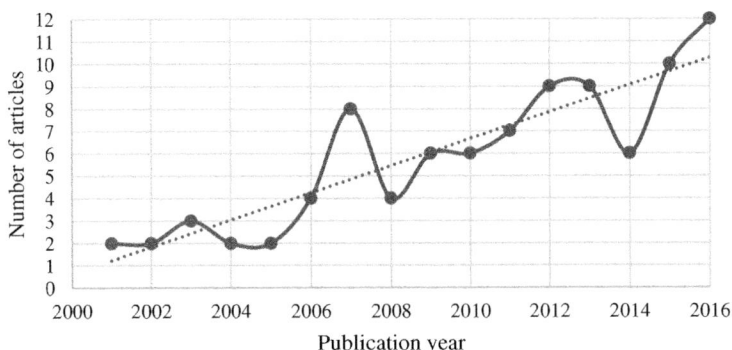

Fig. 11.3 Distribution of articles over time

11.5.3 Labor Rights Violation by Industry

The last two decades have witnessed a growth in anti-sweatshop movements against supply chains rather than individual companies or brands, especially those supply chains operating in labor-intensive industries where some operations require a high degree of manual dexterity such as stitching. Figure 11.4 presents the industries that have been criticized in literature for exploiting workers. Out of all the industries discussed in the reviewed literature, 36% of attention centers on the apparel industry. It should be noted that retailing may overlap with other industries.

11.5.4 Research Methods and Topics

Research methods can be classified into theoretical (e.g. literature review, conceptual, general review) and empirical (e.g. case study, survey, mathematical model) (cf. Jafari 2015). 57 out of the 92 reviewed articles are empirical and 36 are theoretical. Case study is the most common approach in empirical research with a ratio of 27/57.

The main topics discussed in the reviewed articles are summarized in Table 11.3. Unsurprisingly, the mainstream discourse of labor rights

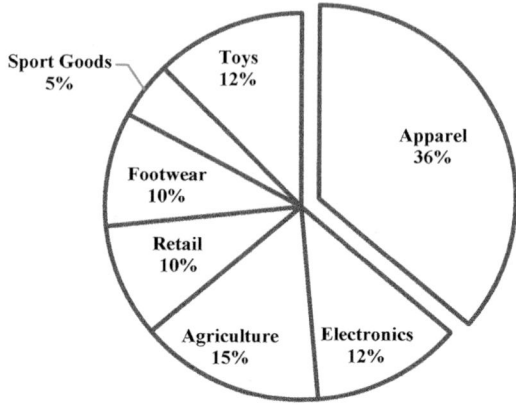

Fig. 11.4 Industry-specific analysis

Table 11.3 The topics covered by the reviewed articles

Topic	Number of articles
Ethical sourcing	11
Compliance and monitoring	11
CSR practices in supply chains	10
Code of conduct	9
Global labor governance	6
Globalization and working conditions	6
Labor standards in industry/country	6
Freedom of association	4
Child labor	4
Labor contracting	4
Female workers	3
Economic/social upgrade	3
NGOs and media	3
Forced labor	3
Industry self-regulation	2
International framework agreement	2
Ethical consumerism	2
Stakeholders management	1
Excessive working hours	1
Labor solidarity	1

centers around the supplier–customer relationship in global context. Although many topics overlap with others, the decision of the author to classify the articles by topic was based on the explicit reference to the topic in abstract and research questions.

11.5.5 Cause-and-Effect Analysis

The identification of root causes for any problem is a key step in understanding it and introducing substantial improvements. One of the most common and practical tools to represent causes of a single issue is a fishbone diagram or a cause-and-effect diagram (Cárdenas et al. 2009). In the context of this research, this method is used to provide a graphical representation of the causes and sub-causes of the violation of labor rights and to show the interrelations between these causes. Although a fishbone diagram is commonly used along with some data eliciting mechanisms such as brainstorming and questionnaires, it is also suitable for showing literature review results. For example, Garg and Garg (2013) used a fishbone diagram to indicate the factors hindering the implementation of enterprise resource planning in the retail industry. Similarly, Shinde et al. (2018) and James et al. (2017) used it to provide information from a literature review. In order to structure the fishbone diagram, multi-stakeholder analysis is used to group the causes under the following categories:

- Worker (the vulnerable laborers)
- Multinational corporation (MNC)
- Supplier (also subcontractors) of MNC
- Authority in the host country (particularly in emerging economics)
- Unions (global and local)
- Other stakeholders (consumers, labor contractors, NGOs, host society, third-party auditors, local and global media).

Figures 11.5, 11.6, 11.7, 11.8, 11.9, 11.10, and 11.11 depict the cause-and-effect analysis for different stakeholders. As some sub-causes relate to

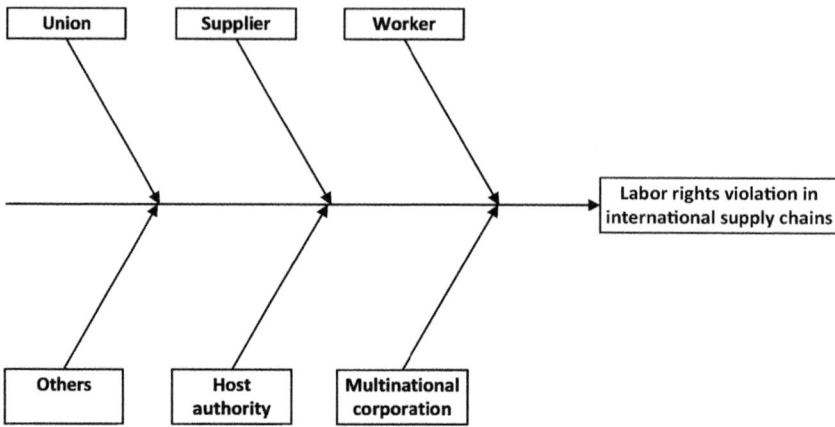

Fig. 11.5 Fishbone diagram

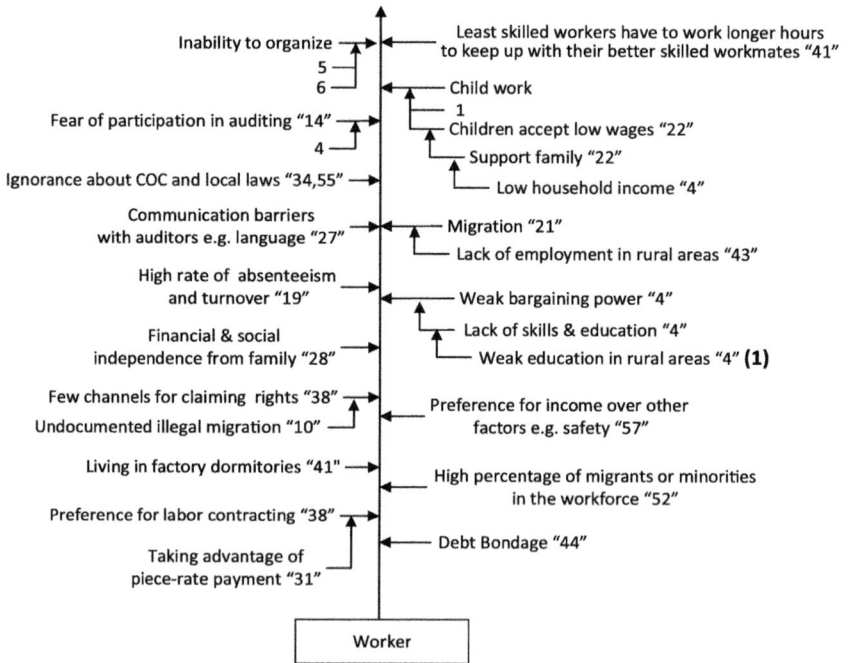

Fig. 11.6 Cause-and-effect analysis for workers

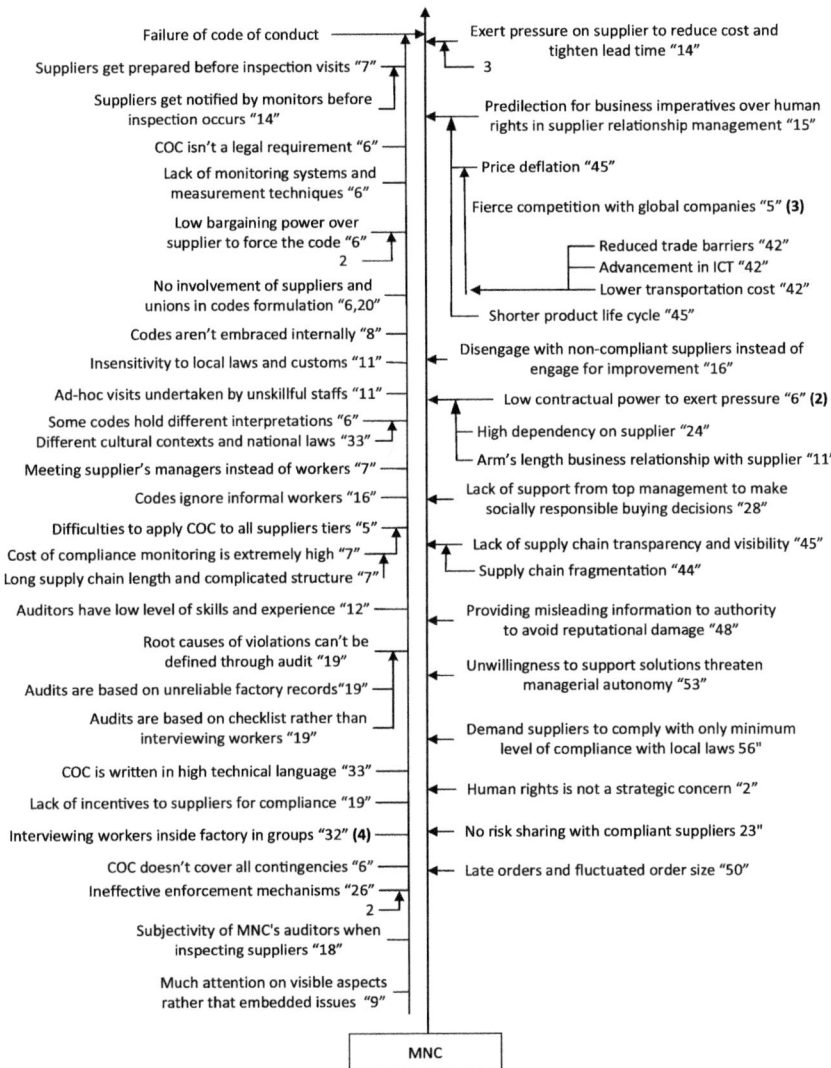

Failure of code of conduct ——————————————
Suppliers get prepared before inspection visits "7"
Suppliers get notified by monitors before inspection occurs "14"
COC isn't a legal requirement "6"
Lack of monitoring systems and measurement techniques "6"
Low bargaining power over supplier to force the code "6"
2
No involvement of suppliers and unions in codes formulation "6,20"
Codes aren't embraced internally "8"
Insensitivity to local laws and customs "11"
Ad-hoc visits undertaken by unskillful staffs "11"
Some codes hold different interpretations "6"
Different cultural contexts and national laws "33"
Meeting supplier's managers instead of workers "7"
Codes ignore informal workers "16"
Difficulties to apply COC to all suppliers tiers "5"
Cost of compliance monitoring is extremely high "7"
Long supply chain length and complicated structure "7"
Auditors have low level of skills and experience "12"
Root causes of violations can't be defined through audit "19"
Audits are based on unreliable factory records "19"
Audits are based on checklist rather than interviewing workers "19"
COC is written in high technical language "33"
Lack of incentives to suppliers for compliance "19"
Interviewing workers inside factory in groups "32" (4)
COC doesn't cover all contingencies "6"
Ineffective enforcement mechanisms "26"
2
Subjectivity of MNC's auditors when inspecting suppliers "18"
Much attention on visible aspects rather that embedded issues "9"

Exert pressure on supplier to reduce cost and tighten lead time "14"
3
Predilection for business imperatives over human rights in supplier relationship management "15"
Price deflation "45"
Fierce competition with global companies "5" (3)
Reduced trade barriers "42"
Advancement in ICT "42"
Lower transportation cost "42"
Shorter product life cycle "45"
Disengage with non-compliant suppliers instead of engage for improvement "16"
Low contractual power to exert pressure "6" (2)
High dependency on supplier "24"
Arm's length business relationship with supplier "11"
Lack of support from top management to make socially responsible buying decisions "28"
Lack of supply chain transparency and visibility "45"
Supply chain fragmentation "44"
Providing misleading information to authority to avoid reputational damage "48"
Unwillingness to support solutions threaten managerial autonomy "53"
Demand suppliers to comply with only minimum level of compliance with local laws 56"
Human rights is not a strategic concern "2"
No risk sharing with compliant suppliers 23"
Late orders and fluctuated order size "50"

MNC

Fig. 11.7 Cause-and-effect analysis for MNC

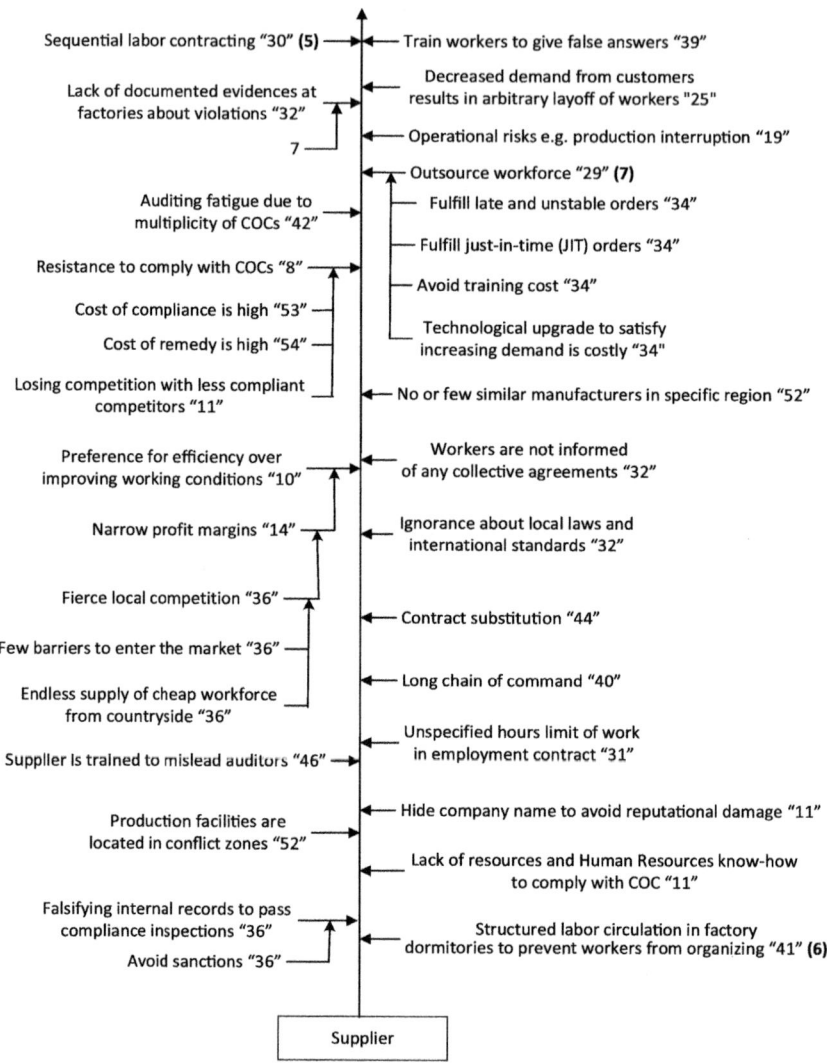

Fig. 11.8 Cause-and-effect analysis for suppliers

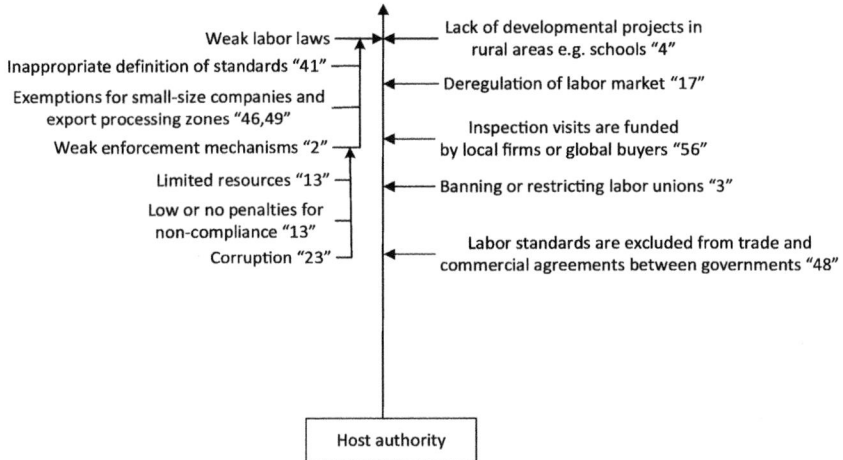

Fig. 11.9 Cause-and-effect analysis for host authority

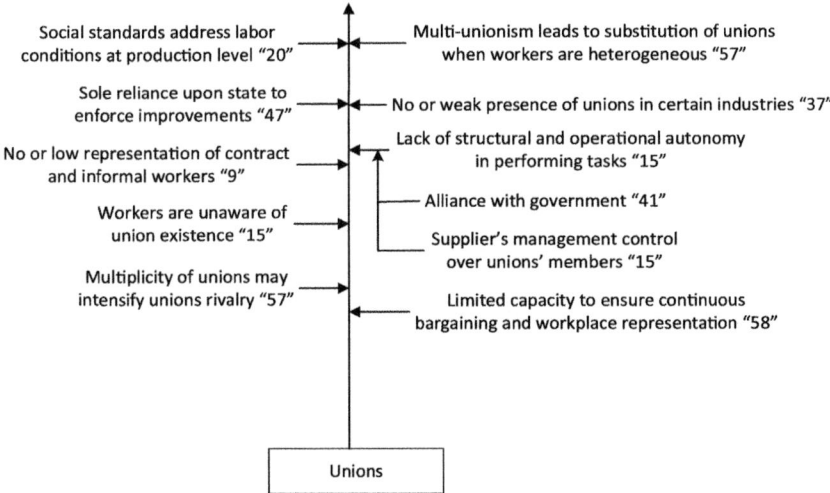

Fig. 11.10 Cause-and-effect analysis for unions

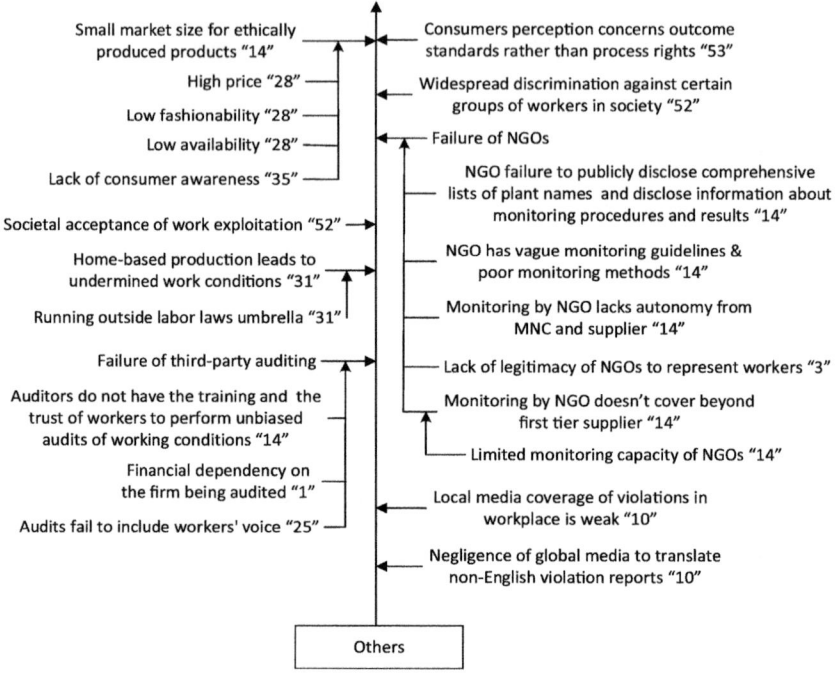

Fig. 11.11 Cause-and-effect analysis for other stakeholders

more than one cause in different categories, a reference coding number is assigned to show such overlapping. For example, sequential labor contracting prevents labor empowerment in the form of self-organizing in a specific industry. Additionally, workers are fearful of participating in compliance auditing at the supplier's site because they are usually interviewed in groups by MNC auditors inside the factory. Thus, they keep silent and do not report any violations in order to avoid retaliation by the management. The number in quotation marks refers to the source in Table 11.4.

11.6 Discussion

The results of the systematic literature review reveal that the issue of labor rights is universal and receiving increasing attention in academia. Notably, the working conditions within the apparel industry

Table 11.4 Sources used to construct the fishbone diagram

(1) Bremer and Udovich (2001); (2) Winstanley et al. (2002); (3) Miller (2004); (4) Becchetti and Trovato (2005); (5) Knorringa and Pegler (2006); (6) Pedersen and Andersen (2006); (7) Prieto-carrón (2006); (8) Boyd et al. (2007); (9) Barrientos and Smith (2007); (10) Frost and Burnett (2007); (11) Lillywhite (2007); (12) Locke et al. (2007); (13) Weil and Mallo (2007); (14) Wells (2007); (15) Yu (2008); (16) Prieto-Carrón (2008); (17) Barrientos (2008); (18) Andersen and Skjoett-Larsen (2009); (19) Locke et al. (2009); (20) Riisgaard (2009); (21) Merk (2009); (22) Zutshi et al. (2009); (23) Oka (2010); (24) Awaysheh and Klassen (2010); (25) Robinson (2010); (26) Thomas (2011); (27) Antonio (2011); (28) Goworek (2011); (29) Barrientos et al. (2011); (30) Taylor (2012); (31) Lund-Thomsen et al. (2012); (32) Anner (2012); (33) Zakaria et al. (2012); (34) Khara and Lund-Thomsen (2012); (35) Gupta and Hodges (2012); (36) Jiang et al. (2012); (37) Klerkx et al. (2012); (38) Barrientos (2013); (39) Lund-Thomsen and Lindgreen (2014); (40) Chan (2013); (41) Smyth et al. (2013); (42) Donaghey et al. (2014); (43) Taplin (2014); (44) Lebaron (2014); (45) Perry et al. (2015); (46) Niforou (2015); (47) Barnes et al. (2015); (48) Rawling (2015); (49) Nadvi and Raj-Reichert (2015); (50) Said-Allsopp and Tallontire (2015); (51) Berliner et al. (2015); (52) Gold et al. (2015); (53) Bartley and Egels-zandén (2015); (54) Hemphill and Kelley (2016); (55) Giri and Singh (2016); (56) Mzembe et al. (2016); (57) Oka (2016); (58) Phillips (2016).

have received the most focus in literature, perhaps due to sustained media interest in this particular industry. The causal relationship between causes and sub-causes is defined by asking "why" questions. For instance, why do laborers prefer working in a labor contracting company (see Fig. 11.6)? One possible reason is that it enables them to take advantage of piece-rate payment to earn more money, in the short-term at least. The cause-and-effect analysis shows that the COC of lead firms plays an essential role in upgrading or downgrading labor rights. Additionally, lead firms should involve different stakeholders such as suppliers, workers, and unions to legitimize their codes in compliance monitoring. Many multi-stakeholder initiatives led by NGOs, such as Fair Labor Association (FLA), have been developed over the last two decades to rectify the drawbacks of MNC codes of conduct. However, such initiatives have received many critiques about their ability to make real changes. There are several reasons for this perspective, as illustrated in Figs. 11.5, 11.6, 11.7, 11.8, 11.9, 11.10, and 11.11.

Consumers can practice their purchasing power through ethical consumerism by boycotting products that are not ethically produced. However, ethical consumerism can be affected by product attributes such as fashionability, price, and availability. The consumer can act as a change agent, especially if vulnerable workers are a part of demand-driven chain. However, consumers can only be influential if they are aware of the exploitative working conditions associated with producing the goods they buy.

In some societies, child labor is socially acceptable, especially in poor areas where it can provide parents with financial assistance. Controversially, if children are not allowed to work in legal business that is governed by local laws, they may have no choice but to engage in illegal businesses such as drug dealing (Arnold and Hartman 2003) or prostitution. Many global companies have realized this issue, and instead of breaking the relationship with the suppliers that employ children, they tend to engage in developing pragmatic solutions.

One of the collaborative solutions between MNCs, NGOs, and suppliers is providing children with an educational opportunity and guaranteed reemployment upon completion of school as well as supporting their families with financial aid (Arnold and Hartman 2003; Zutshi et al. 2009). The cause-and-effect analysis indicates that the relationship between the complexity of the global supply chains and violations of labor rights is directly proportional. Some supply chains involve hundreds of global manufacturers located in different and dispersed geographic areas which makes it nearly impossible for MNCs, NGOs, and labor unions to monitor them all for compliance with COC because of the limited financial and human capacities.

The role of people in advancing the success of CSR initiatives is vital. However, this role is influenced by several factors; these are indicated in Figs. 11.6, 11.7, 11.8, 11.9, 11.10, and 11.11. For example, the high level of education and expertise for workers may reduce the chance of being exploited by the employer. Additionally, auditors of MNCs need to have the knowledge and the expertise to act as innovation agents (Locke et al. 2009) in order to solve issues during auditing visits.

Suppliers may look at workers in dormitories as a buffer workforce that is ready to work longer hours to satisfy increased demand from customers. In many cases, workers are forced to work excessive hours without realizing that they are not obliged to do so because they are unaware of their rights or lack understanding regarding the mechanisms to claim such rights. In the case of informal workers, the scenario is even worse since they are not covered by local labor law which is the first defense line to prevent exploitation by employer.

Additionally, labor contractors provide trained workers to companies to perform certain tasks for a specific period of time. Some businesses may involve different tiers of labor subcontractors (noted in fishbone diagram as sequential labor subcontracting) that results in an aggressive reduction in wages (Taylor 2012).

It could be argued that there is a contrast in whether or not the causes are within the control of the stakeholders. For example, suppliers being ignorant about local labor laws and international standards can be regarded as an in-control cause that can be handled internally through policy development and training (Anner 2012). On the other hand, demand shortfall from global buyers or auditing fatigue requires external interventions and cannot only be treated internally. Furthermore, some causes are driven by market dynamics such as shorter product life cycle and reduction of communication cost due to the advancement in Information and Communication Technologies (ICTs), which force MNCs to adopt collaborative solutions with their suppliers such as the early involvement of the supplier in the product development process through adoption of concurrent engineering or design for logistics approaches (Dowlatshahi 1997), and a Quick Response (QR) to allow real information sharing of customer demand through advanced technologies like barcoding and Electronic Data Interchange (EDI) (Chiu 1995).

Improvement of labor rights is a wicked problem for different stakeholders. For example, buyers prefer gradual improvements over breaking relationship with noncompliant suppliers. In addition, there is no true or false way to make improvements since laborers work in dynamic environments, and the goodness of solutions is usually assessed through longitudinal studies such as periodic interviews with workers. Furthermore, improvements in one dimension can lead to violations in other dimensions. For example, forcing suppliers to eliminate child labor may cause shortage in workforce and subsequently leads to excessive overtime.

The fishbone diagram was established based on different studies that covered several industries and regions. However, some causes may relate to specific contexts. For example, not all countries ban unions and fashionability may not be a key characteristic of all products.

The results provide practitioners and researchers an overview of the possible barriers to improving labor rights in global value chains. Individuals involved in social auditing can reflect the presented findings on their environment and suggest corrective plans. The effectiveness of unions to represent workers is influenced by the factors outlined in Fig. 11.10. Trade union activists should find pragmatic solutions to remove these factors or reduce their symptoms. Researchers can build on the results to further explore the circumstances under which the causes of labor rights violation can be neutralized. Since labor governance is a wicked problem, further research is needed to examine the effects of removing barriers to improving labor rights on workers.

11.7 Conclusion

This chapter aims to highlight the root causes that degrade working conditions in global supply chains using a systematic literature review. For this, causes have been defined from literature and grouped according to an analysis of stakeholders. A fishbone diagram was subsequently constructed to illustrate the causal interrelations. I argue that labor governance in international supply chains is a wicked problem that requires the collaborative efforts of multiple stakeholders to resolve the adverse human rights impacts that stem primarily from trade liberalization and globalization. The systematic literature review affirms that among other industries, the apparel industry seems to be the most notorious when it comes to the violation of labor rights. The review also reveals increasing scholarly interest in this research topic. Additionally, cause-and-effect analysis indicates that different levels of causes for different stakeholders contribute to downgrading labor rights. For instance, failure of COC of lead firms has a major negative impact on labor rights in international supply chains in the sense that it is the main instrument that can be used by lead firms to guard and enhance the basic human rights of workers at suppliers' sites.

It is recommended that the causes or the sub-causes outlined in the fishbone diagram should be empirically examined in more specific contexts. For instance, this could include investigating the factors that may lead to high price and low fashionability of garments by running a questionnaire in a specific region. Understanding the wickedness of labor rights violation requires tools that are capable to cope with complex and dynamic environments. For example, it would be interesting to take the fishbone diagram further and develop a system dynamics model for a specific case or industry to study the interconnections between the causes defined in this chapter.

Acknowledgements The author gratefully acknowledges scholarship support from Kassel University and German Jordanian University. He also thanks the editors and the anonymous referees for their helpful comments.

References

Abidi, Hella, Sander de Leeuw, and Matthias Klumpp. 2014. Humanitarian Supply Chain Performance Management: A Systematic Literature Review. *Supply Chain Management: An International Journal* 19 (5/6): 592–608. https://doi.org/10.1108/SCM-09-2013-0349.

Andersen, Mette, and Tage Skjoett-Larsen. 2009. Corporate Social Responsibility in Global Supply Chains. *Supply Chain Management: An International Journal* 14 (2): 75–86. https://doi.org/10.1108/13598540910941948.

Anner, Mark. 2012. Corporate Social Responsibility and Freedom of Association Rights: The Precarious Quest for Legitimacy and Control in Global Supply Chains. *Politics & Society* 40 (4): 609–644. https://doi.org/10.1177/0032329212460983.

Antonio, K.W. 2011. The Implementation of Social Responsibility in Purchasing in Hong Kong/Pearl River Delta. *Strategic Outsourcing: An International Journal* 4 (1): 13. https://doi.org/10.1108/17538291111108417.

Arnold, Denis G., and Laura P. Hartman. 2003. Moral Imagination and the Future of Sweatshops. *Business and Society Review* 108 (4): 425–461. https://doi.org/10.1046/j.0045-3609.2003.00173.x.

Awaysheh, Amrou, and Robert D. Klassen. 2010. The Impact of Supply Chain Structure on the Use of Supplier Socially Responsible Practices.

International Journal of Operations & Production Management 30 (12): 1246–1268. https://doi.org/10.1108/01443571011094253.

Barnes, Tom, Krishna Shekhar Lal Das, and Surendra Pratap. 2015. Labour Contractors and Global Production Networks: The Case of India's Auto Supply Chain. *The Journal of Development Studies* 51 (4): 355–369. https://doi.org/10.1080/00220388.2014.983908.

Barrientos, Stephanie. 2008. Contract Labour: The 'Achilles Heel' of Corporate Codes in Commercial Value Chains. *Development and Change* 39 (6): 977–990. https://doi.org/10.1111/j.1467-7660.2008.00524.x.

Barrientos, Stephanie, and Sally Smith. 2007. Do Workers Benefit from Ethical Trade? Assessing Codes of Labour Practice in Global Production Systems. *Third World Quarterly* 28 (4): 713–729. https://doi.org/10.1080/01436590701336580.

Barrientos, Stephanie, Gary Gereffi, and Arianna Rossi. 2011. Economic and Social Upgrading in Global Production Networks: A New Paradigm for a Changing World. *International Labour Review* 150 (3–4): 319–340. https://doi.org/10.1111/j.1564-913X.2011.00119.x.

Barrientos, Stephanie Ware. 2013. 'Labour Chains': Analysing the Role of Labour Contractors in Global Production Networks. *The Journal of Development Studies* 49 (8): 1058–1071. https://doi.org/10.1080/0022038 8.2013.780040.

Bartley, Tim, and Niklas Egels-Zandén. 2015. Responsibility and Neglect in Global Production Networks: The Uneven Significance of Codes of Conduct in Indonesian Factories. *Global Networks* 15 (s1): S21–S44. https://doi.org/10.1111/glob.12086.

Becchetti, Leonardo, and Giovanni Trovato. 2005. The Determinants of Child Labour: The Role of Primary Product Specialization. *Labour* 19 (2): 237–271. https://doi.org/10.1111/j.1467-9914.2005.00303.x.

Berliner, Daniel, Anne Regan Greenleaf, Milli Lake, Margaret Levi, and Jennifer Noveck. 2015. Governing Global Supply Chains: What We Know (And Don't) About Improving Labor Rights and Working Conditions. *Annual Review of Law and Social Science* 11: 193–209. https://doi.org/10.1146/annurev-lawsocsci-120814-121322.

Bouchet, Adrien, Mike Troilo, and William Spaniel. 2015. International Sourcing, Social Responsibility and Human Assets: A Framework for Labor Procurement Negotiations in Baseball's Talent Supply Chain. *Corporate Governance* 15 (2): 214–228. https://doi.org/10.1108/CG-09-2014-0108.

Boyd, D. Eric, Robert E. Spekman, John W. Kamauff, and Patricia Werhane. 2007. Corporate Social Responsibility in Global Supply Chains: A Procedural Justice Perspective. *Long Range Planning* 40 (3): 341–356. https://doi.org/10.1016/j.lrp.2006.12.007.

Bremer, Jenifer, and John Udovich. 2001. Alternative Approaches to Supply Chain Compliance Monitoring. *Journal of Fashion Marketing and Management: An International Journal* 5 (4): 333–352. https://doi.org/10.1108/EUM0000000007295.

Cárdenas, Lina Maria, Renzo Shamey, and David Hinks. 2009. Key Variables in the Control of Color in the Textile Supply Chain. *International Journal of Clothing Science and Technology* 21 (5): 256–269. https://doi.org/10.1108/09556220910983759.

Cerchione, Roberto, and Emilio Esposito. 2016. A Systematic Review of Supply Chain Knowledge Management Research: State of the Art and Research Opportunities. *International Journal of Production Economics* 182: 276–292. https://doi.org/10.1016/j.ijpe.2016.09.006.

Chan, Jenny. 2013. A Suicide Survivor: The Life of a Chinese Worker. *New Technology, Work and Employment* 28 (2): 84–99. https://doi.org/10.1111/ntwe.12007.

Chiu, Huan. 1995. The Integrated Logistics Management System: A Framework and Case Study. *International Journal of Physical Distribution & Logistics Management* 25 (6): 4–22.

Cragg, Wesley, Denis G. Arnold, and Peter Muchlinski. 2012. Guest Editors' Introduction: Human Rights and Business. *Business Ethics Quarterly* 22 (1): 1–7. https://doi.org/10.5840/beq20122212.

Delbufalo, Emanuela. 2012. Outcomes of Inter-Organizational Trust in Supply Chain Relationships: A Systematic Literature Review and a Meta-Analysis of the Empirical Evidence. *Supply Chain Management: An International Journal* 17 (4): 377–402. https://doi.org/10.1108/13598541211246549.

Denyer, David, and David Tranfield. 2009. Producing a Systematic Review. In *The Sage Handbook of Organizational Research Methods*, ed. D.A. Buchanan and A. Bryman, 671–689. Thousand Oaks, CA: Sage.

Denyer, David, David Tranfield, and Joan Ernst Van Aken. 2008. Developing Design Propositions Through Research Synthesis. *Organization Studies* 29 (3): 393–413. https://doi.org/10.1177/0170840607088020.

Donaghey, Jimmy, Juliane Reinecke, Christina Niforou, and Benn Lawson. 2014. From Employment Relations to Consumption Relations: Balancing

Labor Governance in Global Supply Chains. *Human Resource Management* 53 (2): 229–252. https://doi.org/10.1002/hrm.21552.

Dowlatshahi, Shad. 1997. The Role of Product Design in Designer-Buyer-Supplier Interface. *Production Planning & Control* 8 (6): 522–532.

Drebes, Maike J. 2014. Impediments to the Implementation of Voluntary Codes of Conduct in Production Factories of the Global South: So Much to Do, So Little Done. *Third World Quarterly* 35 (7): 1256–1272. https://doi.org/10.1080/01436597.2014.926115.

Frenkel, Stephen J. 2001. Globalization, Athletic Footwear Commodity Chains and Employment Relations in China. *Organization Studies* 22 (4): 531–562. https://doi.org/10.1177/0170840601224001.

Frost, Stephen, and Margaret Burnett. 2007. Case Study: The Apple iPod in China. *Corporate Social Responsibility and Environmental Management* 14 (2): 103–113. https://doi.org/10.1002/csr.146.

Garg, Poonam, and Atul Garg. 2013. An Empirical Study on Critical Failure Factors for Enterprise Resource Planning Implementation in Indian Retail Sector. *Business Process Management Journal* 19 (3): 496–514. https://doi.org/10.1108/14637151311319923.

Giri, Amit K., and S.P. Singh. 2016. Labour Standards in Global Value Chains in India: The Case of Handknotted Carpet Manufacturing Cluster. *Asian Journal of Business Ethics* 5 (1–2): 37–52. https://doi.org/10.1007/s13520-016-0052-8.

Gold, Stefan, Alexander Trautrims, and Zoe Trodd. 2015. Modern Slavery Challenges to Supply Chain Management. *Supply Chain Management: An International Journal* 20 (5): 485–494. https://doi.org/10.1108/SCM-02-2015-0046.

Goworek, Helen. 2011. Social and Environmental Sustainability in the Clothing Industry: A Case Study of a Fair Trade Retailer. *Social Responsibility Journal* 7 (1): 74–86. https://doi.org/10.1108/17471111111114558.

Gupta, Megha, and Nancy Hodges. 2012. Corporate Social Responsibility in the Apparel Industry: An Exploration of Indian Consumers' Perceptions and Expectations. *Journal of Fashion Marketing and Management: An International Journal* 16 (2): 216–233. https://doi.org/10.1108/13612021211222833.

Hemphill, Thomas A., and Keith J. Kelley. 2016. Socially Responsible Global Supply Chains: The Human Rights Promise of Shared Responsibility and ISO 45001. *Journal of Global Responsibility* 7 (2): 163–180. https://doi.org/10.1108/JGR-05-2016-0013.

Hu, Yao-Su. 1992. Global or Stateless Corporations Are National Firms with International Operations. *California Management Review* 34 (2): 107–126. https://doi.org/10.2307/41166696.

Jafari, Hamid. 2015. Logistics Flexibility: A Systematic Review. *International Journal of Productivity and Performance Management* 64 (7): 947–970. https://doi.org/10.1108/IJPPM-05-2014-0069.

James, Ajith Tom, O.P. Gandhi, and S.G. Deshmukh. 2017. Assessment of Failures in Automobiles Due to Maintenance Errors. *International Journal of System Assurance Engineering and Management* 8 (4): 719–739. https://doi.org/10.1007/s13198-017-0589-5.

Jiang, Bin, Srinivas (Sri) Talluri, and Tao Yao. 2012. Improving Supplier's Situation Through Supplier Cooperation: The Case of Xintang Jeans Town. *International Journal of Production Economics* 139 (2): 431–437. https://doi.org/10.1016/j.ijpe.2011.03.010.

Kembro, Joakim, Kostas Selviaridis, and Dag Näslund. 2014. Theoretical Perspectives on Information Sharing in Supply Chains: A Systematic Literature Review and Conceptual Framework. *Supply Chain Management: An International Journal* 19 (5/6): 609–625. https://doi.org/10.1108/SCM-12-2013-0460.

Khara, Navjote, and Peter Lund-Thomsen. 2012. Value Chain Restructuring, Work Organization and Labour Outcomes in Football Manufacturing in India. *Competition & Change* 16 (4): 261–280. https://doi.org/10.1179/1024529412Z.00000000017.

Klerkx, Laurens, Pablo Villalobos, and Alejandra Engler. 2012. Variation in Implementation of Corporate Social Responsibility Practices in Emerging Economies' Firms: A Survey of Chilean Fruit Exporters. *Natural Resources Forum* 36 (2): 88–100. https://doi.org/10.1111/j.1477-8947.2012.01440.x.

Knorringa, Peter, and Lee Pegler. 2006. Globalisation, Firm Upgrading and Impacts on Labour. *Tijdschrift voor economische en sociale geografie* 97 (5): 470–479. https://doi.org/10.1111/j.1467-9663.2006.00357.x.

LeBaron, Genevieve. 2014. Subcontracting Is Not Illegal, but Is It Unethical: Business Ethics, Force Labor, and Economic Success. *The Brown Journal World Affairs* 20: 237.

Lillywhite, Serena. 2007. Ethical Purchasing and Workers' Rights in China: The Case of the Brotherhood of St Laurence. *Journal of Industrial Relations* 49 (5): 687–700. https://doi.org/10.1177/0022185607082216.

Locke, Richard, Matthew Amengual, and Akshay Mangla. 2009. Virtue Out of Necessity? Compliance, Commitment, and the Improvement of Labor

Conditions in Global Supply Chains. *Politics & Society* 37 (3): 319–351. https://doi.org/10.1177/0032329209338922.

Locke, Richard M., Fei Qin, and Alberto Brause. 2007. Does Monitoring Improve Labor Standards? Lessons from Nike. *Industrial and Labor Relations Review* 61 (1): 3–31. https://doi.org/10.1177/001979390706100101.

Locke, Richard M., Ben A. Rissing, and Timea Pal. 2013. Complements or Substitutes? Private Codes, State Regulation and the Enforcement of Labour Standards in Global Supply Chains. *British Journal of Industrial Relations* 51 (3): 519–552. https://doi.org/10.1111/bjir.12003.

Lund-Thomsen, Peter, and Adam Lindgreen. 2014. Corporate Social Responsibility in Global Value Chains: Where Are We Now and Where Are We Going? *Journal of Business Ethics* 123 (1): 11–22. https://doi.org/10.1007/s10551-013-1796-x.

Lund-Thomsen, Peter, Khalid Nadvi, Anita Chan, Navjote Khara, and Hong Xue. 2012. Labour in Global Value Chains: Work Conditions in Football Manufacturing in China, India and Pakistan. *Development and Change* 43 (6): 1211–1237. https://doi.org/10.1111/j.1467-7660.2012.01798.x.

Merk, Jeroen. 2009. Jumping Scale and Bridging Space in the Era of Corporate Social Responsibility: Cross-Border Labour Struggles in the Global Garment Industry. *Third World Quarterly* 30 (3): 599–615. https://doi.org/10.1080/01436590902742354.

Miller, Doug. 2004. Negotiating International Framework Agreements in the Global Textile, Garment and Footwear Sector. *Global Social Policy* 4 (2): 215–239. https://doi.org/10.1177/1468018104045110.

Mzembe, Andrew Ngawenja, Adam Lindgreen, François Maon, and Joëlle Vanhamme. 2016. Investigating the Drivers of Corporate Social Responsibility in the Global Tea Supply Chain: A Case Study of Eastern Produce Limited in Malawi. *Corporate Social Responsibility and Environmental Management* 23 (3): 165–178. https://doi.org/10.1002/csr.1370.

Nadvi, Khalid, and Gale Raj-Reichert. 2015. Governing Health and Safety at Lower Tiers of the Computer Industry Global Value Chain. *Regulation & Governance* 9 (3): 243–258. https://doi.org/10.1111/rego.12079.

Niforou, Christina. 2015. Labour Leverage in Global Value Chains: The Role of Interdependencies and Multi-Level Dynamics. *Journal of Business Ethics* 130 (2): 301–311. https://doi.org/10.1007/s10551-014-2222-8.

Ntabe, Eric N., Luc LeBel, Alison D. Munson, and Luis-Antonio Santa-Eulalia. 2015. A Systematic Literature Review of the Supply Chain Operations Reference (SCOR) Model Application with Special Attention to Environmental Issues. *International Journal of Production Economics* 169: 310–332. https://doi.org/10.1016/j.ijpe.2015.08.008.

Oka, Chikako. 2010. Accounting for the Gaps in Labour Standard Compliance: The Role of Reputation-Conscious Buyers in the Cambodian Garment Industry. *The European Journal of Development Research* 22 (1): 59–78. https://doi.org/10.1057/ejdr.2009.38.

Oka, Chikako. 2016. Improving Working Conditions in Garment Supply Chains: The Role of Unions in Cambodia. *British Journal of Industrial Relations* 54 (3): 647–672. https://doi.org/10.1111/bjir.12118.

Pedersen, Esben Rahbek, and Mette Andersen. 2006. Safeguarding Corporate Social Responsibility (CSR) in Global Supply Chains: How Codes of Conduct Are Managed in Buyer-Supplier Relationships. *Journal of Public Affairs: An International Journal* 6 (3–4): 228–240. https://doi.org/10.1002/pa.232.

Perry, Patsy, Steve Wood, and John Fernie. 2015. Corporate Social Responsibility in Garment Sourcing Networks: Factory Management Perspectives on Ethical Trade in Sri Lanka. *Journal of Business Ethics* 130 (3): 737–752. https://doi.org/10.1007/s10551-014-2252-2.

Phau, Ian, Min Teah, and Joe Chuah. 2015. Consumer Attitudes Towards Luxury Fashion Apparel Made in Sweatshops. *Journal of Fashion Marketing and Management* 19 (2): 169–187. https://doi.org/10.1108/JFMM-01-2014-0008.

Phillips, Nicola. 2016. Labour in Global Production: Reflections on Coxian Insights in a World of Global Value Chains. *Globalizations* 13 (5): 594–607. https://doi.org/10.1080/14747731.2016.1138608.

Pilbeam, Colin, Gabriela Alvarez, and Hugh Wilson. 2012. The Governance of Supply Networks: A Systematic Literature Review. *Supply Chain Management: An International Journal* 17 (4): 358–376. https://doi.org/10.1108/13598541211246512.

Posthuma, Anne, and Renato Bignami. 2014. 'Bridging the Gap'? Public and Private Regulation of Labour Standards in Apparel Value Chains in Brazil. *Competition & Change* 18 (4): 345–364. https://doi.org/10.1179/1024529414Z.00000000065.

Prieto-Carron, Marina. 2006. Corporate Social Responsibility in Latin America: Chiquita, Women Banana Workers and Structural Inequalities. *The Journal of Corporate Citizenship* 21: 85. https://doi.org/10.1007/s10551-010-0611-1.

Prieto-Carrón, Marina. 2008. Women Workers, Industrialization, Global Supply Chains and Corporate Codes of Conduct. *Journal of Business Ethics* 83 (1): 5. https://doi.org/10.1007/s10551-007-9650-7.

Rawling, Michael. 2015. Legislative Regulation of Global Value Chains to Protect Workers: A Preliminary Assessment. *The Economic and Labour Relations Review* 26 (4): 660–677. https://doi.org/10.1177/1035304615615513.

Riisgaard, Lone. 2009. Global Value Chains, Labor Organization and Private Social Standards: Lessons from East African Cut Flower Industries. *World Development* 37 (2): 326–340. https://doi.org/10.1016/j.worlddev.2008.03.003.

Rittel, Horst W.J., and Melvin M. Webber. 1973. Dilemmas in a General Theory of Planning. *Policy Sciences* 4 (2): 155–169. https://doi.org/10.1007/BF01405730.

Robinson, Pamela K. 2010. Do Voluntary Labour Initiatives Make a Difference for the Conditions of Workers in Global Supply Chains? *Journal of Industrial Relations* 52 (5): 561–573. https://doi.org/10.1177/0022185610381564.

Said-Allsopp, Muhaimina, and Anne Tallontire. 2015. Pathways to Empowerment?: Dynamics of Women's Participation in Global Value Chains. *Journal of Cleaner Production* 107: 114–121. https://doi.org/10.1016/j.jclepro.2014.03.089.

Schmeisser, Bjoern. 2013. A Systematic Review of Literature on Offshoring of Value Chain Activities. *Journal of International Management* 19 (4): 390–406. https://doi.org/10.1016/j.intman.2013.03.011.

Schrempf-Stirling, Judith, and Guido Palazzo. 2016. Upstream Corporate Social Responsibility: The Evolution from Contract Responsibility to Full Producer Responsibility. *Business & Society* 55 (4): 491–527. https://doi.org/10.1177/0007650313500233.

Shinde, Dnyandeo Dattatraya, Shwetambari Ahirrao, and Ramjee Prasad. 2018. Fishbone Diagram: Application to Identify the Root Causes of Student-Staff Problems in Technical Education. *Wireless Personal Communications* 100 (2): 653–664. https://doi.org/10.1007/s11277-018-5344-y.

Smyth, Russell, Xiaolei Qian, Ingrid Nielsen, and Ines Kaempfer. 2013. Working Hours in Supply Chain Chinese and Thai Factories: Evidence from the Fair Labor Association's 'Soccer Project'. *British Journal of Industrial Relations* 51 (2): 382–408. https://doi.org/10.1111/j.1467-8543.2011.00881.x.

Taplin, Ian. 2014. Who Is to Blame? A Re-Examination of Fast Fashion After the 2013 Factory Disaster in Bangladesh. *Critical Perspectives on International Business* 10 (1/2): 72–83. https://doi.org/10.1108/cpoib-09-2013-0035.

Taylor, Bill. 2012. Supply Chains and Labour Standards in China. *Personnel Review* 41 (5): 552–571. https://doi.org/10.1108/00483481211249102.

Thomas, Mark P. 2011. Global Industrial Relations? Framework Agreements and the Regulation of International Labor Standards. *Labor Studies Journal* 36 (2): 269–287. https://doi.org/10.1177/0160449X10365544.

Weil, David, and Carlos Mallo. 2007. Regulating Labour Standards via Supply Chains: Combining Public/Private Interventions to Improve Workplace Compliance. *British Journal of Industrial Relations* 45 (4): 791–814. https://doi.org/10.1111/j.1467-8543.2007.00649.x.

Wells, Don. 2007. Too Weak for the Job: Corporate Codes of Conduct, Non-governmental Organizations and the Regulation of International Labour Standards. *Global Social Policy* 7 (1): 51–74. https://doi.org/10.1177/1468018107073911.

Wicaksono, Padang, and Lionel Priyadi. 2016. Decent Work in Global Production Network: Lessons Learnt from the Indonesian Automotive Sector. *Journal of Southeast Asian Economies (JSEAE)* 33 (1): 95–110. https://doi.org/10.1353/ase.2016.0006.

Winstanley, Diana, Joanna Clark, and Helena Leeson. 2002. Approaches to Child Labour in the Supply Chain. *Business Ethics: A European Review* 11 (3): 210–223. https://doi.org/10.1111/1467-8608.00279.

Yu, Xiaomin. 2008. Impacts of Corporate Code of Conduct on Labor Standards: A Case Study of Reebok's Athletic Footwear Supplier Factory in China. *Journal of Business Ethics* 81 (3): 513–529. https://doi.org/10.1007/s10551-007-9521-2.

Zakaria, Mohamad, Zanda Garanča, and Abdallah Sobeih. 2012. Cultural and Legal Challenges in Implementing Code of Conduct in Supply Chain Management of Mobile Phone Industries: Sony Ericsson Case Study. *Social Responsibility Journal* 8 (2): 227–241. https://doi.org/10.1108/17471111211234851.

Zimmermann, Ricardo, Luís Miguel D.F. Ferreira, and Antonio Carrizo Moreira. 2016. The Influence of Supply Chain on the Innovation Process: A Systematic Literature Review. *Supply Chain Management: An International Journal* 21 (3): 289–304. https://doi.org/10.1108/SCM-07-2015-0266.

Zutshi, Ambika, Andrew Creed, and Amrik Sohal. 2009. Child Labour and Supply Chain: Profitability or (Mis)Management. *European Business Review* 21 (1): 42–63. https://doi.org/10.1108/09555340910925175.

12

Corporate Wrongdoing and Reputational Risk: A Genealogical Analysis of Toyota's Recall Crisis in 2010

Nobuyuki Chikudate

12.1 Introduction

Ideally, managers should fully grasp the idea of corporate social responsibility (CSR) and the vital role that it plays in strategically implementing business policies and activities and the long-term success of commercial enterprise in the twenty-first century. However, major Japanese corporations, such as Kobelco, Mitsubishi Materials, Mitsubishi Motors, Nissan Motors, Olympus, Subaru, Tokyo Electric Power Company, Toray, Toshiba, Toyota, and others, fail to fulfill their social responsibilities as corporate citizens, and have committed a series of actions which have brought these companies into disrepute. It is true that these companies have engaged in a wide range of negligent activities, wrongdoings, and crimes, with various impacts and victims. However, it seems that two related features are common in the behavior of companies discussed here: (1) inadequate CSR practices before the

N. Chikudate (✉)
Hiroshima University, Hiroshima-City, Japan
e-mail: cikudate@hiroshima-u.ac.jp

© The Author(s) 2019

F. Farache et al. (eds.), *Responsible People*, Palgrave Studies in Governance, Leadership and Responsibility, https://doi.org/10.1007/978-3-030-10740-6_12

exposures of their wrongdoings and (2) poor responses to public criticism up to, and in some cases beyond, the point when the company is dragged into corporate crises. Although these two features have usually been studied as separate categories, either public relations (PR) or CSR, the two features are, I suggest, intricately intertwined. The managers of Japanese corporations that were accused of their wrongdoings may have defined CSR on their own term, created particular views on CSR, and engaged in CSR-related activities years before the "significant" events which led to their corporate crisis. Because of their particular views of CSR, they may also have an inadequate response to public criticisms upon the disclosure of their corporate wrongdoings, and the corporations are subsequently dragged into these crises.

Some practitioners conceive CSR activities as tools to protect organizations against criticism and to influence the external environment (Cornelissen 2011). To do so, they try to intervene into the external environments (or civic societies) and even emasculate the powers of the public who potentially become stakeholders in criticizing the corporations in the spotlight in advance. Consequently, the managers of these corporations may have believed that even though the corporations were involved in wrongdoings, they would not be dragged into the crises; as few stakeholders, especially the media and politicians, offer strong and sustained criticism of corporations in Japanese society.

Toyota's recall crisis in 2010 offers us an opportunity to discuss the validity of this CSR reasoning (Chikudate 2011) and activities related to CSR by carefully examining consequent results. This study does not assume that this CSR reasoning "causes" corporate wrongdoings. However, the managers in Toyota worsened the situations by inappropriately behaving and speaking in public before and upon the exposures of wrongdoings. Such behaviors and speeches may have been informed by their own views on CSR. In this chapter, I conduct an analysis regarding Toyota's history where its particular views and practices relating to CSR and a similar wrongdoing have already been reported years before its recall crisis in 2010.

12.2 Theoretical Frameworks

12.2.1 Corporate Crisis as a Legitimacy Crisis

A corporate crisis can be categorized as specific, unexpected, and non-routine event, or series of events (Ulmer et al. 2011). Furthermore, regardless of the intentionality, if the wrongdoings that are conducted by corporations are observed, it is likely for those corporations to be criticized. Then, they often face social legitimacy crises. During such crises, as public animosity toward a corporation intensifies, it may become the target of *social sanctions*. Such social sanctions are likely to arise in conditions where the general public feels compeled to gather information from events and participate in a rhetorical group to say something to the others or participate in a public debate (e.g., Taylor 2009). Such public debates may not only be held in the traditional media but also using social media, such as Twitter, Facebook, and blogs (e.g., Schultz et al. 2011). Social sanctions may take various forms, such as rejection by opinion leaders, boycotting, and damaging the products/services of focal corporations, hundreds of telephone calls/faxes/emails, among other things.

In these critical situations, the corporations may choose different responses to mitigate criticisms, such as denial, attacking accusers, admitting guilt, and apologizing for misconduct (Benoit 1995). Although many other circumstances intervene, previous stakeholder relations influence the mindsets of some practitioners when choosing responses to the criticisms. In some corporations, PR or crisis management teams are trained and are strategically and proactively prepared for crises. PR practitioners try to establish and maintain a dialogue with the stakeholders about important issues, although this can be a time-consuming process (Cornelissen 2011). In other words, some corporations strategically build a *buffer* against criticism before any crisis arises, and CSR activities play significant roles.

12.2.2 CSR

There is little consensus on definitions and views of CSR (Windsor 2006), but some scholars and practitioners consider CSR activities as a "buffer" against public criticism during corporate crises. Among these perspectives, there are at least two contrastive foundations for reasoning, with respect to CSR: (1) normative or (2) instrumental reasoning. Scholars and practitioners who use normative reasoning tend to consider that *a reservoir of goodwill* that is accumulated though previous CSR activities helps corporations to survive during a crisis (Bhattacharya and Sen 2004). With this reasoning, prior *corporate reputations* and past CSR activities with goodwill have an influence on public attitudes during ongoing corporate crises (Vanhamme and Grobben 2009). Corporate reputation refers to an evaluation of a corporation and its ability to deliver particular goods a perceptual assessment of the corporation, which can be intangible assets for the corporations (Gardberg and Fombrun 2006). The normative reasoning in CSR activities tends to portray corporations creating a public image as honored and responsible citizens in civic societies (Windsor 2006).

On the other hand, practitioners who rely on instrumental reasoning in CSR tend to favor the managing or controlling of interactions with particular stakeholders, rather than including all members of the society. Here, stakeholder refers to "any group or individual who can affect or is affected by the achievement of an organization's purpose" (Freeman 2010, p. 53). As postulated by Friedman (1970), instrumental CSR reasoning justifies socially responsible behaviors solely on economic grounds and puts the priority of profit maximization above anything.

One notable characteristic of instrumental reasoning is that corporations try to prevent the stakeholders' interference with internal operations (Cornelissen 2011) by building buffers against their claims and interests (Freeman 2010). The rationale is that some stakeholders may have an "illegitimate" objective to interfere with the smooth operations of business. Extending this thinking to a corporate crisis, as long as the focal corporations make their critical stakeholder groups inactive, the corporations can be protected from being attacked or criticized.

Especially large corporations receiving increased media coverage who are more likely to have their legitimacy challenged (Deephouse 1996). Such coverage may be biased and filtered (Freeman 2010). That is why Freeman (2010, p. 22) labeled the media as stakeholders, saying, "Little stirs the anger in an executive more than an 'unfair' story in the press." Thus, some executives identify salient stakeholders who actually possess power and have influence on the legitimacy of the focal corporations (Mitchell et al. 1997).

To buffer the claims and interests of these stakeholders, some corporations may focus on strategic maneuvering by attempting to influence the stakeholders' attitudes and opinions (Cornelissen 2011) even before a corporate crisis. With this approach, along with a persuasion strategy, a corporation tries to either insulate itself from external interference or to actively influence stakeholders in its environment through such means as contributions to political action committees, lobbying, advocacy advertising (Cornelissen 2011), and advertising fees for private media in the name of CSR.

It would be true that some managers may mix both normative and instrumental reasoning with regard to CSR in practice. As a result, it may be difficult to discern which CSR reasoning they used. However, if corporations are considered as "anthropomorphized" entities, it may not be so difficult for outsiders of the corporations to discern whether managers of corporations tend to use either normative or instrumental reasoning in relation to CSR activities.

12.2.3 Anthropomorphized Corporations as Citizens

Although corporations exist as legal entities, some legal theorists justify attributing "corporate moral personhood" to corporations (e.g., Ripken 2009) by observing arising incidents of corporate wrongdoings especially since the global financial crises in 2008. According to this view, corporations should be conceived as "moral agents" (Maclagan 2008). Here, it is assumed that a corporation can be personified as a living, mature adult in a highly civilized society (Chikudate 2010). The mature adult in a highly civilized society is referred to as a *citizen*, and thus, some business ethics scholars regard corporations as citizens (e.g., Waddock 2002). This notion of "corporate personhood" has been reinforced to some extent, in the United States at least, by the Supreme Court in Citizens United vs. FEC (Avi-Yonah 2010) which granted corporations many of the same free speech rights as citizens.

Along these lines, corporations are increasingly expected to fulfill the duties of responsible citizens (Waddock 2002), the same way humans are. As for CSR, philanthropic activities to build a reservoir of goodwill are expected for corporations to become honored corporate citizens (Windsor 2006). Thus, if a corporation is honored as a good citizen, its positive reputation would grow in the society. On the other hand, even though the burden of legal responsibility would be obscure (Schultz 1996), the corporations "who" do something wrong could also be held criminally liable for their misdemeanors (Donaldson and Werhane 1988).

As moral agents of corporate citizens, it is ideal for corporations to possess virtue and integrity in their characteristics just like some "human beings" that have the same characteristics. Corporations should also maintain and harness such good characteristics as responsible corporate citizens, and this view is closely intertwined with a normative view of CSR. Being normative in this case means that corporations should *behave as collectively expected* (Habermas 1992) within the given civic societies. Furthermore, corporations should "speak" as collectively expected, which is as responsible citizens in the public sphere, especially when their practices are being questioned by the general public. In this view, a corporation is considered as an agent who actually "behaves and speaks" properly in public (Chikudate 2010; Schultz 1996). In other words, the corporation is "anthropomorphized," or imagined as a singular human entity. The assumption in this idea is that the general public tends to consider any activities of corporate communications, including issued public statements, public behaviors and speeches of corporate executives, press conferences, and others as if "a single human being" behaves or speaks especially when wrongdoings of corporations are exposed (Chikudate 2010). It would be also possible for the outsiders to observe the corporation's own views and definitions of CSR because anthropomorphized corporations actually "spoke" such views/ definitions and behaved accordingly.

12.3 Methods

In this study, I use the Foucaultian method for archival records, also called genealogy. In genealogy, it is assumed that the usage of history is "to help us see that the present is just as strange as the past" (Kendall and Wickham 1999, p. 4). In other words, the researchers use history as a way of diagnosing problems in the present (Kendall and Wickham 1999). Using this approach, the present problem to be discussed in this study is the recall crisis of Toyota.

I do not intend to chronologically detail the events regarding the recall crisis of Toyota in 2010 but instead draw on searches for historical facts regarding Toyota's previous behaviors and speeches as an anthropomorphized corporation, which are publicly available records and archival documents, including Toyota's prior CSR activities behind the scenes. Then, I critically analyze the meanings of several significant events to reveal the latent structure of Toyota's recall crisis in 2010.

12.4 A Genealogical Analysis

12.4.1 Overview of Toyota's Recall Crisis

In 2010, Toyota dearly wanted to end the severest crisis defined by its president, Akio Toyoda, since it was founded (Hōdō Station 2010). Although there had been issues concerning Toyota cars since 2007, Toyota's recall crisis started in the United States in 2009. Toyota received negative media coverage in spring 2010, involving such issues as sticking pedals, sudden acceleration, steering problems, and problems with the electronic control systems of various models (e.g., Saporito 2010). The U.S. media also repeatedly played footage of a horrific crash involving a California highway patrolman, reportedly caused by loose floor mats. Toyota issued recalls on various models on a global scale. As a result, Jim Wiseman, the group vice president for corporate communications at Toyota Motor of America said, "When you're getting three or four hundred [media] inquiries a day, you're just doing your best to keep up with them. I don't think any of us were really prepared in the early stages for how big the onslaught could be" (Liker and Ogden 2011, p. 129). On February 3, 2010, Ray Lahood, the chief of the National Highway Traffic Safety Administration (NHTSA) announced that Toyota cars should not be driven (ABC News 2010b). Thus, Toyota received severe social sanctions.

On February 18, 2010, the U.S. Congress issued an invitation to Toyota to testify at a public hearing. On February 23, 2010, James E. Lentz III (Jim Lentz), President of Toyota Motor Sales U.S.A., testified at the hearing. On February 24, 2010, Akio Toyoda and Yoshimi Inaba (the chief executive of Toyota's United States operations) also testified. Finally, Ray Lahood announced on February 8, 2011, "[…] we feel that Toyota vehicles are safe to drive" (CBS News 2011).

12.4.2 Toyota's Recognition of the Crisis

Jim Lentz testified during the public hearing that Americans were not empowered to authorize any recall decisions in the United States; the authorization had to come from Japan (e.g., News 9 2010b). Many parts of the organization, especially the most senior leadership in Japan, simply did not appreciate the depth of the crisis that Toyota was facing in the United States (Liker and Ogden 2011). In fact, Akio Toyoda retrospectively identified the gap in understanding local conditions and the urgency between regions and headquarters as a major contributor to the evolution of the crisis:

> There was a gap between the time that our U.S. colleagues realized that there was an urgent situation and the time that we realized here in Japan that there was an urgent situation happening in the United States. It took 3 months for us to recognize that this had turned into a crisis. In Japan, unfortunately, until the middle of January, we did not think that this was really a crisis. (Liker and Ogden 2011, p. 28)

Then, the question to be asked is, "Did Toyota really not prepare for the crisis and/or did they do something through their CSR activities?" As for CSR activities in the United States, some of the U.S. media disclosed

Toyota's political donations (e.g., CBS News 2010) aside from paying a lot of taxes, hiring U.S. workers, and philanthropic activities. In fact, Toyota's CSR activities seem to be based on their own views and definitions of CSR.

12.4.3 Toyota and CSR: The Public and Private Face of Corporate Policy CSR

Anthropomorphized Toyota defined CSR years before the crisis. It is true that Toyota boasted on its homepage about its CSR policy of being an ecologically and environmentally friendly company by producing energy-efficient cars (Toyota Motor Corporation 2008). Toyota also stated, "Honor the language and spirit of the law of every nation and undertake open and fair corporate activities to be a good corporate citizen of the world" (Toyota Motor Corporation 2018) as one of its guiding principles. The company (2008) also announced that their code of ethics and CSR principles were in accordance with Keidanren (Japan Business Federation) (2017), which have institutionalized practices among 1350 representative companies in Japan. Keidanren represents the club for elite Japanese companies, and Toyota was proud of having its former president being now Keidanren's president. This means that Toyota tried to identify itself as the face or leader of elite Japanese corporations. In the official version of Keidanren's code of ethics and CSR principles, ethics, being moral, green, sustainable, and such, were the common terms stated (Keidanren 2011). On October 26, 2010, Hiromasa Yonekura, former chairperson of Keidanren and former president of Sumitomo Chemical, however, disclosed his definition of CSR, "For individuals and corporations, political donation is one aspect of CSR. As long as [politicians] receive it, we are very happy to offer them to our advantage" (*Nihon Keizai Shimbun Morning Issue* 2010, p. 3). This view of CSR was, in fact, consistent with the statement of Hiroshi Okuda, Toyota's former CEO and president. On May 27, 2003, Hiroshi Okuda announced "We are willing to give political donations by evaluating the policies of each political party" (*Asahi Shimbun Morning Issue* 2003, p. 8). Hiroshi Okuda was also the chairman of Keidanren before Hiromasa Yonekura. Here, it would be inferred that the managers of Toyota may have incorrectly defined political donations as an aspect of CSR, however Toyota's managers did not perceive the definition as incorrectly. In fact, Toyota's political donations in the United States reflected this view.

Besides political donations, the tracing of historical facts of anthropomorphized Toyota's speeches in public years before its recall crisis in 2010 indicates that Toyota's CSR activities include the following: (1) doing some of the groundwork to charm the salient stakeholders who exerted their influence on Toyota, (2) sidelining stakeholders who are critical about Toyota, and (3) self-justifying Toyota's operations while disregarding the law in the process.

12.4.4 Charming the Salient Stakeholders

Anthropomorphized Toyota often disclosed its instrumental CSR orientation in its support for salient stakeholders who were potentially useful to the company. Former CEOs and presidents of Toyota, including Fujio Cho and Katsuaki Watanabe, who represented Toyota in the public eye openly supported the candidates belonging to Liberal Democratic Party (LDP) during the national election in 2005; they mobilized the managers of Toyota and its suppliers in the Toyota Kingdom located in Aichi prefecture where many local residents were affiliated with Toyota (Yokota and Sataka 2006). Thus, Toyota identified LDP as one of the salient stakeholders who could be strong supporters for Toyota, and Toyota did have an influence on Japan's politics and tried to shape Japan's public policies via its relationship with the LDP.

12.4.5 Japanese Private Media That Were Sidelined by Toyota

Toyota also tried to manage and control the Japanese media (stakeholders) that were potentially critical about Toyota for their own purposes. On November 12, 2008, at a meeting in the Prime Minister's Office,

Hiroshi Okuda, who served as the chair for the Informal Assembly for Planning Public Health and Labour Policy, said:

> I am personally angry. Partly with the newspapers, but largely with the private TV stations, where a few guys show up in programs from morning to night to criticize the Ministry of Public Health, Labour, Welfare, Insurance and Pensions...Shall I retaliate?...To be honest, the big corporations would not let them appear on TV. It is obvious that the sponsors of such TV programs are not big corporations (such as Toyota) but small pachinko parlors [semi-gambling places], saunas or udon noodle [fast food] shops in the provinces [of peripheries in Japan]. (*Asahi Shimbun Morning Issue* 2008, p. 38; *Nihon Keizai Shimbun Morning Issue* 2008, p. 5)

Asahi Shimbun Morning Issue (2008, 38) provided further details, as follows. One of the attendees at the meeting criticized Hiroshi Okuda, "Would you stop sponsoring the media if they criticized you? That's overkill!" Worse, Hiroshi Okuda, who was furious, countered, "In reality, it is already happening" in front of the media. Therefore, because of the shortage of advertising fees in the Japanese private media after the financial crisis in 2008 (e.g., *Shukan Diamond* 2011), such a rhetorical performance created a certain image of Toyota; an arrogant, large corporation to whom other members of society have to bow.

In fact, because of this rhetorical performance of the former CEO and president of Toyota in public and Toyota's advertising fees to private media in Japan, some Japanese journalists may have constructed a certain reality. Soichiro Tahara, a pundit and journalist in Japan, let something slip when he introduced Seiji Maehara, Minister of Land, Infrastructure and Transportation, on his live show covering Toyota recall crisis in 2010; "In Japan, nobody [especially LDP politicians who have benefitted through Toyota's donations and the private media in Japan] has anything negative to say about Toyota except you, Sir, Mr. Maehara [belonging to Democratic Party of Japan]" (Sunday Project 2010).

Indeed, Japanese *private* media rarely reported the incidents in the United States. The media organization that scooped the Toyota crisis was in fact NHK, the public media in Japan. NHK camera crews interviewed

Akio Toyoda during the Davos conference of the World Economic Forum. Then, the same interview was aired by ABC News (2010a) in the United States on January 29, 2010, because ABC is an affiliate of NHK. Under these circumstances, Japanese executives in Toyota headquarters may have miscalculated that their belief of sustaining the buffer from the accusations from private media in Japan could be also applied to the public media even in Japan and U.S. media whose legitimacy and journalistic ethics were not influenced by advertising fees.

12.4.6 Toyota's Self-Justifying Attitudes

Because of instrumental CSR activities, Japanese executives in the Toyota headquarters may have been confident in maintaining the company's legitimacy in the early stages of its crisis before 2010. Their version of reality about the situation was as follows; *the nature of the problems was merely a technical matter of floor mats, and the majority of accidents were attributed to the mishandling of the drivers.* For example, when a delegation of the NHTSA visited Toyota headquarters in Japan, the executives in charge of product quality tried to justify their position. During the press conference on February 9, 2010, Shinichi Sasaki (vice president in charge of quality control) confessed, "Regarding the floor mats [that caused the pedals to stick], our univocal explanation [to the delegation of the NHTSA in December 2009] was that American customers simply did not use the mats appropriately. Then we received severe criticism and were asked, 'Does Toyota still think that way?'" (A to Z 2010). Toyota was reluctant to issue the recalls. From this moment, Toyota, whose top quality control officer never questioned Toyota's legitimacy, had to go through the battle with NHTSA, the U.S. authority for regulation.

Toyota behaved in a similar way before as battling with NHTSA in 2009 and was already charged in Japan due to similar recall problems. Archival records showed that before the public accusations against Toyota from 2010 to 2011, three Toyota managers were sent the papers pertaining to a criminal case to the public prosecutor's office in 2006 because of its mishandling recalls of Hilux, station wagons (*Asahi*

Shimbun Morning Issue 2006). A driver who drove a Hilux was killed because of its deficient steering relay rod, and there were at least 11 claims about the same deficiency. However, Toyota hid this for 12 years. Toyota submitted an investigation report to Ministry of Land, Infrastructure and Tourism (MLIT), the supervising agency, although Toyota justified its position of quality control (*Asahi Shimbun Evening Issue* 2006). In other words, something may have already been wrong inside Toyota before 2010. It is true that Toyota's recall crisis in 2010 occurred in the United States and not in Japan, and that the Toyota Japanese executives in charge may have been different from those in charge of the recall case of 2006 in Japan. However, from these historical records, it becomes obvious that anthropomorphized Toyota's self-justifying attitudes may have led the corporation to disobey the laws and regulations in given societies because it was consistent and did not change from 2006 to 2009 to 2010.

12.4.7 Toyota's Human-Like Attitudes and Rhetorical Performances

Such self-justifying attitudes manifested in the very crucial moments of speaking to the public because the attitudes of anthropomorphized Toyota were consistent. On February 3, 2010, talking about the loss of function or delaying of brake action in the Prius, Shinichi Sakaki said, "[There is no mechanical problem with the Prius], it is a matter of [the driver's] feeling…Since Toyota's customers get used to the feeling of Toyota, they may feel something wrong once something different happens" (*Asahi Shimbun Morning Issue* 2010). A public comment made by another Toyota executive had the same connotation. During the press conference on February 4, 2010, concerning the Prius anti-lock braking system (ABS), Hiroyuki Yokoyama (managing director) said, "There may be incompatibility between the drivers' senses and the movements of the car. If drivers have not experienced such phenomena before, they may feel anxious" (News 9 2010a). Because Toyota executives rarely needed to communicate with stakeholders whose influence was not controllable (Linstead 2001), it is obvious that these executives revealed that they were suffering from a condition of collective myopia, defined as "the situation in which members of certain communities or organizations are able to make sense and give sense in each context in which they live but are not able to monitor the emerging order or patterns as a whole created by themselves" (Chikudate 2002, p. 294). In collective myopia, the way they make sense of and explain issues which do not include customers in their limited contexts within their Toyota castle. That is why they spoke as representing Toyota to the public in their attitudes of anthropomorphized company without any hesitation. Furthermore, the displayed attitudes were consistent. Jim Lentz reflected, "As I look at where we were in the past, what had become… with our success…as a company, we had a little bit of an attitude. Arrogance is probably the best explanation" (Liker and Ogden 2011, p. 177). Thus, anthropomorphized Toyota held arrogant characteristics, resulting in the company's behavior and speeches that were no longer like that of a responsible corporate citizen, even though they have also engaged in some philanthropic activities, such as CSR practices.

12.4.8 Unanticipated Enemies

With their previous instrumental CSR practices and stakeholder management, Toyota's Japanese executives may have held false beliefs that Toyota was able to control accusations through the Japanese politicians. However, the speeches of anthropomorphized Toyota that were embodied by its two executives brought the anger of Seiji Maehara upon themselves. On the evening of February 5, 2010, Seiji Maehara held a press conference and overtly criticized Toyota for failing to consider the perspective of its customers (MLIT 2010). During the TV program, *Sunday Project*, he said, "It was wrong for the company to hide the recalls. It is necessary to create social systems that impose *social sanctions* on a company that hides recalls and that stimulate the willingness of companies to recall" (Sunday Project 2010). Toyota's Japanese executives would have hardly anticipated this accusation of the Japanese minister.

The accusation against Toyota by an authoritative figure in Japan resulted not only from inappropriate public comments by Toyota's executives but also from Toyota's prior political involvements as part of its CSR activities. Toyota's former CEOs and presidents openly supported LDP candidates during elections, and Hiroshi Okuda publicly expressed his support for LDP (*Nihon Keizai Shimbun Morning Issue* 2003). However, there was a real power shift from LDP to the Democratic Party of Japan in the national election in 2009. Thus, Toyota bred the grounds potentially harming the company in the future with their own views of CSR and behaviors/speeches of anthropomorphized Toyota that were embodied by the company's three former CEOs and presidents. As a result, Akio Toyoda, the successor of these three CEOs and presidents, confessed during the interview that no matter how Toyota explained in logical and engineering manners, Toyota will always be criticized by the public (Kinoshita 2010). Then, the only rescue for Toyota was to play the role of a responsible corporate citizen, showing emotive and moral characteristics by switching its responses to public criticism to *corporate apologia*, a strategic crisis communication through apology (Hearit 1995). Finally, Toyota agreed to pay a record fine to the U.S. government for its irresponsible behavior to end its crisis in 2010.

12.5 Conclusion

In this chapter, I have shown the results of a genealogical analysis on Toyota's own definition of CSR and CSR-related activities before its recall crisis in 2010. There is no doubt that Toyota evolved into a global corporation of technological innovation and contributed to the economy of each society, for instance, by hiring many workers, purchasing from local suppliers, paying corporate taxes, and engaging in philanthropic activities. Besides these activities, Toyota prepared for the crisis by building buffers against the accusations of key stakeholders. However, these preparations did not work as expected both in the United States and Japan. The overconfidence of having a buffer led Toyota executives in Japan to make inadequate judgments on the ongoing situations in the United States and Japan. The overconfidence also led Toyota's Japanese executives to be arrogant, and anthropomorphized Toyota displayed arrogance through its behavior and speeches. Finally, rhetorical performances of Japanese executives have put Toyota into a position where the only strategic response for the corporation was *apologia*.

It would be easy for managers of large corporations to practice CSR by connecting the conception of strategic management with the mentalities of warlords who tend to attribute anything with either "win or lose" or the hegemony/power. Then, Toyota lost the battle. Therefore, the biggest lesson to be learned from Toyota's recall crisis in 2010 is that doing groundworks of silencing "voices" by instrumental activities is not as effective as how the managers of large corporations have assumed.

A further interesting observation is that Toyota's recall crisis in 2010 was a mere beginning of exposing the wrongdoings by major auto manufacturers in the global market, including General Motors, Volkswagens, and Daimler-Bentz. Perhaps a similar pathology of Toyota, collective myopia, may also have resided as a *resident pathogen* (Reason 1990) that is potentially harmful to an entire system in the systems of global car manufacturers even in the western societies (Chikudate 2015). Thus, the managers in multinational corporations should appreciate humanist knowledge, such as ethics, rhetoric, and communication, besides global strategy/marketing, innovation, and other subjects if they still wish to fully grasp the concept of corporate citizens whose activities should conform to normative CSR reasoning.

References

A to Z. 2010. "A to Z," aired by *NHK*, February 20.

ABC News. 2010a. "ABC News," aired by *ABC*, New York, January 29.

ABC News. 2010b. "ABC News," aired by *ABC*, New York, February 3.

Asahi Shimbun Evening Issue. 2006. Toyota Seisaikin Shiharai [Toyota Paid Fine], May 19.

Asahi Shimbun Morning Issue. 2003. Kigyo no Seijikenkin Fukkatsu o Aratamete Hyoumei Okuda Keidanren Kaichō [Reviving Manifestation of Political Donation, Okuda Chairperson of Keidanren], May 28.

Asahi Shimbun Morning Issue. 2006. Toyota 96nen ni Kairyōhin [Toyota Remodeled in 1996], July 12.

Asahi Shimbun Morning Issue. 2008. Kōrōshō Tataki Ijyo Masukomi ni Hōhuku demo [Abnormal Media Basing Against Ministry of Health, Labour and Welfare. So Shall I Retaliate on the Media?], November 13.

Asahi Shimbun Morning Issue. 2010. Toyota Kanban nimo Kizu [Stain on Toyota's Reputation], February 4.

Avi-Yonah, Reuvan S. 2010. Citizens United and the Corporate Form. *Wisconsin Law Review* 4: 999–1047.

Benoit, William L. 1995. *Accounts, Excuses, and Apologies: A Theory of Image Restoration Strategies*. Albany, NY. State University of New York Press.

Bhattacharya, C.B., and Sanker Sen. 2004. Doing Better at Doing Good: When, Why, and How Consumers Respond to Corporate Social Initiatives. *California Management Review* 47: 9–24.

CBS News. 2010. Toyota Has Donated to Investigating Reps. Last modified February 23. https://www.cbsnews.com/news/toyota-has-donated-to-investigating-reps.

CBS News. 2011. Electronics Not at Fault in Toyota Deaths. Last modified February 8. https://www.cbsnews.com/news/electronics-not-at-fault-in-toyota-deaths.

Chikudate, Nobuyuki. 2002. Collective Myopia and Disciplinary Power Behind the Scenes of Unethical Practices: A Diagnostic Theory on Japanese Organization. *Journal of Management Studies* 39: 289–307.

Chikudate, Nobuyuki. 2010. Reinterpreting Corporate Apologia as Self-Discipline. *Corporate Communications: An International Journal* 15: 397–409.

Chikudate, Nobuyuki. 2011. Collapsed Buffer, Reputation, and Instrumental CSR: Toyota Recall Crisis in 2010. Paper presented at CSR Communication Conference, Amsterdam, October 26–28.

Chikudate, Nobuyuki. 2015. *Collective Myopia in Japanese Organizations: A Transcultural Approach for Identifying Corporate Meltdowns*. New York: Palgrave Macmillan.

Cornelissen, Joep. 2011. *Corporate Communication: A Guide to Theory and Practice*, 3rd ed. London: Sage.

Deephouse, David L. 1996. Does Isomorphism Legitimate? *Academy of Management Journal* 39: 1024–1039.

Donaldson, Thomas, and Patricia Werhane. 1988. *Ethical Issues and Business*. Englewood Cliffs: Prentice Hall.

Freeman, R. Edward. 2010. *Strategic Management: A Stakeholder Approach*. Cambridge: Cambridge University Press.

Friedman, Milton. 1970. The Social Responsibility of Business Is to Increase Its Profit. *The New York Times Magazine*, September 13: 32–33, 122, 124, 126.

Gardberg, Naomi, A., and Charles, J. Fombrun. 2006. Corporate Citizenship: Creating Intangible Assets Across Institutional Environments. *Academy of Management Review* 3: 329–346.

Habermas, Jürgen. 1992. *Postmetaphysical Thinking*, trans. William M. Hohengarten. Cambridge: Polity Press.

Hearit, Keith M. 1995. 'Mistakes Were Made': Organizations, Apologia, and Crises of Social Legitimacy. *Communication Studies* 46: 1–17.

Hōdō Station. 2010. "Hōdō Station," aired by *TV Asahi*, March 3.

Keidanren. 2011. Keidanren Homepage. Accessed September 1, 2011. http://www.keidanren.or.jp/indexj.html.

Keidanren. 2017. Keidanren Homepage. Accessed August 9, 2017. http://www.keidanren.or.jp/en/profile/pro001.html.

Kendall, Gavin, and Gary Wickham. 1999. *Using Foucault's Methods*. London: Sage.

Kinoshita, Takayuki. 2010. *Toyoda Akio no Ningen-ryoku* [Characteristics of Akio Toyoda]. Tokyo: Gakken Publishing.

Liker, Jeffery K., and Timothy N. Ogden. 2011. *Toyota Under Fire*. New York: McGraw Hill.

Linstead, Stephen A. 2001. Rhetoric and Organizational Control: A Framework for Analysis. In *The Language of Organization*, ed. Robert Westwood and Stephen Linstead, 217–240. London: Sage.

Maclagan, Patrick. 2008. Organizations and Responsibility: A Critical Overview. *Systems Research and Behavioral Science* 25: 371–381.

Ministry of Land, Infrastructure and Tourism (MLIT). 2010. Press Conference on February 5. Accessed September 1, 2010. http://www.mlit.go.jp/report/interview/daijin100205.html.

Mitchell, Ronald K., Bradley R. Agle, and Donna J. Wood. 1997. Toward a Theory of Stakeholder Identification and Salience: Defining the Principle of Who and What Really Counts. *Academy of Management Review* 22: 853–886.

News 9. 2010a. "News 9," aired by *NHK*, February 18.

News 9. 2010b. "News 9," aired by *NHK*, February 24.

Nihon Keizai Shimbun Morning Issue. 2003. Ichiban Hachō Au no wa Jimin [The Most Favorite Is LDP], October 21.

Nihon Keizai Shimbun Morning Issue. 2008. Kōrōshō Tataki Okudashi Ijo [Ministry of Health, Labour and Welfare Bashing, Abnormal Mr. Okuda], November 13.

Nihon Keizai Shimbun Morning Issue. 2010. Minshu Keizaikai ni Sekkin [DPJ Approaches Business World], October 27.

Reason, James. 1990. *Human Error*. Cambridge: Cambridge University Press.

Ripken, Susanna. 2009. Corporations Are People Too: A Multi-dimensional Approach to the Corporate Personhood Puzzle. *Fordham Journal of Corporate & Financial Law* 15: 97–177.

Saporito, Bill. 2010. Toyota's Brown Engine. *Time Magazine (Asian ed.)*, February 22: 2–16.

Schultz, Friederike, Sonja Utz, and Anja Goritz. 2011. Is the Medium the Message? Perceptions of and Reactions to Crisis Communication via Twitter, Blogs and Traditional Media. *Public Relations Review* 37: 20–27.

Schultz, Pamela D. 1996. The Morally Accountable Corporation: A Postmodern Approach to Organizational Responsibility. *The Journal of Business Communication* 33: 165–183.

Shukan Diamond. 2011. Shimbun, Terebi Shōsha Naki Shōmōsen [Newspapers, TV, War of Attrition Without Winners], January 15: 28–65.

Sunday Project. 2010. "Sunday Project," aired by *TV Asahi*, February 28.

Taylor, M. 2009. Civil Society as a Rhetorical Public Relations Process. In *Rhetorical and Critical Approaches to Public Relations II*, ed. Robert L. Heath, Elizabeth L. Toh, and Damion Waymer, 76–91. New York: Routledge.

Toyota Motor Corporation. 2008. CSR Policy: Contribution Towards Sustainable Development. Accessed September 30, 2008. http://www.toyota.co.jp/en/vision/sustainability/index.html.

Toyota Motor Corporation. 2018. Guiding Principles at Toyota. Accessed June 11, 2018. http://www.toyota-global.com/pages/contents/company/vision_philosophy/pdf/guiding_principles.pdf.

Ulmer, Robert R., Timothy L. Sellnow, and Matthew W. Seeger. 2011. *Effective Crisis Communication: Moving from Crisis to Opportunity*, 2nd ed. Thousand Oaks: Sage.

Vanhamme, Joëlle, and Bas Grobben. 2009. Too Good to Be True! The Effectiveness of CSR History in Countering Negative Publicity. *Journal of Business Ethics* 85: 273–283.

Waddock, Sandra A. 2002. *Leading Corporate Citizens: Vision, Values, Value Added*. Boston: McGraw-Hill.

Windsor, Duane. 2006. Corporate Social Responsibility. *Journal of Management Studies* 43: 93–114.

Yokota, Hajime, and Makoto Sataka. 2006. *Toyota no Shoutai* [Toyota's True Characteristics]. Tokyo: Kabushikigaisha Kinyobi.

Index

Printed by Printforce, the Netherlands